RADICAL PHILOSOPHY

2.14
Series 2 / Spring 2023

Robot Makes Free **Daniel Nemenyi**	3
Why the customer is always right **Eric-John Russell**	21
History and revolution in Debord's *The Society of the Spectacle* **Tom Bunyard**	36
The toxic ideology of longtermism **Alice Crary**	49
Antagonisms between bourgeois and coalitional formations **Roderick Ferguson**	58
Whose movement is it anyway? **Gail Lewis**	64
Health without security? An interview with Mark Neocleous **Mark Neocleous with Sam Kelly**	75

REVIEWS

Nathan Brown, *Rationalist Empiricism: A Theory of Speculative Critique* **Daniel Sacilotto**	89
Louis Menand, *The Free World: Art and Thought in the Cold War* **Josefine Wikström**	95
Timothy Bewes, *Free Indirect: The Novel in a Postfictional Age* **Carson Welch**	99
Boris Groys, *Philosophy of Care* **Maria Walsh**	101
Ntina Tzouvala, *Capitalism as Civilisation: A History of International Law* **Aziz Rana**	105
Jill Godmilow, *Kill The Documentary* **Stefanie Baumann**	108
Thomas Lemke, *The Government of Things: Foucault and the New Materialisms* **Deren Ertas**	111
Moritz Altenried, *The Digital Factory: The Human Labour of Automation* **Yari Lanci**	115
Russell Muirhead & Nancy L. Rosenblum, eds., *A Lot of People are Saying* **Michael F. Miller**	118
Description of a Self-Portrait: Jean-Luc Godard, 1930-2022 **Christa Blümlinger**	122

Editorial collective
Claudia Aradau
Brenna Bhandar
Victoria Browne
David Cunningham
Peter Hallward
Stewart Martin
Lucie Mercier
Daniel Nemenyi
Hannah Proctor
Rahul Rao
Martina Tazzioli
Chris Wilbert

Engineers
Daniel Nemenyi
Alex Sassmanshausen

Cover image
Peter Hallward

CC BY-NC-ND
RP, Spring 2023

ISSN 0300-211X
ISBN 978-1-914099-03-8

Robot Makes Free
The Leibnizian cryptowar of Norbert Wiener
Daniel Nemenyi

> The world of the future will … not [be] a comfortable hammock in which we can lie down to be waited upon by our robot slaves.
>
> — Norbert Wiener, *God and Golem,* Inc.

The word 'robot' entered the English language just over a hundred years ago, on 9 October 1922. It arrived with a Broadway production of the play in which it was coined, *Rossum's Universal Robots (R.U.R.)* by Czech writer Karel Čapek, which immediately captured the *Zeitgeist* and was being performed in theatres around the world as quickly as it could be translated.[1] Though the conceptual drama and its author may have been lost to popular memories (beyond Central Europe at least), the spectre of its neologism – *robot* – which in the play signifies a 'race' of artificial humans who turn against their creators, haunts the world ever more with each milestone that today's revolutions in 'machine learning' bring. This begs a question: beyond science fiction and beyond techno-utopias – what is signified by the concept of a robot?

An ontological other out for your bread, a failed simularum of authentic existence – fembots, Chinese, autists – and the cyborgs that we anyway all are.[2] These are the three employments of 'robot' (always undefined) I found in the archive of a certain magazine that has existed for half its life, namely *RP*, yet none get at the concrete sense of power there originally and in its richest philosophical discussion since: the cybernetics of Norbert Wiener. This article shall discuss each in turn. Alas the concept of the robot has emptied out and lightened up. Perhaps this has something to do with the fact that the other side of Paulo Virno's observation that one thing an AI cannot fake is having a 'good sense of humour' is that, in at least a certain popular unconscious, the robot has become the paradigmatic *object* of humour:[3] a classically Bergsonian being of mechanical inelasticity in movement, voice and intellect where one expects the pliableness of a living being.[4] Think *L'uomo meccanico*, the Tin Man, Robby the Robot, C-3PO, the Roomba vacuum cleaner, etc.

The original play had no such slapstick. It is true that Čapek did consider the play 'a comedy, partly of science, partly of truth', and that his characters represent rigid archetypes expressed univocally by their names – Dr Rossum, the inventor of the robot, from the Czech for intelligence (*rozum*), Busman represents businessmen, Domin from Latin *dominus* and 'robot' from a root meaning drudgery, forced labourer, orphan or slave – the German *Arbeit* shares the same root. But as Ivan Klíma shows, Čapek intended their one-dimensionality to imitate the 'simple, calm, direct classical farce' of Plautus' comedy *The Brothers Menaechim*, wherein each 'character is assigned from the outset a single interest … no turning points, no changes, no psychological development at all.' The joke is in the irreversibility of humanity's self-destruction, of some 'terrible machinery [that] must not stop, for if it does it would destroy the lives of thousands. It must, on the contrary, go on faster and faster'.[5] It is the worker's soul which is slowing this machinery down, the dross of their 'feelings of altruism and camaraderie, all familial, poetic, and transcendental feelings'. For to the boss:

> Everything must be speeded up … The workers' question is holding us back. The worker must become a machine, so that he can simply rotate like a wheel. Every thought is insubordination! … A worker's soul is not a machine, therefore it must be removed. This is my system … I have sterilized the worker, purified him.[6]

These words actually preempt *R.U.R.* by nearly a decade, hailing from the short story 'The System' (1911) which Karel Čapek co-authored with his brother Josef, who would later suggest the word 'robot' to name *R.U.R.*'s soul-stripped – hence purely machine – workers. Likewise, *R.U.R.*'s 'robots' are just artificial humans lacking a natural sense of humanity, sterile and pure workers produced en masse by the play's eponymous corporation. Yet between these two texts, between 1911 and 1920, a noticeable gear has shifted in Čapek's writings. The violence is of another order – World War I has taken place. The System has *actually* tried to strip the soul from the worker. Millions who might otherwise have been part of an international class struggle have been reduced to killing machines, butchering one another on an industrial scale for the narrow and conflicting interests of their rulers. The system in question, which was clearly capitalism, is now more general. *R.U.R.* implicates not only capitalism and the State but, as a comedy of science and truth, also a certain potential of humanity as such.

In Čapek's play the R.U.R. Corporation manufactures artificial humans who have no desire, no will to speak of: fleshy – chemical and biological, not mechanical – but cattle-like 'living machines' who the corporation brags can be fed 'on pineapples, straw, whatever you like.' The best of these 'robots' work relentlessly for twenty years before being 'used up', in which time they have been two-and-a-half times more productive than a naturally-born human. By radically undercutting the price of labour, orders are placed by corporations and governments for such soulless 'shadows of man' by the hundreds of thousands until they replace human labour altogether. A (purportedly) rare number of these robots suffer an episode of 'teeth gnashing', whose obscenity – a hint at a soul? – means they get sent immediately to the 'stamping mill' for termination. They go indifferently. Though the General Manager of R.U.R. nurtures a Fully Automated Luxury Communist ambition[7] to turn 'the whole of mankind into an aristocracy nourished by millions of mechanical slaves', the birth rate of humanity crashes to nil since it has no work to sustain itself, and its armed uprisings are stamped out by impossible robot armies bought by governments to protect their economies.

It has been argued by Louis Chude-Sokei that *R.U.R.* represents a late imperial anxiety of slave rebellions in the vein of Mary Shelley's colonially-minded *Frankenstein*.[8] Yet were Čapek to have wanted White audiences to identify with the naturally-born humans of the play who end up wiped out by the robots' genocidal war of liberation, he would have surely depicted them as morally superior to their slaves-turned-exterminators. Instead *R.U.R.* presents natural humans as liable to becoming *equally* servile to the interests of capital as its artificial ones. Human statecraft as secure in the pockets of blinkered corporate agendas. Human shareholders as hell bent on the 'dream of dividends, and their dividends are the ruin of mankind'. The robot's justification for eventually murdering all natural humans is not entirely unfounded, all things considered: 'Slaughter and domination are necessary if you would be human beings. Read history.' I take Čapek's point to be that you don't need to be born in a factory – or of a certain race – to be a robot, you just need to turn in your soul and rotate like a wheel. The natural humans who represent the interests of capital and state are no less 'robots' than the robots themselves. This is to say that in its origin the robot is *not* the fiction of a fascist imagination, but the fiction of fascists imagined: a premonition seen in WWI by two brothers who would come to lead Czechoslovakia's cultural resistance to Fascism until their demise under its shadow: Josef, who coined the word 'robot', perishing in the concentration camp system whose gates bore those terrible – yet poignant – words, '*Arbeit Macht Frei*'.

Machine, machine, machine

If *R.U.R.*'s robots are vaunted as products of 'modern engineering' but hail from the technical imaginary of an era when the Ford assembly line was barely seven years old, today they should be reconsidered in light of the techno-scientific revolution that has since taken place. Cybernetics. The 'information revolution' or, in Einstein's words, the 'information bomb' which exploded into history during the following World War but whose consequences are only starting to be felt.[9]

No less a figure than the father of cybernetics – MIT physicist Norbert Wiener – delivered a prologue to the MIT drama society's performance of *R.U.R.* on 5 May 1950, the thirtieth anniversary of the original. Wiener's book *Cybernetics, or Communication and Control in the Animal and the Machine* (1948; 1961) had only just introduced the public to the logical and programmable computer, to information as a statistical quanta inverse to entropy, to the analogy of homeostasis in the organism and negative feedback in a machine, to the possible simulation of nervous systems, to a universal ontology of things defined by their communication and self-regulation. It concluded with a chapter that touched on the social and political consequences of this revolution, an argument drawn out in the sequel *The Human Use of Human Beings: Cybernetics and Society*, whose first edition (*HUHB*a) was to be published imminently to wild critical and commercial success. Though there is no mention of Čapek or robots in either *Cybernetics* or *HUHB*, both books develop a theory of a 'new Fascism' rendered possible, inevitable even, by cybernetic machines, a theory that is carried to its conclusion in Wiener's final book, *God and Golem, Inc.* (1964).[10] The cover of the first edition of *HUHB*a depicts two figures merged inside a rotating pinion, a circular gear – immanent to it and supplying its force. This is unlike the Tramp in Chaplin's *Modern Times* who gets trapped *between* gears and thereby within a system he in fact transcends, but exactly as the Brothers Čapek put it in 'The System', the worker having become a machine which 'simply rotate[s] like a wheel'. Wiener uses his *Prelude to* R.U.R. to introduce his socio-political argument, which begins by distinguishing Čapek's robot from the cybernetic robot and its philosophy:

> When the play was written, the automatic machine was still in its infancy, or perhaps it is even better to say was still in its gestation. Since then, we have had not merely a succession of automatic machines, but a philosophy of automatic machinery itself.[11]

The following article will discuss what such a 'philosophy of automatic machinery' – a cybernetic philosophy of robots – entails.

Functioning automatic

In truth, except for in that early paper and his *Prelude to* R.U.R. Wiener hardly uses the word 'robot'. Perhaps because of his education in philosophy – he read Plato in Greek as a child, philosophy for his PhD under Josiah Royce and George Santayana, and sat in lectures by William James, Bertrand Russel and Edmund Husserl – he uses a classical term far richer in philosophical significance with roots in Aristotle: 'automatic machine'. In his *Prologue for* R.U.R. Wiener clearly aligns robots and auto- matic machines by claiming that Čapek wrote his play while 'the automatic machine was still in its infancy, or perhaps it is even better to say was still in its gestation.' Wiener swaps out Čapek's robot for what may seem a quaint phrase – automatic machine – but in doing so only increases its intensity.

If 'automatic machine' sounds quaint we can at least in part thank the marketing departments of so many car and arms dealers who have glibly replaced 'automatic' with 'autonomous'. Wiener was consistent in avoiding such a collocation, employing autonomy sparingly and never affirmatively as an attribute of machines.[12] For him, the robot is not *auto-nomos*, subject of its own laws, rather it is precisely that which has to have laws prescribed to it by another, which has no autonomy to speak of. His use instead of 'automatic' for machines accords to the classical tradition of an accidental cause whose end may seem to be intrinsic but is in fact entirely auxiliary. The motor cause in all such cases is *automaton*, quite literally *auto-matên*, 'by itself in vain', an accident caused by a pure motor cause.[13] Aristotle distinguishes *automaton* ('chance', according to its conventional translation) from *tuchê* ('fortune') as an accidental cause that has involved an incidental element deliberation, for example someone who decides to take a stroll and, as fortune would have it, bumps into someone who owes them money. To Aristotle the capacity for decision-making sets one animal, the hu-

5

man, above all others as a political animal, as that whose nature affords a life that need not be confined to mindless automatism; or *should* not be so, for the very flourishing of life is at stake in the activity of training oneself – and one's citizens, for a government – to act evermore virtuously. (*Nicomachaen Ethics*, 1103a21-1103b6.) An automatic machine is *a priori* a being which moves but without a capacity to choose its own ends.

Wiener presses this Aristotelian point in his *Prelude to R.U.R.*. Referring to the opening scene of *R.U.R.* where orders are received for robots by the tens-of-thousand – a Fordist model of mass-production – Wiener notes that the coming aeroplane factory would need 'two dozen Mark 18 assembly-line robots' alone: plus one human: a 'taping expert' to 'tell the machine what it has to do'. The automatic machines Wiener describes may be able to build aircraft but they are not autonomous, they need someone to programme them, to decide their *telos finalis*. A few robots may be able to build fleets of aeroplanes, but they are still the puppets of a programmer. The engineer governs the automatic machines.

Automatic joy

Wiener followed in the tradition of those who build automata in the image of nature. Switching on his flashlight and yelling 'Here, Palomilla!', a motorised buggy drove onstage. Palomilla could steer towards his torch (Moth-mode) or away from it (Bedbug), behaviours determined by a feedback loop involving photosensitive cells on either side of her neck. She was a hoot – *The Harvard Crimson* reported that Palomilla drove into the stage curtain repeatedly and acted with 'at least as much decision and far more speed than an earthworm'.[14] Sensitive to her comicality, Wiener beckoned the audience to consider not 'the particular facial resemblance of this machine to a living organism' – to laugh with Bergson at the one who with mechanical rigidity imitates the fluidity of the living – but its 'soul, and what it does and how it behaves'. The soul of Palomilla was its attempted replication of an inner behaviour essential to organic life, not a superficial appearance.

Principally, the machine was not actually meant to represent a moth or bedbug at all.[15] Rather, by continuously correcting its orientation to balance the intensity of light upon its two photocells it was to model the vital principle discovered by Claude Bernard which would be named 'homeostasis' by the Harvard physiologist Walter Cannon, whose protégé Arturo Rosenblueth would diagnose the overshooting of Wiener's groundbreaking WWII aircraft flight predicting machine as akin to a hand doomed to swing past its object due to cerebellar damage, or a resting hand's Parkinson's shake – both, failures of compensation, debts paid too much or too little.[16] The engineering vocabulary for such self-regulation and overcompensation in machines had already been established by Bell Labs in the 1920s with respect to amplifiers – 'negative' and 'positive feedback', the former since unwanted signals are progressively removed from an output before it is fed back in again as an input, the latter since they are left to accumulate – think of the screech from a loudspeaker when a microphone inputs the speaker's output back into itself over and over.[17] The immediate invention of the collaboration between the physicist Wiener and the physiologist Rosenblueth, together with engineer Julian Bigelow, was a new homology of machine and organisms based on the identification of homeostasis and negative feedback, intention tremors with positive feedback.[18] Palomilla's superficially-comedic indecision, her bouncing into walls, represent both kinds of physio-machinic pathology; her demonstration during Wiener's *Prelude to* R.U.R. being one of the very first public demonstrations of the new age of cybernetic automatic machinery which we see everywhere today.

That the essence or 'soul' of a mechanical automata may appear homologous to the mechanism of an organism involves a second philosophical signification – an aesthetico-cognitive sense – latent within some of the earliest discussions of automata in Greek thought. Wiener seems to touch on this in *Cybernetics* when he writes,

> At every stage of technique since Daedalus or Hero of Alexandria, the ability of the artificer to produce a working simulacrum of a living organism has always intrigued people. This desire to produce and to study automata has always been expressed in terms of the living technique of the age.[19]

That the makers of automata have always drawn 'intrigue', as Wiener says, echoes Hero of Alexandria's own depiction at the start of his opus *On Automata* (approx. 50-100CE) that people consider the makers of automata, ' "wonder-workers [*thaûmatourgous*]" because of the astounding character of the spectacle.'[20] Certainly the automata of the Hellenic world's foremost engineer were wonderful spectacles in a quotidian sense: one involved a mechanical Dionysus walking about with a fennel staff that spurted out milk while he poured libations of wine to dancing Bacchantes and the thunder of falling lead balls.[21] However, to follow Francesco Grillo, there is also a philosophical sense to the 'wonder' that Hero inspired with his automata.[22] This wonder goes beyond that which Aristotle argues is at the root of our enjoyment of 'automatic marionettes' (and philosophy too) early in the *Metaphysics* (983a11-15 and 982b12-21): the aporetic wonder of being dumbfounded by a mechanism's operation which leads to trying to figure it out. Wonder in this sense is the servant of knowledge. Elsewhere, Aristotle offers another explanation whereby the pair are equals: the delight in an imitation of nature itself, man's being 'the most imitative creature in the world', and through the appreciation of a work which imitates nature, a pleasure which 'is one at the same time learning' and is available universally even to the non-philosopher (*Poetics*, 1448b6-20). Aristotle adds that the source of the pleasure of such mimesis is not in the sensible charms of the organism copied, nor the skill of the artisan who copies them, but in the understanding itself of the 'original realities' and 'links of causation' that the mimic representation proffers (*Parts of Animals*, 645a7-15). The 'intrigue' that Wiener refers to as having always been drawn by the makers of automata from the production of the 'working simulacrum of a living organism' derives from the appreciation of the automata's mimesis of nature and the intricacy of the mechanisms at stake.

Today, it would be impossible to feel the wonder that Hero describes about his own automata. They were powered by counterweights of flowing mustard seed and millet.[23] The same goes for the clockwork automata envisaged by Leibniz and his contemporaries, from Thomas Boyle who insisted on a univocal explanation of corpuscles and the inner workings of a clock, to Descartes who held no doubt that 'when swallows come in spring, they operate like clocks. The actions of honeybees are of the same nature', to Hobbes' animals composed of 'springs and wheels as doth a watch'.[24] The aesthetico-cognitive pleasure of automata as such may be transhistorical, but the possibility of its effect is historically determined, and consequently so.

To every age, a distinct 'living technique', Wiener argues, one defined by an archetypical machine – an 'operative image'[25] – whose 'soul' acquires the status of an essential foundation upon which all knowledge of nature stands. He divides the modern era into three such ages: an age of clocks, one of thermodynamic engines and an age of cybernetic machines (specifically, I would argue, the internet).[26] Through cybernetics, Wiener claims to resolve the inadequacies in the thermodynamic operative image. How so?

Full of negentropy

Wiener attributes the prime enunciation of the thermodynamic operative image to Erwin Schrödinger's famous 1944 depiction of life as that which, through metabolism, 'delays the decay into thermodynamical equilibrium (death)'.[27] Some read Schrödinger's thermodynamic negative entropy (later contracted as 'negentropy') as contemporary to cybernetics. This is a misunderstanding. For the sake of clarity and to see how Wiener replaces Schrödinger's image with a cybernetic one, it is worth recapping the modalities and stakes of the problem of entropy in thermodynamics.

The conventional illustration of this begins with a box of billiard balls. Same size, shape, weight and hardness, different colours. On the left of the box white balls are stacked, on the right, black. At this point there is a *disequilibrium* in the dispersion of colours. The box has an *order* to it. It is a state that you are unlikely to find in the universe; its natural occurrence would be highly *improbable*. Now, if you shake the box, soon the balls will be evenly jumbled. No more separation of colours, a *disordered* grey mass like the static of an analogue TV, an *equilibrium* of colours. This is the most *probable* state in the universe. If you did want to see their original ordered disequilibrium again you better be prepared to keep shaking indefinitely.

Now replace shaking balls with a real thermodynamic system. An isolated chamber of atoms, hot and fast ones on the left, cool and slow on the right. The difference in temperature can be exploited to do things, to work – the system is an ordered disequilibrium. Given some time, the atoms would mix themselves up throughout the chamber just like the shaken box of balls. How wrong the ancient atomists were to hold that like attracts like!

The total energy of the system would remain the same, since according to the first law of thermodynamics (the principle of conservation of energy) the amount of energy in the universe can neither increase or decrease, but its conversion back into an ordered and usable energy would be exceptionally unlikely (second law of thermodynamics). It energy has not been destroyed but wasted, dissipated, subject to 'disgregation' or 'entropy'. This is the tendency of everything in the universe, the thermodynamic arrow of time points to a deathly equilibrium of all things, the lifeless 'heat death of the universe'.

Why then is there not only something, but constant regeneration and life? Schrödinger answers that life is that which feeds upon external sources of energy, like a chamber whose entropy naturally increases unless a load of atoms of a different temperature are injected in. Organisms to him are defined by their consuming the universe, metabolising things that hold a calorific value and converting them into waste. Foodstuffs constitute, according to him, 'negative entropy', since they reduce the entropy of the organism and so push back its death; their spent form which the organism emits he calls 'positive entropy'. The operative image here is clear: organisms are thermodynamic engines whose life consists in burning fuel.

Wiener picks out a flaw in this in his critique of bio-physicist Nicolas Rashevsky, but I would argue the glove was made to fit Schrödinger.[28] If the very ruling principle of the thermodynamic operative image is the energy's conservation and degradation of energy into heat, then why, for the same amount of work, Wiener presses, do engines burn so hot while organisms keep so relatively cool? Where is all the radiation and heat from their work?

Wiener anticipates that Schrödinger might reply that there is an essential difference between the chemical energy of an organism and that of an engine. If the analogy can even survive such a distinction, then how can it account for the analogy of brain and nervous system? Wiener rebukes: Are we to construe the organism as outputting thought 'in the form of energy, as the muscle puts out its activity'?[29] The precise wording Wiener employs suggests that he may have had in mind an attack on phrenology by the nineteenth-century American anatomist Thomas Sewall, who lambasted the phrenological analogy of brain and muscle which lead its adherents to believe that, like a large muscle, the bigger the brain the greater its power.[30] Wiener's point is that energetic power is an inappropriate measure of the capacities of a brain and as such these mechanists of the 'age of steam engines' can no more than the clockwork-minded Cartesians account for the 'coupling' of body and mind.

Photos of *R.U.R.* from the Theatre Guild production at the Garrick and Frazee Theatres, New York, 1922/23. Scans by Tobias Higbie.

Against Schrödinger Wiener instead offers a new operative image for an 'age of communication and control': the brain *qua* computer – and not only because of their analogous capacities for logical reasoning, of the realisation of Leibniz's *Machina Ratiocinatrix* in the Turing machine.[31] Instead, by emphasising the parallels of the brain and just-invented digital computer's low energy consumption, Wiener displaces the thermodynamic principle of energy conservation as such. For even if the colossal first digital computers of the 1940s consumed, says Wiener, 'a quantity of energy which may well be measured in kilowatts ... the energy spent per individual operation is almost vanishingly small, and does not even begin to form an adequate measure of the performance of the apparatus'.[32] The work of digital computers and brains needs an altogether new scale of measurement. A new value.

Not *energy*. Certainly not the *mechanical force* of the Cartesian age – Wiener: 'the mechanical brain does not secrete thought "as the liver does bile," as the earlier materialists claimed' (another quote seemingly from the anti-Phrenologist Sewall, though it carries an echo of Pierre Jean Georges Cabanis too).[33] No, *information*. The automaton of today can be neither clock nor engine, but cybernetic machine. Hence Wiener's notorious injunction:

Information is information, not matter or energy.[34]

But what is information? Wiener identifies it with 'negative entropy', using Schrödinger's formulation although in a distinctly unreified sense. Man cannot live *on* negative entropy alone, as to Schrödinger, but one does live *by* negative entropy. Wiener's information as negative entropy depends on an inventive reading of a thought experiment involving the chamber of atoms by James Clerk Maxwell.

Maxwell supposed that entropy could be reversed given an imaginary scenario of a divider inserted into the chamber with a door small enough to fit a single atom, and a doorkeeper or 'pointsman' – William Thomson (Lord Kelvin) nicknamed it the Maxwell Demon – who opened it for hot particles travelling from one side and cold particles from the other. Given such a demon, half of the chamber would gradually fill with hotter particles, the other cooler, and the entropic tendency of the system could be reversed, without the addition of an external source of energy.[35] Maxwell intended his demon to accentuate its own absurdity: such a being or mechanism would be impossible, and even more so following the quantum mechanical discovery, writes Wiener, that the very perception of an atom would increase its energy and change its course.[36] The Maxwell demon is doomed to remain a thought experiment which illustrates the necessity of the degeneration of all systems.

Yet more interesting than jettisoning Maxwell's thought experiment altogether, Wiener says, is to answer the question it poses: How would such a hypothetical demon know to open or close the door in the first place?

The cybernetic answer was revolutionary.[37] Some kind of physical process, radiation say, could be read by a (hypothetical) demon as a channel, a message, from which it could derive knowledge – *information* – about the particle: its position, trajectory and speed. Knowing these, the demon could know when to open and close the door so as to bring about order. The quantity of information the demon has about the particles directly corresponds to its capacity to reverse the entropy of the chamber. Information hence measures the statistical possibility of the negation of entropy – a probability since the second law of thermodynamics does not exactly assert the impossibility of heat returning to energy, but the extreme improbability of its so doing. If entropy constitutes the extent to which a condition is stable, probable, disordered, homogeneous and dead, then information measures its instability, improbability, order, difference and life.[38]

Wiener could now subsume Schrödinger's depiction of life as negative entropy, but do so in a radically original way. It is a thing's capacity for *information* which determines the extent to which it is alive. Organisms live not merely because their environment provides them with energy which they consume like an engine, but more fundamentally because they adapt themselves to their environment by drawing adequate information from it. The essential quality of life is not metabolism, but homeostasis. Wiener stresses that the energy the demon receives from the world, the particle's radiation, is 'far less significant than the transfer of information'.[39] In this way he resolves the problem of why brains and computers are so unlike engines in that their output far exceeds their energy input. Energy is an inappropriate measurement of the work of nervous systems and computers. Instead, the age of cybernetic machines is premised on *information*.

We might note that this is why apologists for the vast energy consumption of computationally-expensive processes such as cryptocurrency mining and machine learning frequently retort that energy cannot be used to value the work of such processes, only information can. Their fallacy lies in a failure to consider whether their so-called 'information' will ever be able to reverse the heat death of the system named Earth that their computations are contributing to, and if not whether it is actually no more than a perhaps beautiful mode of entropy, like a glimmer of petrol on the surface of a stream. This is the junction at which cybernetics came to peel off especially in the 1960s into those who 'went off into computers' and 'input-output', as Margaret Mead and Gregory Bateson describe computer science, and ecologists like themselves who recognised Wiener's cybernetics to be 'the science of the whole circuit.'[40] Unfortunately, many ecologists came to mirror the mistakes of such 'computer scientists' by rejecting the conceptual value of information to ecology outright.

Dancing mechanic

The discovery of the statistical concept of information as negative entropy allows Wiener to formulate a new 'operational image' and 'working simulacra of a living organism', or what Heidegger calls the 'fundamental science' of the age.[41] To live is to possess a greater degree of information than the entropic forces of death about. Yet Heidegger failed to appreciate the philosophical foundations that Wiener had laid, framing cybernetics as sovereign of just the positive sciences. Instead his cybernetics should be read as a system of thought in the vein of Leibniz's monadology, to which it can be read as a reply. Today this much is becoming increasingly acknowledged, for one through the work of Yuk Hui,[42] while Wiener's recognition of Leibniz as founding the principles of digital computing continues to be detailed by works such as the recently published collection *Leibniz on Binary: The Invention of Computer Arithmetic*, edited by Lloyd Strickland and Harry R. Lewis (2022).[43] What is not so appreciated is how Wiener's cybernetics not only stands upon but then usurps the *Monadology*, and how information is premised *critically* upon Leibniz's theory of perception, and cybernetic control on its notion of domination.

Wiener bestowed various honorifics upon Leibniz – 'patron saint for cybernetics', 'in more than one way, the intellectual ancestor of the ideas of this book [*The Human Use of Human Beings*]' – but beneath these the critical relation between cybernetics and the monadology surfaces precisely in Wiener's discussion of the Maxwell demon:

> In the long run, the Maxwell demon is itself subject to a random motion corresponding to the temperature of its environment, and, as Leibniz says of some of his monads, it receives a large number of small impressions, until it falls into 'a certain vertigo' and is incapable of clear perceptions. In fact, it ceases to act as a Maxwell demon.[44]

This is a reference to Leibniz's depiction of death as '*un vertige*' in which substances (monads) are unable to distinguish their perceptions, when monads see nothing but 'a vast number of *petites perceptions*' as when 'we continuously spin around the same direction' (*M*21).[45] Wiener reads the Maxwell demon and thereby information directly with respect to Leibniz's infinitesimal notion of perception, and thereon he launches his attack.

Let us briefly summarise what Leibniz's theory of perception entails, since it is key to Wiener's theory of information. In the *Monadology* every substance is a so-called 'monad' which mirrors the entire universe from a singular perspective defined by the relative clarity and confusion of its infinite perceptions. Only the primitive monad of God clearly and distinctly perceives – in Leibniz's language 'apperceives' – every perception. All others are subject to an infinity of perceptions which they know only in the most confused of senses, as well as perhaps a few which they do apperceive. The distinction between mere perceptions and apperceived perceptions (or simply apperceptions) allows Leibniz to posit substances as subject to infinite degrees of perception. This departs from Descartes who held only three: the confused and obscure perception of sensation, the clear and obscure perception of pleasure and pain, and – for human souls – the clear and the distinct perception of the substances (mind, body, God), number, duration and so on.[46] Even the primitive monads of stones will receive an infinity of perceptions, but the higher monads of animals and humans may also distinctly apperceive some. These undulate throughout their life, coming and going, though a human may raise their apperceptive potential, may potentialise itself, through the embrace and study of its divinely chosen world, and moreover through inventing automata: through 'imitating something of [the system of the universe] through smaller scale constructions (*échantillons architectoniques*) of their own' and thereby making of itself 'a little divinity of its own sphere' (*M*21). We live and we *live* to the extent that we apperceive.

Hence to suffer an abject lack of apperceptions is a kind of death – as it is for Wiener's Maxwell demon. So-called 'death' to Leibniz is a stupor, dream or a fainting fit from which nothing is remembered. Truly, monads only die if God would decide to annihilate them by miracle; what 'death' *really* is is a descent into a vertiginous coma-like confusion: 'an infinity of little perceptions all at once, in which there is no single one which is clearly distinguished from the others' (*M*21). Life cannot escape death, it emerges out of it to the extent that its apperceptions 'fold' out of its perceptions.

Leibniz's concept of death is the basis upon which Wiener, in the passage above, can depict the Maxwell demon who 'ceases to act as a Maxwell demon' – who dies – as akin to a monad who 'falls into "a certain vertigo" and is incapable of clear perceptions.' Wiener is aligning the entropy of the dead Maxwell's demon with the apperceptionless perceptions of the dead monad, and so vice versa, the information or negative entropy of the living demon with the apperception of the monad. *Information with apperception and entropy with mere perception*. For the cybernetician the informationalising/apperceiving Maxwell demon is more than a thought experiment, it is the living organism as such. In the same way that the monad comes to life when apperceiving, comes to death when it cannot, Wiener carries on to define living beings as 'metastable Maxwell demons', as *beyond* (meta-) the condition of deathly entropic stability.[47] To this Leibnizian Wiener, a being's drawing of information from undifferentiated entropy constitutes its temporary relief of life from death.

Hook up

If the claim that the modern concept of information is based in Leibniz's theory of perception seems bold, consider that Wiener had already demonstrated familiarity with Leibniz's notion in his remarkable (though unremarkably neglected) philosophical entries for the 1918-1920 *Encyclopedia Americana*. An entire entry – 'Apperception' – constitutes an intervention by the young Wiener into the conflation into the single word 'perception' of both the vague and imperfect apprehension of things and the clear and self-conscious apprehension of them – or what Leibniz calls apperception – by the day's Anglo-American psychological orthodoxy.[48] Against them he invokes first Leibniz's theory of perception and then its contemporary psychological inheritors, Johann Wilhelm Wundt, Friedrich Herbart and William James. Much of the entry reads as though about cybernetics: the depiction of how, for Herbart, the incursion of a new idea into the mind 'disturbs the equilibrium', the turn to James' depiction of infant consciousness as 'a big, blooming, buzzing confusion', the formal situation of the monadology as the origin in need of return; but also the stress upon – and departure from – the windowlessness of monads; their being, the young Wiener notes, 'with no reference whatever to the apprehension of external things.' Wiener in his cybernetic writings would emphasise exactly this point too: Leibniz's windowless monads are like, he writes, 'little figures which dance on the top of a music box ... [they] have no trace of communication with the outer world, except this one-way stage of communication with the pre-established mechanism of the music box.'[49]

Whereas in the young Wiener's 'Apperception' entry he speaks through the voice of others and leaves moot the consequences of opening the hermetic monad's perception onto an outside world, *Cybernetics* with all its drumming apocalypticism constitutes a profound reflection on what it means for the monad to have windows, on the splitting open of Leibniz's 'true atom'.

Control: one can neither talk seriously about apperception nor information without also appreciating what is entailed by the second verb in the title of Wiener's opus *Cybernetics, or Communication* and Control *in the Animal and the Machine* and how it derives by necessity from Wiener's monstrous adoption of Leibniz's theory of apperception as the foundation of his – our – concept of information.

Recall that for Leibniz the 'Perfect agreement of all, which have no communication with each other, could come only from a common cause': God.[50] Wiener sees this point as pertinent enough to *Cybernetics* to elaborate:

Each [monad] lives in its own closed universe, with a perfect causal chain from the creation or from minus infinity in time to the indefinitely remote future; but closed though they are, they correspond one to the other through the pre-established harmony of God.'[51]

This causal chain from every monad to God cannot be mechanically explained via a transfer of force or energy from one to the next, since monads do not interact with one another. Rather they possess an internal principle of change, an 'appetite', which consists in a striving from one perception that God has pre-inscribed in them to another. Their perceptions are internal, their causes *intra*-substantive, not inter (*M*7). How is it then possible for a monad to seem as though it acts upon another? Leibniz's answer is that the links of a 'golden chain' that make monads seem as though they determine one another are their relative explanatory capacities, their relative degree of apperception with respect to one another.

This chain is organised in a pyramid. Since to Leibniz apperception involves clarity about the divine wisdom instilled in every aspect of the universe, the golden chain involves a hierarchy of monads which, ascending from so many coma-like vertigo-suffering bare monads to the primitive monad of God who perfectly apperceives everything, can ever more clearly explain why something is as it is, or better, why it is so so as to contribute to God's plan for the best of possible worlds. The hierarchy of the universe is ordered according to the capacity of all substances to decipher (apperceive) God's infinitely detailed cryptogram. In this sense we can say that the monad of the mind causes those of the fingers and toes to swim in the sea because, although the digits merely perceive the infinite ripples and contours of the water, the mind has a greater degree of clear and distinct perceptions (a more active appetite) than the confused and relatively passive digits, so it can offer a better explanation than them. The toes in turn can better explain the perceptions of their hairs, and so on *ad infinitum*. A monad's greater degree of apperception relative to another constitutes its *domination* over it. As Leibniz says, 'considered in terms of the monads themselves, domination and subordination consist only in degrees of perception.'[52]

Leibniz's taxonomy is a cascading pyramid of determination in its triple sense of knowledge, power and will, with the primitive monad of God at its apex, the bare monads of minerals and plants at its base with animals above them, and human souls organised in between. This is not only a pyramid of knowledge, but also inalienably domination and subordination. *Of power*. But of course, only by analogy since Leibniz's windowless monads cannot, in fact, inter-communicate with or control one another.

What happens when the older Wiener retains Leibniz's logic of apperception but plugs photocells into the monads, such that the *analogy* of communication with others is rendered *actual*? When windows are punched into the monad, and its apperceptions involve others? What are the consequences of all this for the cybernetic automatic machine and its world?

Playing yourself

Wiener offers a certain kind of structure as an answer, with a set of rules, which is to say a kind of a game, but this is neither the structure of the structuralists nor the game of game theory. Critiquing his contemporaries, it is something of his own.

Wiener's critique of Structuralism is targeted at Benoît Mandelbrot and Roman Jakobson, the former having copy-edited the original *Cybernetics* manuscript and the latter having collaborated with Wiener on a stochastical study of phonemes in Russian after inheriting a Professorship in Slavic languages at Harvard in 1949,[53] a post established for Wiener's eminent father Leo Wiener who held it for the greater part of half-a-century.

In an addition to the second edition of *The Human Use of Human Beings*, published in 1954, Wiener reflects that Mandelbrot and Jakobson,

> consider communication to be a game played in partnership by the speaker and the listener against the forces of confusion, represented by the ordinary difficulties of communication.[54]

He explains this with recourse to an argument which he attributes to Mandelbrot, which itself draws from Shannon's work on the optimum redundancy of letters in 'A Mathematical Theory of Communication' (1948). Through computational analysis, Mandelbrot, he writes, shows how natural languages tend towards an optimal distribution of word lengths, which implies that they have over time undergone a process of natural selection. This is, as opposed to artificial languages like Esperanto where no such optimal distribution of word lengths is to be found. Wiener writes that this natural 'attrition of language', a phylogenetic homeostasis of words, implies that languages evolve towards a sort of 'optimum form of distribution' through the processes of guarding against confusion. The words in languages naturally evolve towards states ever richer in information.

This being the case, Wiener argues, the 'philosophical assumption' of Mandelbrot's 'ordinary' and 'normal' linguistic game theory is that the 'major opponent of the conversant is the entropic tendency of nature itself'. The structuralist deployment of information treats languages as though the actual speakers who constitute them are no more than nature passively awaiting an adequate linguist. The structuralists play a game against the universal tendency of nature to deteriorate into entropy.

What right does Wiener have to depict these structural linguists as game theorists? For one thing because, while Wiener was revising *HUHB* Mandelbrot himself was doing so. In 'An informational theory of the statistical structure of languages' (1953) Mandelbrot writes of the 'association of language to a game', specifically with the famous game of Ferdinand de Saussure's *Course in General Linguistics* in mind: chess.[55] He invokes Saussure's depiction of chess as being, 'like an artificial realization of what language offers in a natural form' – an argument supported by three premises.[56] First, the state of the board at any one moment corresponds to the state of a language. Second, both language and chess depend on unchangeable conventions which pre-exist and persist through every game and conversation. Finally, a single move can 'revolutionize the whole game'. Thereby Saussure introduces his signature distinction between conventional 'diachronic' linguistics, which concerns the past and future 'evolutionary phase' and 'historical grammar' of a language, and his own 'synchronic' linguistics, which concerns the present arrangement of language-states. In structural linguistics as in chess, Saussure argues, it only matters what happened ten-moves prior in as much as this diachronic fact led to the current synchronic state of the game.

Central to Wiener's critique of Mandelbrot and Jakobson's structural cybernetics is Saussure's admission that his analogy between language and chess has one weakness – the need to imagine in language an 'unconscious or unintelligent player' who makes their moves like the player in chess.[57] The players of the structuralist game are relegated to external diachronic forces as much as the previous moves are just historical events. They are not exactly irrelevant, since 'a language can only be compared to the idea of the game of chess taken as a whole, including both [synchronic] positions and [diachronic] moves',[58] but external forces and past moves come under a lesser class of analysis. The actual game of a chess game for Saussure has little to do with the two players; it resides in the analyst's reading of the current field of play. Lévi-Strauss puts this fact succinctly in *The Story of Lynx* (1991) when he answers the question of who the opponent of the structuralist anthropologist is: 'We play against myths'.[59] The opponent of the structuralist game is no more the natural entropy of ignorance, and while '[ignorance] plays a difficult game', Wiener writes, 'he may be defeated by our intelligence as thoroughly as by a sprinkle of holy water.'[60]

In the *Human Use of Human Beings* Wiener names the opponent of structural analysis an 'Augustinian evil': natural entropy, mere ignorance, epistemological lack, where 'the black of the world is negative and is the mere absence of white'.[61] He identifies it with Einstein's formulation, 'God may be subtle, but he isn't plain mean'; and it is the evil of Leibniz's theodicy, the good deriving from apperception of God's creation, evil ignorance thereof.[62] In truth Wiener formerly saw himself as battling the same enemy, as evidenced by a letter he wrote in August 1933 with an eye to events in Europe:

> Knowledge is a good which is above usefulness, and ignorance an evil, and we have enlisted as good soldiers in the army whose enemy is ignorance and whose watchword is Truth. ... This is of course the point of view of the German liberal scholar of the middle of the last century ... All modern professional scholarship is the heir of that Germany.[63]

For Wiener this calling would not survive the coming war wherein he would be enlisted to develop an apparatus that could shoot down Nazi aeroplanes, the evil of bombs pouring from the sky; an *enemy bomber* whose possible future points of interception are not only subject to the entropy of uncertainty, given the mores, the character, of their aircraft's signature flying pattern, but whose pilot's cunning evasive manoeuvres strive to confuse their enemy's attempts to decipher a targetable position. The opponent here is very much not nature. It is an enemy who actively resists. Who encrypts their signature and attacks their enemy's capacity to forcefully decrypt it through disinformative behaviour. The dance of the enemy aircraft and anti-aircraft battery does not just involve coding and decoding, as per Mandelbrot and Jakobson's playerless structural cybernetics, but of enciphering, disinformation and cryptanalysis (surveillance). Not the darkness of entropy as the lack of informational light but, as Wiener puts it, 'white and black belong to two opposed armies drawn up in line facing one another.'[64] Communication as conflict between enemies who 'bluff' and employ 'jamming forces in order to adapt themselves to new communication techniques', enemies who actively seek to plunge each other into confusion.[65]

A game of six halves

At stake is not merely information or communication theory, but cryptology: a martial paradigm which construes its enemy to be, Wiener says, a 'Manichean evil'. Modern cryptology is the study both of *cryptography*, which concerns the techniques of mathematically encrypting and decrypting messages (cryptograms) between friends so as to be unintelligible to enemies, and *cryptanalysis*, the techniques of forcefully breaking open the cryptograms of an enemy so as to strengthen one's position, as well as its inverse *disinformation* ('pseudography'?), the meta-technique of distributing false-messages and false-cryptograms into the enemy's internal communications so as to divide their very coherence and even their very ability to distinguish friend from foe, rendering them a weaker player. This final side is why, according to Chelsea Manning in a recent *FT* interview, 'The Russians are spending way more on spreading disinformation [in Ukraine] than on trying to obtain secrets.'[66] By contrast information theory only involves an encoding and decoding which does not take the friend-enemy distinction into account, and therefore 'the political' which is established on this distinction (Carl Schmitt). Whereas the Augustinian paradigm of information theory conceives the passive darkness of ignorance to be its opponent, the Manichean involves an enemy who actively resists, a real opponent in a struggle for domination within a cryptological field of battle.

In war, diplomacy, politics, law, business – in the war-diplomacy-politics-law-business of actually constituted science – the negation of entropy of one is the amplification of entropy of another. The greater the surveillance into the bomber's imminent position, of the cryptoanlysed information, the greater the control over it, the closer it draws to death. In such conflict the light of one is the darkness of another; the Manichaean struggle is a zero-sum-game.

Wiener's critique of the apolitical game theory of the structuralists leads to his critique of Game Theory proper, John von Neumann and Oskar Morgenstern's simultaneously nascent science. In *HUHB* he broaches this via Claude Shannon[67] – but not the Shannon of 'A Mathematical Theory of Communication' (1948), the sun around which information theorists tend to revolve. Rather the Shannon of 'Communication Theory of Secrecy Systems' (1945 but classified until 1949), a product of his wartime work mathematically proving the security of Roosevelt and Churchill's encrypted telephone line.[68] In this paper, which establishes modern cryptology as a statistical discipline and lays the foundations for his theory of information, Shannon explicitly depicts the relation between cipher designer (*cryptographer*) and breaker (*cryptanalyst*) as a game which accords with that of von Neumann and Morgenstern's theory of strategic games, one played between mutual 'enemies'.[69] In turn, the founders of Game Theory had depicted the fundamental questions essential to all games of strategy as being in a more abstract sense essentially cryptological too:

> How does each player plan his course, i.e. how does one formulate an exact concept of a strategy? What information is available to each player at every stage of the game? What is the role of a player being informed about the other player's strategy? About the entire theory of the game?[70]

Von Neumann and Morgenstern's Game Theory is cryptological in that it involves a contest between players over each other's information. Not merely the synchronic arrangement of chess pieces but of each other's plans and diachronic future moves: not for the sake of intellectual curiosity but to predict, outmanoeuvre and beat them. Stabilised in the grave, *pax perpetua*. Critiques abound of the rational self-interested subjectivity assumed by conventional Game Theory – Wiener's is internal to his philosophical system. 'Naturally', Wiener writes, 'von Neumann's picture of the player as a completely intelligent, completely ruthless person is an abstraction and a perversion of the facts.'[71]

His argument is that given that the struggle for life *over one another* is determined by a zero-sum cryptological struggle over information, it should not be assumed that all players have equal capacities for play, equal knowledge from which to extrapolate one another's moves: 'It is rare to find a large number of thoroughly clever and unprincipled persons playing a game together.' Instead an exponential disequilibrium of capacities should be assumed, one that skews control to the information-rich with respect to the information-poor. Wiener calls the former knaves, the latter fools:

> Where the knaves assemble, there will always be fools; and where the fools are present in sufficient numbers, they offer a more profitable object of exploitation for the knaves. ... [T]he fool operates in a manner which, by and large, is as predictable as the struggles of a rat in a maze.[72]

Since predictability is aligned with entropy in Wiener's information theory, the fool is closer to disorganisation and death. The knave is their opposite: so organised, unpredictable and alive to the fool that their moves increasingly stupefy. Adam Curtis' *Hypernormalisation* (2016) portrays such a knave in Vladislav Surkov, whose ideological and practical support of Putin's regime entailed his 'play with and undermin[ing of the Russian people's] very perception of the world, so they are never sure of what is really happening ... [A] strategy of power which keeps any opposition constantly confused. A ceaseless shapeshift[ing] that is unstoppable because it is indefinable.'[73] Von Neumann and Morgenstern's Game Theory presumes their players to be stable equals: the subjects of Wiener's cybernetic game theory are locked into rendering one another more or less capable players. Given that there is an infinite quantity of information to be accumulated, that according to Wiener's system 'no man is either all fool or all knave', the best one can say is that the game is always open to be played, however skewed against the information-poor it may become, however much their opportunity for control tends towards zero.

Shoshana Zuboff's notion of 'surveillance capitalism' touches on this dynamic while putting the cart before the horse.[74] Any economic system would have to contend with the potential for an accumulation of information and imbalance of capabilities the cybernetic game of control involves. The surveillance that she dwells on is only one type of move in a game which also involves encoding, decoding, encryption, decryption and disinformation. Both surveillance and disinformation imply each other as violent acts against an enemy whose goal is the relative gain of control, the former an accumulation through theft, the latter a diminishing through poison. To dwell solely on surveillance, as Zuboff does, is to solve one of six sides of a Rubik's Cube, and to focus only on capitalism is to play for one row. The relative degree of power is what is at stake, not just the accumulation of secrets, which is why Wiener's critique leads him to foresee it giving rise to not only a new kind of capitalism but a new kind of Fascism as well as its concomitant subjectivity, the automatic machine.

Machine à gouverner

Clearly we are no longer in the land of Leibniz's Best of Possible Worlds.

When Wiener renders actual Leibniz's analogy of the intercommunication of substances, when he shows that due to the emergence of the cybernetic operative image the beings who waltz upon the music box do so by actually apperceiving one another not by acting out an infinitely-detailed script that a benevolent God has authored in them at the beginning of time, Wiener replaces Leibniz's pyramidal preestablished harmony of all beings with, to use André Robinet's phrase, a 'tangle of interconnected myriagons'.[75] Not a horizontal plane à la Hardt and Negri but an infinity of pyramids in every direction. To reinterpret cybernetician Warren McCulloch's neologism which is currently enjoying a moment of vogue, a 'heterarchy' not a hierarchy, one in which, as Bruno Latour puts it, any 'harmony is postestablished locally'.[76] If in Leibniz each monad only acts *as if* it apperceives the other, but truly acts out a script chosen by God for its role in the play, The Best of Possible Worlds, the older Wiener realises that if monads *actually* apperceive one another, the single God-pinched hierarchy is smashed to an infinity of hierarchies, and with this not only divine authorship but all sense of benevolence in the universe too. Instead of seeming to dominate one another in a single great pyramid, these actual intercommunicating beings actually do so. The game for Leibniz is in the Augustinian deciphering of the infinitely detailed pyramid; for Wiener it is a total, Manichean, cryptological state of conflict – what may be called a 'cryptowar'.[77]

Wiener declares the horizon to which the Manichean cybernetic age tends a '*machine à gouverner*', taking the phrase from Dominique Dubarle, a Dominican theologian whose *Le Monde* review of *Cybernetics* he uncharacteristically reproduces across three pages of *The Human Use of Human Beings*.[78] Dubarle defines the *machine à gouverner* – Wiener leaves it untranslated – as a 'State apparatus covering all systems of political decisions'. This is a machine with 'enormous privileges' which will render 'the State as the best-informed player at each particular level'; being so advantaged in the six sides of the cryptowar that it will 'permit the State under all circumstances to beat every player of a human game other than itself by offering this dilemma: either immediate ruin, or planned cooperation.' It constitutes no less than a 'A great World State' and 'a world worse than hell for every clear mind' – no less than the rise of a 'prodigious Leviathan' compared to which that of Hobbes was 'a pleasant joke.'[79] Wiener and Dubarle envision the great cryptological machines of our day: of the Five Eyes, China, Russia, Israel and so on, each of which is shrouded in a secrecy which only admits meaningful competition from state cryptological players or their servants, or from internal leakers to which the cryptological friend/enemy distinction will be applied, especially to those at the bottom (Edward Snowden) but also at the top (Hillary Clinton's server).

Simondonians take note! What is it that Dubarle says the *machine à gouverner* gathers its information about and strives to control, abstractly? None other than, writes Dubarle, '*les réalitée humaines*'. The cybernetic Leviathan's awesome power over humans is derived from its being a Maxwell's demon of human realities. In *this* sense we can say that the reality of humans is distinct from the *machine à gouverner*: they relate through competition and are not on the same side. Yet this very exteriority, this capacity to think relations of conflict involving a 'colossal state machine ... [which is] quite possibly being planned by a secret military project for the purposes of combat and domination', writes Wiener in 1950,[80] is what Simondon considers problematic. He denounces the separation of human and machinic realities as expressions of a 'primitive xenophobia', 'facile humanism' and a 'system of defence against techniques'. *Les réalitée humaine* is essential to *les réalitée technique*! To deny this is to be alienated from the essential technicity of life; to impose 'purely mythical and imaginery' relations of competition and domination between humans and machines. To render 'machines in the service of man' is to reduce them to slaves argus Simondon, 'in the belief that the reduction to slavery is a sure way to prevent any rebellion.'[81] It is, for Simondon, to reduce them to the mythical creature of the robot.

Wiener's problematic however was never about an autonomous machine enslaving humans. It was about humans *using* others as if they were machines, controlling them such that they become as automatic as Palomilla was organic. Hence the title of his second cybernetic book which he had wanted to call *Cassandra* or *Pandora* as a wake up call to humanity (if a tragically unheeded one) until his publisher demurred, and which was instead titled *The* Human Use *of Human Beings*.[82] It is about humans *using* each other as machines, and about a virtuous *human* use for each other as *humans*. Certainly, in his *Prelude to* R.U.R. Wiener entertained the kind of sci-fi claim about machines enslaving humans that would have made Simondon squirm:

> Machines demand to be understood, or they will take the bread from the mouths of workers. Not only that, but they demand that we understand man as man, or we shall become their slaves and not they ours.

Doubtless also he considered real the danger of automation to human employment – just a few days after his *Prologue for* R.U.R. he declared that American labour would soon become so superfluous that whole industries would have to be nationalised and a 'Socialistic state' be imposed.[83] However the major threat of machines that he returns to consistently in his cybernetic writings is that humans will become stupefied through losing the game of secrecy, lies and bluff which cybernetics affords. They would lose all capacity for choosing their own ends and would become automata, dependent on superiors for programming.

In his last book *God and Golem,* Inc. (1964), Wiener describes being familiar with a certain kind of engineer and manager, mostly within America, which he has come to call a 'gadget worshipper'. Such a 'devoted priest of power' strives to create workers who are 'capable of great industry but of little independent initiative. ... Meek, self-effacing, and wholly at his disposal ... Limbs at the disposal of his brain.' They serve those above them entirely and shirk all personal responsibility. Chance, superiors, unquestionable policies and 'a mechanical device which one cannot fully understand but which has a presumed objectivity' – an apt description for a popular understanding of today's machine learning algorithms – are all claimed as responsible instead. The gadget worshipper is precisely the figure who in the earlier cybernetic writings he derides as 'not in their full right as responsible human beings, but ... cogs and levers and rods' with respect to which 'it matters little that their raw material is flesh and blood'.[84] Finally in this text Wiener not only refers to *R.U.R.* in print – 'such subordinates are contemplated by Čapek's play' – but he also gives an example of one: Adolf Eichmann.[85]

Daniel Nemenyi is a research fellow at the Leuphana Institute of Advanced Studies (LIAS) and a member of the Radical Philosophy *editorial collective.*

Notes

1. Walter Prichard Eaton, *The Theatre Guild: The first ten years* (New York: Brentano's, 1929), 66, 113, 253.

2. By my count *RP*'s roughly 1,500 contributors have referred to robots in these three ways. First, as an ontological other, primarily an economic one, against whom humans must compete ('Will a robot take *your* job?', asks Amelia Horgan in *RP* 2.11). Second, an existential sense whereby the robot is a standardised, reactionary and failed simulacrum of a qualified existence, in the sense that for Penelope Deutscher, Simone de Beauvoir oft portrays women who 'reduce themselves to robotic, slick or passive stereotypes of femininity' (*RP* 96); or C. W. Mills admonishes 'cultural domination' for producing 'cheerful robots' (Vincent di Norcia, *RP* 12); and Mary Daly, according to Jean Grimshaw (*RP* 49), depicts male interactions as tending to leave women 'lobotomised, moronised, robotised; as fembots, as the "puppets of Papa", even as "mutants"'. In the hands of the Western right, this existential sense has from the start had an acutely Sinophobic signification, from *The Times* being quoted back in *RP* 8 as depicting 'the ordinary Chinese' as 'robotised like an army' to the implicitly robotic way in which compliance to Covid-19 restrictions has been racialised in the West (Jana Cattier, *RP* 2.12). Related, it pertains to the trope of a neurodivergent Other, in the sense that Paulo Virno identifies the autist with the humourless AI (Jeremy Gilbert, *RP* 154). Third, a broadly-'cybernetic' position which acknowledges as historical fact and universal political theatre our '*robotically adjusted life*', in Achille Mbembe's words (*RP* 200); a position comparable to Donna Haraway's cyborg (Marsden, *RP* 78) no less than Claudia Aradau and Mercedes Bunz's depiction of 'AI [as] a distributed sociotechnical system' (*RP* 2.12); and Finn Brunton's playful dialogue with a chatbot of his own creation (*RP* 164), all of which deny the ontological separation and moral priority of human before their machines.

3. Jeremy Gilbert, 'Having a laugh', *Radical Philosophy* 154, 2009, 62–64.
4. Henri Bergson, *On Laughter*, trans. Cloudesley Brereton and Fred Rothwell (London: Macmillan, 1921), 9–10.
5. Ivan Klíma, *Karel Čapek: Life and Work*, trans. Norma Comrada (North Haven: Catbird Press, 2001), 78–84.
6. ibid., 72–73.
7. Aaron Bastani, *Fully Automated Luxury Communism: A Manifesto* (London: Verso, 2019)
8. Louis Chude-Sokei, *The Sound of Culture: Diaspora and Black Technopoetics* (Middletown, Conncticut: Wesleyan University Press, 2016), 63–68.
9. Paul Virilio, *The Information Bomb*, trans. Chris Turner (London & New York: Verso, 2000), 135.
10. Norbert Wiener, *The Human Use of Human Beings: Cybernetics and Society*, 1st ed. (London: Eyre / Spottiswoode, 1950), 60–61, 102, 209, 214.
11. Norbert Wiener, *Prologue for* R. U. R. *(5 May 1950)*, https://archivesspace.mit.edu/repositories/2/archival_objects/151494, Cambridge: MC22, box 29b, folder 657, MIT, MIT Archives, Cambridge, MA.
12. See for example, Norbert Wiener, *The Human Use of Human Beings: Cybernetics and Society*, 2nd ed. (London: Sphere Books, 1954), 157.
13. *Dictionary of Untranslatables: A Philosophical Lexicon*, ed. Barbara Cassin et al., trans. Steven Rendall et al. (Princeton and Oxford: Princeton University Press, 2014), 534.
14. Paul W. Mandel, 'Cabbages & Kings: Deus ex Machina', The Harvard Crimson, 10 May 1950, https://www.thecrimson.com/article/1950/5/10/cabbages-kings-plast-friday-and/; W. K., 'Revival of R. U. R. With New Prologue: Presenting Palomilla As Plato Said', *The New York Times* (New York), 7 May 1950, accessed 9 August 2017, https://www.nytimes.com/1950/05/07/archives/revival-of-rur-with-new-prologue-presenting-palomilla-as-plato-said.html. See the remarkable collection of photos and texts relating to Wiener's moth/bedbug at: Reuben Hoggett, '1949 – Wiener's Moth "Palomilla" – Wiener / Wiesner / Singleton', Cybernetic Zoo, 9 September 2009, https://cyberneticzoo.com/cyberneticanimals/1949-wieners-moth-wiener-wiesner-singleton/.
15. Wiener, *HUHBa*, 192–195; Wiener, *HUHBb*, 142–145; Ronald R. Kline, *The Cybernetics Moment: Or Why We Call Our Age the Information Age* (Baltimore: John Hopkins University Press, 2015), 76–77.
16. Norbert Wiener, *I Am a Mathematician: The Later Life of a Prodigy* (Cambridge, MA: MIT Press, 1956), 252–54.
17. H. T. Friis and A. G. Jensen, 'High frequency amplifiers', *The Bell System Technical Journal* 3, no. 2 (1924): 181–205; H. S. Black, 'Stabilized Feedback Amplifiers', *Bell System Technical Journal* 13, no. 1 (January 1934): 1–18.
18. First was published in, Norbert Wiener, Arturo Rosenblueth and Julian Bigelow, 'Behavior, Purpose, Teleology', *Philosophy of Science*, no. 10 (1943): 18–24.
19. Norbert Wiener, *Cybernetics: or Control and Communication in the Animal and the Machine*, 2nd ed. (Cambridge, MA: MIT Press, 1961), 39. Daedelus is depicted in both Plato's *Euthyphro* (11d4) and *Meno* (97d4) as having invented statues which moved of their own accord, as well as the wooden cow which was so realistic that the Cretan Bull would mate with it and thereby cunning Pasiphaë who was hiding inside. (Diodorus Siculus, *Bibliotheca historica* 4.77).
20. Hero of Alexandria, *On Automata*, 1.1, 1.7. Translation of Francesco Grillo, 'Hero of Alexandria's Automata: a critical edition and translation, including a commentary on Book One' (PhD thesis, University of Glasgow, 2019), http://theses.gla.ac.uk/76774.
21. Hero, *On Automata*, I.
22. ibid., 114-17.
23. ibid., 1.9.
24. G. W. Leibniz, *Philosophical Papers and Letters*, 2nd ed., ed. and trans. Leroy E. Loemker (Dordrechy, Boston & London: Kluwer Academic Publishers, 1969), 460; Peter R. Anstey, *The Philosophy of Robert Boyle* (London: Routledge, 2000), 55–60; René Descartes, *The Philosophical Writings of Descartes*, trans. John Cottingham, Robert Stoothoff and Dugald Murdoch (Cambridge: Cambridge University

Press, 1984), I.99–108; Thomas Hobbes, *Leviathan*, ed. Richard Tuck (Cambridge: Cambridge University Press, 1996), 9.

25. Norbert Wiener, *God and Golem*, Inc. (London: Chapman & Hall, 1964), 37.

26. Daniel Nemenyi, 'What is an internet? Norbert Wiener and the Society of Control' (PhD thesis, Kingston University, 2018).

27. Erwin Schrödinger, *What is Life? The Physical Aspect of the Living Cell* (Cambridge: Cambridge University Press, 1992), ch. 6; Wiener, *Cybernetics*, 11, 41.

28. Wiener, *Cybernetics*, 40–42. That Wiener here singles out the pioneering mathematical biophysicist Nicolas Rashevsky as such a 'conservative physiologist' is interesting given Rashevsky's groundbreaking neural network model having become a staple concept of the early cybernetic group via Walter Pitts (his student) and Warren McCulloch, and from there into machine learning and the very architecture of the internet today. A critical juncture worthy of future consideration. See, Tara H. Abraham, '(Physio)logical circuits: The intellectual origins of the McCulloch–Pitts neural networks', *Journal of the History of the Behavioral Sciences* 38, no. 1 (2002): 3–25, https://onlinelibrary.wiley.com/doi/abs/10.1002/jhbs.1094.

29. Wiener, *Cybernetics*, 42, 132.

30. Thomas Sewall, *An Examination of Phrenology: In Two Lectures*, 2nd ed. (Boston: D. S. King, 1839), 59.

31. 'We have already spoken of the computing machine, and consequently the brain, as a logical machine. ... Here the chief work is that of Turing['s 'On Computable Numbers with and Application to the Entscheidungsproblem' (1936)]. We have said before that the *machina ratiocinatrix* is nothing but the *calculus ratiocinator* of Leibniz with an engine in it; and just as modern mathematical logic begins with this calculus, so it is inevitable that its present engineering development should cast a new light on logic.' Wiener, *Cybernetics*, 125.

32. ibid., 42, 132.

33. ibid. Sewall considers a possible phrenological position that, '[the brain] is a secreting organ, and elaborates thought *as the liver does bile* from the blood'. That it can be coherently deployed doubly both to depict the operational image of the clock as well as that of thermodynamics, as described above, may be in lieu of its own echo of Pierre Jean Georges Cabanis' earlier more mechanically cause-and-effect description of the liver and brain as activated by food and impressions, respectively, which cause them to produce bile and thought. See, Sewall, *An Examination of Phrenology*, 59, emphasis added; Georges Canguilhem, 'The brain and thought', trans. Steven Corcoran and Peter Hallward, *Radical Philosophy*, 148 2008, 7–18; and Pierre Jean Georges Cabanis, *Rapports du physique et du moral de l'homme*, 3rd ed., vol. 1 (Paris: Hacquart, 1815), 127–28.

34. Wiener, *Cybernetics*, 132.

35. J. C. Maxwell, *The Scientific Letters and Papers of James Clerk Maxwell*, ed. P. M. Harman, vol. II (Cambridge: Cambridge University Press, 1995), 366–67; P. M. Harman, *The Natural Philosophy of James Clerk Maxwell* (Cambridge: Cambridge University Press, 1998), 138–389, 204.

36. Wiener, *Cybernetics*, 57–58. Wiener himself made fundamental contributions to the study of the movement of particles in the 1920s (the 'Wiener process' or 'Brownian motion'), Wiener, *I Am a Mathematician*, 37–39.

37. I do not wish to imply that the invention of a relation between information and entropy was Wiener's alone. Rather, his role is part of a succession of analyses effectively kicked off by Leo Szilard's 1929 paper, 'On the Decrease of Entropy in a Thermodynamic System by the Intervention of Intelligent Beings'. See, Harvey S. Leff and Andrew F. Rex, eds., *Maxwell's Demon: Entropy, Information, Computing* (Bristol: Adam Hilger, 1990).

38. According to Claude Shannon's simultaneously discovered concept of information, information is instead identified with entropy and probability, and opposed to noise, thereby taking the opposite sign. I leave this for another day, but to say that Wiener and Shannon consider the disagreement 'purely formal' and 'complimentary', respectively. See, Kline, *The Cybernetics Moment*, 15.

39. Wiener, *Cybernetics*, 58.

40. Margaret Mead, Gregory Bateson and Stewart Brand, 'For God's Sake, Margaret', *CoEvolutionary Quarterly*, no. 10 (June 1976): 32–44.

41. Martin Heidegger and Joan Stambough, *On Time and Being* (New York: Harper & Row, 1972), 58; Martin Heidegger, *Zollikon Seminars: Protocols—Conversations—Letters*, ed. Medard Boss, trans. Franz Mayr and Richard Askay (Evanston, Il: Northwestern University Press, 2001), 95.

42. Yuk Hui, *Recursivity and Contingency* (London: Rowman & Littlefield, 2019), 119–22.

43. Wiener, *Cybernetics*, 125.

44. ibid., 58.

45. Translations of the *Monadology* based on, G. W. Leibniz, *Leibniz's Monadology: A New Translation and Guide*, ed. and trans. Lloyd Strickland (Edinburgh: Edinburgh University Press, 2014).

46. Descartes, *Discourse on Method*, *The Philosophical Writings of Descartes*, I.38–39.

47. One laments the fact that so much scholarship treats metastability as having been coined by Gilbert Simondon, who would have certainly inherited the concept from Wiener's discussion of the Maxwell demon in Wiener, *Cybernetics*, 58–59.

48. *Apperception*, in *Encyclopedia Americana*, vol. 2 (New

York & Chicago: The Encyclopedia Americana Corporation, 1918), 82–83, by Norbert Wiener.
49. Wiener, *Cybernetics*, 41; Wiener, *HUHBb*, 22–23.
50. Lloyd Strickland, ed. and trans., *Shorter Leibniz Texts* (London: Continuum, 2006), 76. See M38.
51. Wiener, *Cybernetics*, 41.
52. G. W. Leibniz, *The Leibniz-Des Bosses Correspondence*, trans. Brandon C. Look and Donald Rutherford (New Haven: Yale University Press, 2007), 257.
53. David Mindell, Jerome Segal and Slava Gerovitch, 'From communications engineering to communications science: Cybernetics and information theory in the United States, France, and the Soviet Union', in *Science and ideology: A comparative history*, ed. Mark Walker (London: Routledge, 2003), 80; Bernard Dionysius Geoghegan, 'From Information Theory to French Theory: Jakobson, Lévi-Strauss, and the Cybernetic Apparatus', *Critical Inquiry*, 2011, 110; Wiener, *HUHBb*, 162.
54. ibid., 92–93.
55. See the footnote in, Benoît Mandelbrot, 'An Informational Theory of the Statistical Structure of Language', in *Communication Theory*, ed. Willis Jackson, Applications of Communication Theory, Institute of Electrical Engineers, London, 22–26 September 1952 (London: Butterworths Scientific Publications, 1953), 489; Mandelbrot, 'Contribution à la théorie mathématique des jeux de communication', *Comptes rendus de l'Académie des sciences*, 234, (1952), 1345–1347.
56. Ferdinand de Saussure, *Course in General Linguistics*, ed. Charles Bally and Albert Sechehaye, trans., with an introduction, by Wade Baskin (New York, Toronto & London: McGraw-Hill Book Company, 1959), 88–89 and 110.
57. ibid., 89.
58. Ferdinand de Saussure, *Writings in General Linguistics*, trans. Carol Sanders (Oxford: Oxford University Press, 2006), 143–44.
59. Claude Lévi-Strauss, *The Story of Lynx*, trans. Catherine Tihanyi (Chicago & London: University of Chicago Press, 1995), xi–xvii.
60. Wiener, *HUHBb*, 34.
61. ibid., 165.
62. 'One can also say that the absence of good is an evil and that the absence of evil is a general good.' G. W. Leibniz, *Political Writings*, ed. and trans. Patrick Riley (Cambridge: Cambridge University Press, 1988), 55.
63. Norbert Wiener, *Letter to Paul de Kruif*, Cambridge: MIT Archives MC22, box 2, folder 38, 3 August 1933.
64. Wiener, *HUHBb*, 164.
65. ibid., 113, 162–3.
66. 'Lunch with the FT: Chelsea Manning', *FT Weekend* 10/11 December 2022, 3.
67. I read *HUHBb*, 153, as referring to, C. E. Shannon, 'Communication Theory of Secrecy Systems', *Bell System Technical Journal* 28, no. 4 (1949): 663, 704.
68. See Kline, *The Cybernetics Moment*, 31–35.
69. Shannon, 'Communication Theory of Secrecy Systems', 663, 704.
70. John von Neumann and Oskar Morgenstern, *Theory of Games and Economic Behavior*, 3rd ed. (Princeton: Princeton University Press, 1953), 5.2.1, 47.
71. Wiener, *Cybernetics*, 159–60.
72. ibid.
73. Surkov himself considers the situation reversed: the people as entropy which the State must control. He identifies entropy with chaos, turbulence and instability – which is a mistake or, more likely, a ruse. The chaos of entropy, according to Wiener's cybernetics, is one of sameness, 'de-differentiation', death and utmost probability, which is to say precisely the controlled condition that a Putinist like Surkov would desire from Statecraft. Vladislav Surkov, '*Kuda delsia khaos? Raspakovka stabil'nosti*' [Where has chaos gone? Unpacking stability], *Aktual'nye kommentarii*, 20 November 2021, https://actualcomment.ru/kuda-delsya-khaos-raspakovka-stabilnosti-2111201336.html; Wiener, *HUHBb*, 15, 85.
74. Shoshana Zuboff, *The age of surveillance capitalism* (London: Profile, 2019).
75. André Robinet, *Le Défi Cybernétique: L'automate et La Pensée* (Paris: Gallimard, 1973), 114.
76. Warren S. McCulloch, 'The Heterarchy of Values Determined by the Topology of Nervous Nets', *The Bulletin of Mathematical Biophysics* 7, no. 4 (December 1945): 227; Bruno Latour, *The Pasteurization of France*, trans. Alan Sheridan and John Law (Cambrdige, MA & London: Harvard University Press, 1988), 164.
77. Daniel Nemenyi, 'Submarine State: On secrets and leaks', *Radical Philosophy*, 193 Sept/Oct 2015, 2–8.
78. Pierre Dubarle, 'Une nouvelle science: la cybernétique – Vers la machine à gouverner...', *Le Monde*, 28 December 1948, Wiener, *HUHBb*, 180.
79. ibid.
80. Wiener, *HUHBa*, 209.
81. Gilbert Simondon, *On the Mode of Existence of Technical Objects*, trans. Cécile Malaspina and John Rogove (Minneapolis, MN: Univocal, 2017), 15–17.
82. Kline, *The Cybernetics Moment*, 80.
83. *The Tech*, 70.27, 12 May 1950, 1.
84. Wiener, *HUHBb*, 161, 157.
85. Wiener, *God and Golem*, Inc., 58–61.

Why the customer is always right
Debord's spectacle as the rationalisation of mimesis
Eric-John Russell

> I once knew a monster who said she could not read Proust because there were no figures in Proust with whom she could identify.
>
> Theodor W. Adorno

With this seemingly off-the-cuff anecdote, Adorno, lecturing on the topic of aesthetics in 1958, gave illustration to a critique of a certain kind of aesthetic reception, or against the idea that art must be commensurate or conform to the experiential familiarity of the viewing subject. Throughout his writings, one finds recurrent concern with the problem of aesthetic relativism: that the criterion of evaluating works of art ought to defer to judgments of taste, and therewith to an insatiable subjectivity that demands art 'give' them something. It is the insistence that works of art blend completely into the closed surface of immediate experience, consonant with meagre perceptions of an easily recognisable reality and preformation mechanisms of subjective reaction, allowing people to 'cheaply unburden themselves' through identification.[1] For Adorno, aesthetic experience limited to such a subjective reflex, a provision expected in return for given attention, elicits, at base, that loathsome idea of exchange, an ethos that *the customer is always right*.

For Adorno, when the mimetic component of aesthetic experience is reduced to mere duplication or replication of empirical reality and *a priori* categories of perception, to the exercise of just recognising the always already familiar, we have entered the arena of the 'culture industry', where art fails to demarcate itself adequately from the schematism of an administered world of commodity relations, liquidating the boundary between itself and reality, most enticingly, for example, when 'based on a true story'.

A social world economically structured around an omnipresent compulsion for identification with the immediate appearances of everyday reality has perhaps, alongside the work of Adorno, one of its most incisive diagnoses in the work of Guy Debord and his concept of the society of the spectacle. In two hundred and twenty-one short theses, Debord's *The Society of the Spectacle* (1967) outlines a peculiar form of domination developed through the autonomy of the commodity economy within the capitalist mode of production, in which people come to *identify* with the appearances of social life, under compulsion to recognise themselves and their needs within the dominant images, representations and appearances produced by commodity society – including today the avatars, emojis, gifs, memes, hashtags and, what Hegel might have called, other picture-thinking units of digital communication. Just as Narcissus fell victim to his own reflection, helpless to tear himself away from the grip of identification, so too are human beings within the spectacle captivated by their own mirror image. Against the need for social reassurance and recognition, nothing is worse than failing to be noticed.

As will be explored in the following essay, Debord's concept of the spectacle incorporates what Joseph Gabel termed *Identitätszwang* – that is, the compulsion for identification. Yet the literature on Debord that has taken more seriously his debt to Hegelian and Marxist thinking has tended to emphasise not the significance of *identification* within the logic of the spectacle, but rather the importance of *separation*.[2] And for good reason: the social cohesion of the society of the spectacle is produced through separation. It is a social separation of human beings from their own activity, falsified into appearances operating outside of their control. For Debord, the 'triumph of an economic system founded on separation leads to the *proletarianization of the world*'.[3] Characteristic here is, of course, a relation of dispossession, a detachment, dislocation or bifurcation of the proletariat from its own conditions of existence, subject to forces experienced as coercively imposed upon it. Yet the phenomena of separation and alienation, conceived here as an antimonic distanciation, is only part of Debord's critical diagnosis. There is also comfort to be drawn in the recognitive relations to the immediacies of the world, however inverted and torn asunder they may be by the heteronomy of the capitalist mode of production. For Debord, the society of the spectacle, as the form capitalism took over the twentieth century, has inaugurated *universal* modes of pathological identification, mechanisms of recognition not easily dismissed under the rubric of a hostile schism. Single recourse to the framework of division risks failing to grasp the spectacle as the 'the social *organization* of appearances' and the ways in which human beings are entangled in its reproduction.[4]

The spectacle refers to the nature of capitalist society as a structural totality, the total result of social objectification including both processes of human activity and the immediate appearance of that externalised social reality. With the increasing fragmentation of human experience through the capitalist division of labour and the structuring of social relations through the form of the commodity, the spectacle for Debord reconstitutes a *unitary* social life from its separated and disjointed moments, albeit at the level of appearance. In a word, while separation remains 'the alpha and omega of the spectacle',[5] and is its basis insofar as it is the development of the commodity-capitalist economy and its requisite class division, the spectacle nevertheless obtains a certain unity-in-separation, a complex logic beyond the scope of the present essay yet concomitant with both Marx's critique of political economy and Hegel's notion of speculative identity.[6]

This is where Debord's analysis makes considerable strides beyond the young Marx and Georg Lukács' concept of reification. That is, the spectacle comprises an integrative socialisation, cohering through a principle of identity, soliciting not only *passive* contemplation from the standpoint of spectators, but also *active* and participatory identification, with individuals 'recognizing [themselves] in the dominant images of need'.[7]

The Society of the Spectacle expounds not simply a social situation in which fragmentation abounds without any reconciliation between subject and object, but rather, as a 1966 article from issue 10 of *Internationale Situationniste* makes explicit, a reconstructed 'lost paradise of unitary societies ... a reality entirely reduced to the quantitative, thoroughly dominated by the principle of identity'. As the article continues, the logical principle of *identity* has found its 'appropriate realisation in the commodity-spectacle'. The 'flat and disincarnated positivity' installed by the commodity-spectacle thereby realises identity not simply as an illusory fantasy but actual through the formalisation of social relations by exchange.[8] There is a principle of identity between spectacle and spectators whereby the former furnishes the latter with an entire purview of social possibility and satisfaction, and, at its most nefarious, compels the latter to collapse into the former without remainder.

It will be the argument of the following essay that the mode of identification constitutive of the society of the spectacle is best illustrated through the concept of *mimesis*, that is, we will give greater focus to the overwhelming social mandate for pathological identification, equivalence and mimetic adaptation to the dominant appearance-forms of capitalist society. We will proceed through discursive variations on the critical usage of the concept of mimesis, particularly through the work of Adorno, but also with regard to the writings of Roger Caillois and Joseph Gabel, all of whom can provide insight into the role of mimetic behaviour within Debord's concept of the society of the spectacle.

The aim is to advance the concept of mimesis as a critical framework for understanding spectacular domination. More broadly however, the essay also seeks to establish a firm continuity between Debord's diagnosis and the first generation of Frankfurt School critical theory, specifically the work of Adorno. It is not sufficiently recognised that Debord ought to reside in that same tradition of working out a critical theory of society based on the dynamics of commodity exchange. It will be demonstrated that it is not simply the case that what binds the work of Debord to the critical theory of the Frankfurt School is a common concern over generic issues of alienation and reification, or that both merely scrutinise more closely how human beings subordinate themselves to things. It is more specifically in the spectacular logic of identification, of rendering commensurable *like with like* as the rationalisation of mimesis, so central to Max Horkheimer and Adorno's *Dialectic of Enlightenment*, that Debord's critical theory finds accord with the early Frankfurt School.

The rationalisation of mimesis

Walter Benjamin famously inquired into the historical development of the mimetic faculty, and whether or not there might be a decay or transformation of this natural comportment. As he writes, 'neither mimetic powers nor mimetic objects have remained unchanged over time [and that] on the whole, a unified direction is perceptible in the historical development of the mimetic faculty'.[9] It is within Benjamin's broader proposition – that the mimetic faculties have anthropologically undergone a kind of decomposition – that mimesis can begin to emerge as a critical heuristic, to discover how mimetic behaviour becomes entangled with modern forms of domination and corresponding forms of anxiety and psychological disorder.

Horkheimer and Adorno's *Dialectic of Enlightenment* traverses the history of the mimetic faculty in and through a critique of rationality, specifically situated within a subject's relationship to the objective world, one for which the movement of imitation, going back to Aristotle, is based on an instinct expressed in the relation of a subject towards an object.[10] This subject is the consciousness of an ego that rests its identity on reason, while the object amounts to that which is different, incommensurable and nonidentical. Imitation becomes the disposition for experiencing an object, one for which the subject seeks likeness in order to rationally grasp the object.

For Adorno and Horkheimer, the history of the mimetic faculty is inextricably tied to the history of rationality itself, a development which witnesses the scientifically rationalised bourgeois subject of the late eighteenth century emerge from an incipient self that is characterised by magical practices of the myth-oriented subject of primeval societies. This admittedly speculative history of rationality consists in a development of man's relation to, and domination of, nature, whose objectification is grounded in myth. *Dialectic of Enlightenment* traces the manner in which the rationality of enlightenment thinking is not simply opposed to myth but already located within the phenomenon of myth as the first effort at grasping one's object in order to dominate it out of the compulsion for self-preservation. In a word, it is fear that initiates imitation. The self wants to become *like* the objective power it fears. Mimetic behaviour becomes the protective self-defence mechanism for a self adapting to its environment. This process consists in the mastering of nature, whereby an emerging self gradually establishes itself in opposition to nature and, in this objectification, the self projects personifications upon nature as possessing 'powers', thereby grounding myth as an object of knowledge. The constitution of myth thereby emerges as the rationalisation of man's fear of nature and efforts at self-preservation.[11] Myth seeks to report, narrate and explain the phenomena of nature as an external force.

The phase of mythology proceeds in accordance with this development of human beings adapting to the power of gods through the medium of sacrifice in order to ensure self-preservation.[12] The consciousness of myth as such consists in the compulsion of owing something to the gods, a ritualistic mode of communication with the deity that, for Adorno, prefigures exchange relations. The self-preservation of mythic society comes to depend on a form of exchange with the mythic forces in the form of sacrifice, executing a communication with the projected deities. Sacrifice is thereby the result of human beings mimetically adapting themselves to nature in order to escape its hostility, developing the logic of self-preservation into the realm of commensurability.

Yet for Adorno and Horkheimer, enlightenment thinking does not abolish the practice of mythic sacrifice but facilitates its transformation into formalised exchange relations. Whereas what Adorno and Horkheimer call the 'magical phase' of mimesis witnesses sacrifices made in order to influence natural or transcendental powers, the exchange relation constitutive of its 'historical phase' refers to the rational self seeking its own preservation. For Adorno, the regimentation of mimesis is myth undergoing increased rationalisation. The models of myth become replicated within instrumental reason as the perfection of man's domination of nature. This 'historical phase' consists in the ascendency of an instrumental rationality whereby bodily adaptation to nature characterising the magical phase is replaced by conceptual identification. The natural must be absorbed into utility through the sanitising channels of a conceptual order. The mimetic replication of a thoroughly administered society becomes adaptation to a petrified objective world. Here, the structure of self-preservation becomes the barbaric content of empirical life.

Through this philosophical anthropology, mimetic adaptation is no longer focused on communicating with natural or transcendental powers, but towards the omnipotent power of the social whole, still nevertheless carrying forward the centrality of sacrificial exchange. Here, sacrifice progressively requires an accurate calculation of quantities and proportions, a rationalised magnitude of exchange, thereby anticipating the use of money. As such, sacrifice can be described as the defining experience in which the first practical roots and ideological precursors of economic practice appear, one for which self-preservation and survival came to depend on pacts, contracts and more formalised modes of exchange with both mythical forces and other clans. Myth, it can be said, facilitating the development of the exchange relation, functions to conceal the cunning of exchange, that is, a pervasive form of social mediation increasingly dominated by the principle of equivalence and identity.[13] Within the exchange relation, sacrifice comes to be quantified, calculated, rationalised and standardised under the logic of universal commensurability. Through this process, the objective forces of natural powers are supplanted by society itself as the external force over and against the individual. Here, the dynamic of myth is reproduced through its deification. In a word, modernity becomes mythic. Instead of a subordination to magical or mythical forces, there is now a subordination to a rationality which attains mythic proportion as it imposes a 'civilizing process'.

Mimicry as a renunciation of the self

Motivated by the fear of death, society perpetuates the threat from nature as a permanent, organised compul-

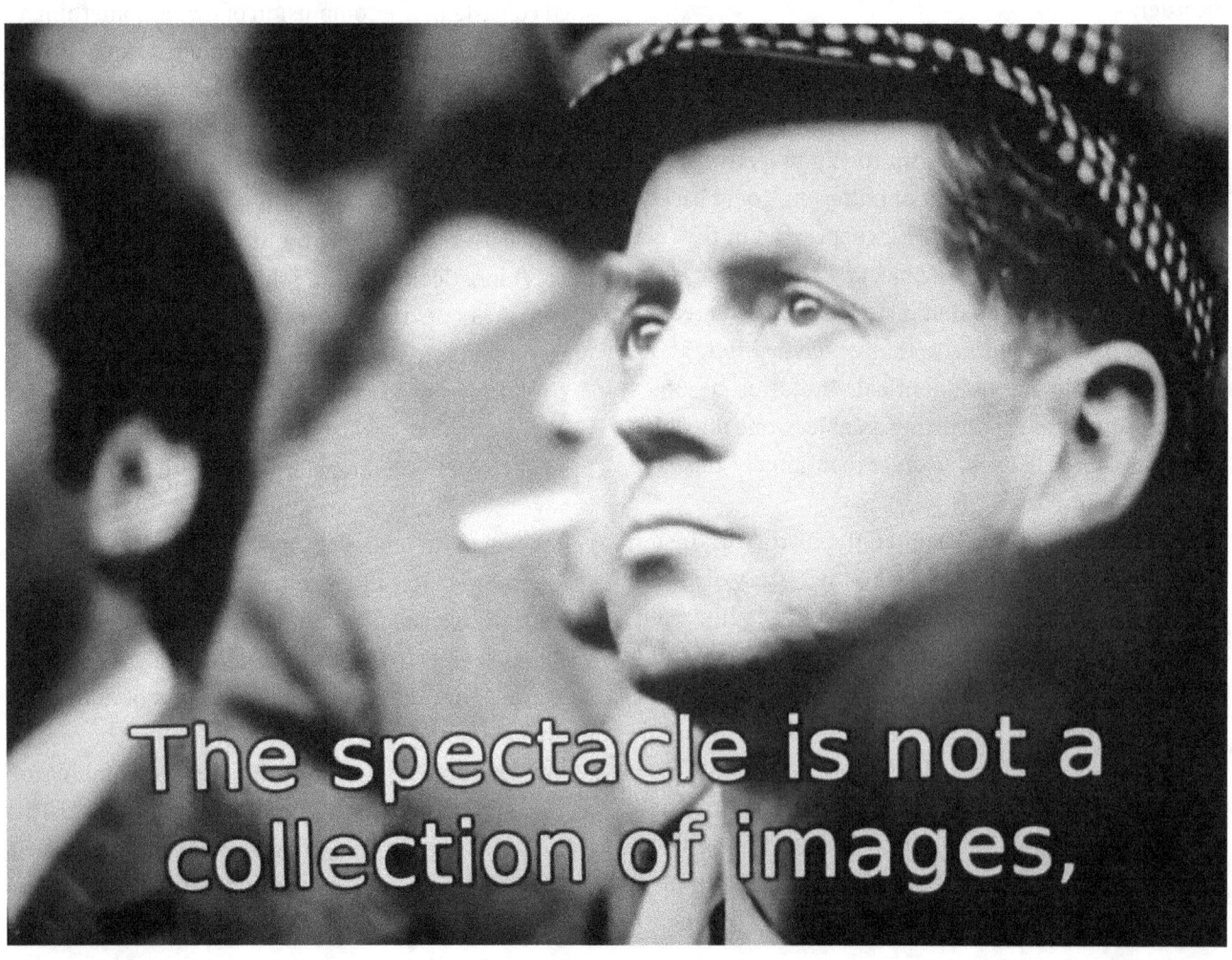

sion, a systematic self-preservation repetitively carried out with regularity and preserved under mythic proportions. Here, as a central theme in the process of the rationalisation of mimesis, equality commands a mode of adaptation that witnesses an identity of the world with the subject. Thought comes to subsume difference under identity, equalising particulars under a universal. This process subsumes diversity within a unity, then into commensurable equivalence, finally engendering concretely applied notions of calculability and exchange. Controlled or regimented mimesis therefore induces the subsumption of difference under sameness, an adaptation and identification with forces of domination. The transformation of the faculty for establishing sameness consists in the transition from an adaptation of likeness to a subsumption of equivalence. 'Judgment is no longer based on a real act of synthesis but on blind subsumption.'[14]

Yet Adorno and Horkheimer also describe the rationalisation of mimesis as patterned after biological mimicry, that is, as the mere replication or copying of the external environment in order to better equip oneself in the face of objective forces. This process of adaptation internalises a dominant rational order that, through its increasing estrangement from nature, itself reverts to a frigidly objectified and lifeless nature. The subject comes to mimic its own rationalised contortion of nature. The mimesis of an increasingly objectified, cold and inorganic nature – that is, the mimesis of death – functions as a defence mechanism against the dissolution of the newly acquired rational and self-sustained self. 'They reproduce within themselves the insatiability of the power of which they are afraid.'[15] Mimicry thereby consists of an estrangement of the self, a movement of complete subordination of human beings to a dominated objectivity.

In his 1935 essay 'Mimicry and Legendary Psychasthenia', Roger Caillois transposes the phenomena of mimicry from the world of zoology to a set of pathological disorders characterised by phobias, obsessions, compulsions or excessive anxiety, an analysis thematically consistent with Adorno and Horkheimer's account of mimicry but with a different emphasis. Caillois begins with various forms of mimicry employed in the animal kingdom either to surprise prey, to escape the sight of a predator or to frighten it away by deceptive appearance, as well as the employment of disguises and the resemblance of different species.[16] Instances of homomorphic adaptation of form between an organism and its surroundings are subsequently brought within the realm human experience, conceived as pathological, specifically with what Caillois describes as 'a real *temptation by space*'.[17]

For Caillois, within represented space, the organism is not the origin of coordinates, but merely one point among others on a horizontal and vertical plane. '[I]t is dispossessed of its privilege and literally *no longer knows where to place itself*.'[18] In this dispossession, space becomes a devouring force, pursuing, swallowing and digesting individuals. The result is a certain depersonalisation through the mimetic assimilation to space, a point sociologically registered by David Riesman in his 1950 study *The Lonely Crowd*, a work that was important for Debord.[19] Similar to Caillois, Debord also identifies the encroachment of spatialisation as significant for the theory of the spectacle, an important lineage connecting his own writings to the work of Lukács. Both conceive reification as entailing the degradation of time's fluidity to an abstract spatial dimension for which its 'qualitative, variable, flowing nature ... freezes into an exactly delimited, quantifiable continuum filled with quantifiable "things" ... in short, it becomes space'.[20] Debord explicitly describes the reduction of space and time to an abstract common denominator, a '*spatial alienation*, whereby a society which radically severs the subject from the activity that it steals from him separates him in the first place from his own time'.[21]

But for Caillois, this form of adaptation is concomitant with a decline in the feeling of personality and life of the individual, or a generalisation of abstract space at the expense of the individual. The instinct for self-preservation thus leads to an instinct for self-renunciation. The individual 'tries to look at *himself from any point whatever in space*. He feels himself becoming space, *dark space where things cannot be put*. He is similar, not to something, but just *similar*'.[22]

Once nature is rendered into an object of mechanical rationality, to mimetically adapt to it – in Caillois' case, to space in the abstract – is to internalise its inanimate significance. Mimicry, again, becomes the adaptation to a lifelessness in the interest of self-preservation. It is the synchronisation of the self with an estranged world. Like a moth to a flame, it becomes *Identitätszwang*. Yet the faculty of mimesis remains in the interest of self-preservation, such that 'the tribute life pays for its continued existence is adaptation to death'.[23]

Schizophrenic mimesis

Within what Caillois calls legendary psychasthenia, the individual, through its mimetic faculty, seems to lose ground and is diminished, caught in a blurred boundary between itself and its surroundings. This form of adaptation cultivates and arouses within the individual *equivalent behaviour*, a pathological phenomenon Caillois borrows from the phenomenological psychiatry of Eugène Minkowski, who heavily influenced one of the Debord's inspirations for *The Society of the Spectacle*, namely the work of Joseph Gabel.[24] Debord's reliance on Gabel's *False Consciousness: An Essay on Reification* (1962) for the concept of the society of the spectacle is, however, remarkably absent from the literature. Gabel draws a parallel between ideology and schizophrenia, an association that Debord relates directly to the concept of the spectacle and its development of the exchange process, which elevates to the level of the whole the axiom of identification. It is therefore crucial to examine Gabel's thesis since Debord adopts a number of its insights.[25]

Through a synthesis of Lukács' theory of reification, Karl Mannheim's concept of total ideology and the interwar existential and phenomenological psychiatry of Minkowski and Ludwig Binswanger, Gabel provides a psycho-sociological theory of consciousness, specifically through a parallel between a reified relation to the world and a clinical psychiatric condition of schizophrenia, both sharing a rationality which, similar to Caillois, subordinates temporal experience to excessive spatialisation. Here, reification is said to be analogous to schizophrenic symptoms and, as a result, the aporetic gap between subject and object is filled with pathological identification. Gabel's term for this process, adopted from Minkowski, is *morbid rationalism*.

This 'loss of vital contact with reality' is for Gabel a tenet of reification as a condition of schizophrenia.[26] As Gabel summarises in his preface: 'Defined as an *individual form of false consciousness,* schizophrenia finds a new nosological unity centred on the concept of morbid rationalism within the framework of a unitary conception ("total concept") of alienation, capable of embracing both its social forms and its clinical aspects.'[27] Such phenomena occur for Gabel through processes of repetition, imitation, utopian fixation and temporal irreversibility, all of which can be derived from formal axiological structures as structures of social reality.

Gabel's 'Marxian theory of mental derangement' concerns a deterioration of the dialectic between subject and object, or more specifically, an identification between a subject and its world[28] – an insight taken up by Debord. It is an integrative process that renders the world into a spatialised and axiological experiential structure. Reification, as schizophrenic in nature, tends towards the spatialisation of duration, and 'concludes with the principle of axio-dialectical equivalence'.[29] Gabel's nosological account of reification unfolds a morbid rationalism that pivots upon a preponderant function of identification. Invoking an idea of 'false identification', which in turn produces 'false differentiation', this mechanism, dependent on the degree of accumulated aggression, can assume the form of either an absolute or relative identity. In either case, the 'human spirit's appetite for identity' transitions into an uncompromising rationalism whose logical structure, often expressed in forms of analogy, symbolism, caricature and stereotypy, sanctions non-differentiation while proliferating dichotomies.[30]

It is Gabel's concept of *Identitätszwang* – again, the compulsion or obsession for identification – that is important for our investigation. The identificatory and egocentric logic of the schizophrenic orientation to the world unifies subject and predicate under its morbid rationalism. This 'great *leveling*' procures a 'universe without frontiers',[31] a flat earth with neither mountains nor oceans and which has eradicated any central point of reference.[32] In the concluding chapter of *The Society of the Spectacle*, Debord employs Gabel's concept of *Identitätszwang* as a 'virtual identification',[33] an injunction set in motion by the spectacle:

> The spectacle erases the dividing line between self and world, in that the self, under siege by the presence/absence of the world, is eventually overwhelmed; it likewise erases the dividing line between true and false, repressing all directly lived truth beneath the *real presence* of the falsehood maintained by the organization of appearances.[34]

For the omnipresence of the spectacle, identifications between self and world, subject and object, appearance and essence and, ultimately, truth and falsehood reign. Furthermore, as '[t]he role of the look in paranoid madness is notorious',[35] the spectacle assimilates and reflects back objectivity in and through its deranged gaze.[36] What it sees is the triumphant procession of a world that it itself has created. However, despite the fact that Debord occasionally makes reference to alienated individuals, the schizophrenic agent, in this correlation with Gabel, is not the spectator but the spectacle itself in its totality. As Debord writes in his archival notes on Gabel, 'thus the whole spectacle, being organized collectively, is a socially hallucinating fact'.[37] Writing further in a May 1969 letter to the Italian section of the Situationist International, Debord claims the ninth chapter of *The Society of the Spectacle*, 'considers all of spectacular society as a psychopathological formation'.[38] Thus it can be said that Debord utilises Gabel's analysis as a macro condition for society at large, not for a particular pathological agent. It is a schizophrenic structure beyond individual psychology and subsisting at the level of the social whole.[39] It is for this reason that any obsolescence of Gabel's psychoanalytic theory is secondary to Debord's adoption of the latter's ideas for a diagnosis of larger social tendencies.[40] As a structure subsisting at the level of the whole, Debord, within his notes on Gabel, makes the distinction between production and consumption along the respective lines of the spatialised time of schizophrenia and the destructured time of maniacal hysteria: 'In short, the SduS would be schizophrenic in production – including the production of the spectacle to the partial recipient; the visible [apparent] spectacle – and hysterical in all of its consumption'. And yet not completely adopting such a schematic, Debord also reverses the relation further on in his notes: 'Or it can be said that the spectacle (consumption) is schizo, but that its production is maniacal.'[41]

It is clear that, for Debord, the society of the spectacle adopts a schizophrenic structure. It is, as he himself says when quoting Gabel, 'quite another level of pathology', in which 'the abnormal need for representation here compensates for a torturing feeling of being at the margin of existence'.[42] Further, with regard to the distinction between truth and falsehood, Gabel examines the erasure of definitive limits on the true and the false characteristic of fantasy pseudology, itself a variation on hysteria whose 'theatrical consciousness ... destroys the subject-object dialectic by causing the subject to disappear (whilst the lie destroys it by reifying the object) [and] ends in the same psychological and moral result as the lie, despite the possible congruence of its assertions with reality'.[43] The schizophrenic structure of the spectacle thereby collapses the distinctive boundaries between the true and the false through the hysterical pattern of pseudology, a perversion of the mimetic faculty where individuals are rendered commensurate with the appearances that surround them. Pathological identification through the rationalisation of mimesis characterises the logic of the society of the spectacle, itself part, as Debord derives from Gabel, of a schizophrenic structure whose morbid rationality perpetuates 'generalized autism',[44] in and through its maleficent organisation of appearances, which exude overwhelming radiance. As Debord writes of the spectator, '[t]he need to imitate ... is indeed a truly infantile need, one determined by every aspect of his fundamental dispossession'.[45]

Pathic projection

A month after *The Society of the Spectacle* was published, Debord wrote to the American section of the Situationist International, claiming that the primary task of their organisation 'is to produce the most adequate critical theory'.[46] It would not be the only time Debord would characterise the critique of the society of the spectacle as a critical theory: 'In 1967 I wanted the Situationist International to have a book of theory ... impos[ing] its victory on the terrain of critical theory.'[47] Despite these references, his own direct relation to the critical theory coming out of Frankfurt via the Institut für Sozialforschung are few and far between. Yet it is known that Debord's personal library contained copies of Adorno and Horkheimer's *Dialectic of Enlightenment* and Marcuse's *One-Dimensional Man* and *Eros and Civilisation*. Additionally, Debord's archive notes include comments on Adorno's 'Music and Technique', whose French translation appeared in the 1960 issue of *Arguments* no. 19.

Even if it would be too much to say that the work of Debord and Adorno were like two ships quietly passing in the night, Debord's concept of the spectacle shares a number of important continuities with Adorno's work. For example, Adorno begins *Minima Moralia* with formulations that strongly accord with ideas found in *The*

Society of the Spectacle, most notably with an observation that the relation between the economy and life proceeds by debasing the latter to a form of appearance of the former. It is a development for Adorno in which 'life has become appearance'. Further on, 'people cling to what mocks them confirming the mutilation of their essence by the smoothness of its own appearance.'[48] For both Adorno and Debord, we discover again *Identitätszwang* – the social compulsion to identify with the surrounding world and its concurrent injuries to subjectivity.

One of the most potent convergence points observed by commentators between Adorno and Debord is the critique of industrial culture.[49] Here, in the case of cultural phenomena within capitalist society, products of leisure become pre-digested and standardised, whose various media elicit mass psychological behaviour for which base survival and integration assume the form of satisfaction. Yet it is often ignored how such a diagnosis does not rest on a simple one-way framework in which a juggernaut of commodified culture merely imposes its contours upon otherwise *tabula rasa* spectators. On the contrary, we find a form of pathological projection in which *people strive to adapt* to a schematism accompanied by a set of ready-made reactions to the cultural products on display, with their empty promissory notes designed to indefinitely prolong an unsublimated anticipation of pleasure, depleting the already scarce psychological resources of weak egos.

Accommodating various layers of behavioural response patterns, the cultural products of the spectacle refine their ability to directly identify reality *with* its representation. The more densely and completely its techniques duplicate empirical objects, the more easily it creates the verifiable conviction that the world outside is a seamless extension of the one which, for example, has been revealed in the cinema. Herein lies the spectacle as geared to mimetic regression, to the manipulation of repressed impulses to copy. Its orientation is to anticipate the spectator's imitative practice by giving the appearance of agreement. Yet the entire system is justified on the basis of an infantile public, which the system itself has created. Again, it is a customer-demand ethos that *appearances be made relatable*.

This physiognomy of reification consists in a mixture of, on the one hand, streamlining photographic hardness and precision and, on the other, an individual's pathological identification with standardised formulas and clichés. Here, the revelation of barbaric existence and the objective legitimation of its meaning are given direct exposition, that is, *spectacularised*. Recall that the spectacle is a structure of reification in which human beings 'recognize', as Debord writes, their 'own needs in the images of need proposed by the dominant system.'[50] For both Debord and Adorno, reification thereby comprises a mechanism of identification through the continuous presentation of what exists as the sole possible horizon and as objects of pathological projection. Everything is reduced to recognition, to 'whatever the camera reproduces',[51] therefore stunting the power of discernment in an emaciation of human perception through its *Identitätszwang*. Human comprehension comes to require only a quick and observant mind, while at the same time it debars thinking so that fleeting facts aren't missed. In a word, a primacy of alertness is necessary, even if in a state of perpetual distraction.

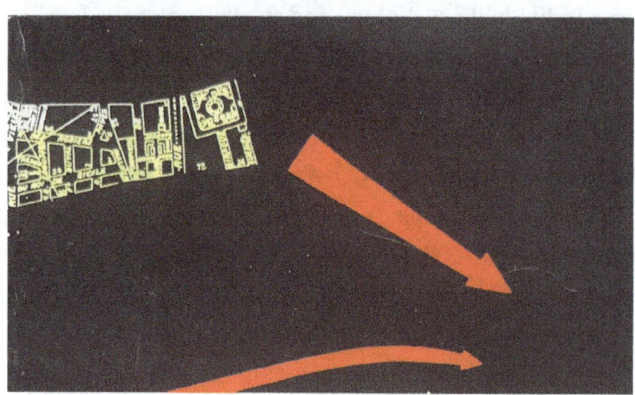

For Adorno, specifically in the case of photography and film, the resulting reification of the audience is a degradation of human perception. It does this, first and foremost, through a certain *domesticated naturalism* to which the photographic image is disposed, infusing empirical life with meaning: 'the duplicity of which viewers can scarcely see through because the nightclub looks exactly like the one they know.'[52] Again, here the spectacle need only display the reigning actuality through individualised cultural products under an 'ideal of naturalness'. 'Such a photological proof is of course not stringent, but it is overpowering.' Like the culture industry, the spectacle upholds the world in reverence as its own object, under the 'demand for pitiless clarity'. As Adorno continues: 'It exploits the cult of fact by describing bad existence with utmost exactitude in order to elevate it into the realm of facts.'[53] These comments are consistent with Debord, insofar as the spectacle employs 'a sort of flat, positivistic exactness',[54] in which 'everything is reduced to a satisfying positivity [which in turn] justifies its own existence tautologically by the mere fact that it exists, which is to say that it is granted *recognition* within the spectacle'.[55]

The pathological projection constitutive of the society of the spectacle is inadvertently described throughout *Dialectic of Enlightenment*. Yet if readers of the book remain content to draw similarities between Adorno and Debord from the chapter 'The Culture Industry' alone, the centrality of *Identitätszwang* for the diagnosis will never emerge. It is rather the case that the full significance of the critique of industrial culture – how pathic projection, as its fundamental theoretical core, is what most precisely establishes the continuity between Adorno and Debord's social diagnoses – only comes to fruition in the subsequent chapter, 'Elements of Anti-Semitism'. There Adorno and Horkheimer invoke a psychoanalytic theory of false-projection as the repression or reversal of mimesis, whereby 'if mimesis makes itself resemble its surroundings, false projection makes its surroundings resemble itself'.[56] Here, the rationalisation of mimesis is translated into a pathic character trait of the reified consciousness, a self which is mimetically structured by the society it inhabits, for which it then projects its psychosomatic damages back onto the world. This process of replication emerges as fundamental to the rationalised mimetic faculty, whereby volatile inwardness is displaced onto the world at large and reconstituted in its own degraded image. Within human history, as the faculty of projection of the self is increasingly controlled, its degeneration into a false projection emerges, such that the subject is unable to return to the object what it has received from it, and as such, can no longer reflect upon the object nor itself.

This process heralds the omnipotence of the rational subject, investing 'the outside world boundlessly with what is within itself; but what it invests is something utterly insignificant, … a grim praxis unilluminated by thought'.[57] The subject renders the world the mere occasion for its delusion, calibrating social experience towards a primacy of the *inner*, essentially fragmenting objectivity itself. The modern subject positions himself at the centre of the world, dislocating gods, nature and all other metaphysical totalities and yet maintains the adaptation to myth insofar as its neuroses are the result of its drive for self-preservation. As Debord writes, in the spectacle, 'the most modern is also the most archaic'.[58] Or as stated within issue eight of *Internationale situationniste*: 'The spectacle is nothing but secularized and fragmented myth.'[59] The world is perceived only insofar as it corresponds to the subject's blind purposes of self-interest, the cold means of their self-preservation, and to be touched by this world awakens in them only shame and rage, exemplified, for Adorno and Horkheimer, in the doctrine of the idiosyncratic image of the Jew that appears to refuse full assimilation, that is, as deficient adaptation.

The analysis of anti-Semitism pivots on the rationalisation of mimesis, driven by the urge of sameness and the sanctioned rage of the collective body. It is a 'situation in which blinded people, deprived of subjectivity, are let loose as subjects.'[60] It is here worth repeating that such a dynamic – in which damaged subjects are 'let loose' – cannot be captured within a framework that upholds 'passivity' as the sole criterion by which individuals take in the world.[61] There is nothing 'simply passive' about the march of Brownshirts, nor the (however meagre) agency allotted to composing a Spotify playlist. Mimetic adaptation, which, in the case of Adorno, is the diagnostic for grasping the continuity between industrial culture and fascism, requires active participation. The volatile interiority of such damaged subjects, under the mandate that the world ought to mimetically adhere to and resemble the blind sequencing of their own lifeless and rational omnipotence, correspondingly receives validation for their own pathologies, since their system of delusional neurosis is declared true to a reality that has, in truth, become thingified. The world becomes an extension of the subject's delusion, a paranoiac fixation for creating everything in its own image, imbuing the outside world with stereotypical formulae. It is worth repeating: *the customer is always right.*[62]

Against recognition

Lukács tells us that in the commodity, 'the worker *recognises* himself' in objectified form, that its consciousness is 'the *self-consciousness of the commodity*'.[63] Discovered here is the kernel of how recognitive relations can be pregnant with various pathological relations to both oneself and the outside world, not simply however as a phenomenon of 'inter-subjective relations' or moral transgressions, but as an objective characteristic of capitalist commodity production, that is, in the way in which this society has transformed the mimetic faculty of human beings. If for Axel Honneth recognition precedes cognition, then mimesis is a precondition for recognition since to recognise is to identify familiarity within an environment of difference.[64] Not only for ethical bonding, but recognition can also be a proviso for hatred and indifference,[65] or, following Adorno and the spectacle's solicitations as described above, identification with the aggressor as a self-defence mechanism.

Relations of recognition adequate to the inverted world of the commodity and its spectacularisation are embedded within the rationalisation of mimesis, that is, 'imitation as absolute'.[66] Here a defensive anxiety retains the individual's propensity for fierce competition while seeking social acclaim and recognition. This is compounded by a dependence on vicarious warmth provided by others, yet alongside a fear of dependence. It is a tension not reducible to a personality structure but emboldened by a society that rewards pseudo self-insight, calculating seductiveness, nervously self-deprecating humour, a ravenous craving for notoriety while contemptuous of others and insatiably hungry for emotional experiences.

It is the difference between being an individual and being individuated that marks the regression into an empty yet grandiose self for which the world is only its mirror; in a word, the collapse of the boundary between the self and the world. These developments accelerate and intensify, in a dense interpersonal and interconnected society, with the proliferation of visual and audio images permeating everyday experience, wherein, it can be argued, the preoccupation of the self with the self has become total.

The identity of a subject that wishes to recognise itself everywhere links directly with the principle of equivalence paramount in a society dominated by the autonomy of exchange value. Accordingly, nowhere has the abolition of hierarchy been more successful than in the realm of taste. It is through the universality of equivalence that every cup of coffee risks being watered down for commercial interests. Equality becomes a principle of levelling mediocrity as the barometer of cultural advance.

Against vertically organised traditional broadcasting and informational services, the spectacular horizontalism of digital communication and its lateral organisation, its direct and instantaneous communication throughout the globe, is infused with economic imperatives of commensurable uniformity and transparency. Here the right to self-definition comes to trump all other rights: a struggle over attentive constituencies and self-identification. The result is an overwhelming, however subtle, demand for branding, a staple not just of the market, but of politics as well: it is crucial to stay on message and to prize that communication over content. Both a voting drive and an iPhone advertising campaign compete in the field of expeditious ideas, brand consistency and repetitive jingles.

Two desiderata of its stimuli are to provoke the recipient's attention while doing so in 'recognisable' language. To simply recognise the melody of a pop song is enough to afford it grandeur. Thinking becomes the mechanism of identification taking place under the appeal and veneration for unlimited transparency and communication. Yet to stand out is only to accord with the repetitive mechanisms of distributing standardised material, or what Adorno refers to as 'plugging' as 'the literal repetition and inexorable representation of endless sameness'.[67] Here, the success and popularity of a particular product derives directly from the phenomenon of repetition and '[i]ts fame is only the sum-total of these very announcements'.[68] Youtube, Instagram and TikTok personalities are a case in point in which the developing technological standards democratise chances of success simply as a result of the proliferation and extension of the cultural schematism. The success of any 'influencer' does not derive from any cultural 'pioneering' but is predominantly the result of pre-existing standardisation and algorithmic strategising. The velocity of ever-nuanced variations on standardised and administrated experience emerges as more crucial than any of its individual products. The unending stream of social media feeds, with one entry deserving far less than the perpetual current of the whole, remains exemplary of this dynamic. In this way, the inattentive attention of retention today is only 'the *recognition* of a sequence of identical pattern'.[69]

A criterion of cultural success requires flat objectivity, a structure of recognition that habituates the viewer with content already known. 'Recognition becomes an end instead of a means',[70] which finds of course various expressions. We can hum a catchy toothpaste melody and solidify a vague remembrance. We can straightforwardly identify with a film's protagonist with earnest awareness. We can find belonging through labelling staples such as associated references, allusions, affinities, milieus and hashtags. We can find reassurance in that which we've already internalised. In all cases, leisure today has never been more devoid of laziness. It takes strenuous efforts to harmonise with our surroundings.

The result mocks the precarious self-sufficiency of the spectator who is trained in recognising the already familiar conditions of its base existence. Total technological replication of empirical reality, through an infinite abundance of information, is its aim. Within photography and film especially, the eye cannot compete with this situation and the spectator resolves to find only verification of itself in all of its contortions such as the lack of spatial depth, of scale or an inhuman tempo. Like the lives we live, a relation between foreground and background becomes increasingly difficult to discern. There can be no suspense, only anxiety, when our engagement with detail amounts only to the apprehension of a nasty residue of photochemical processes and pixel saturation, an absolute emaciation of perception. Everything is reduced to recognition, a substitute for contemplation and patient reflection.

Within both the culture industry and the spectacle, the resemblance of art and life has become rationalised mimesis, the mere replication of empirical reality. Its 'technicolour heroes do not allow us to forget for a second that they are normal people'.[71] When they don't furnish models of the good life, they will at least extend solidarity and 'relatable' hardship, often reaffirming doctrines of empowerment and exonerating our own situation. Through entertainment, 'art abandons the attempt to weave illusions around the audience and to present a heightened version of reality, it tries [instead] to close the gap between audience and actors.'[72]

A waning belief in the objectivity and reality of the external world corresponds to an identification with a reality furnished by materials of advertising and mass industrial culture, with themes and dramatic tropes of popular film and television, fragments torn and assembled from a vast range of cultural traditions. On the whole, 'the affirmation and intellectual duplication of what exists anyway become pseudo-culture's own content, proof of its legitimacy'.[73] We rally in the form of pop music, mimic the intonations of comedians, dream in the style of a video game. The mechanical reproduction of culture, with its proliferation of images and the rapid sequence of their incessant generation, brings the rationalisation of mimesis to prominence as a damaged form of relations of recognition.

A faithful portrait

For Adorno, mimesis, 'which reaches back into the biological dimension',[74] consists of a thoroughly participatory attitude toward reality for which the subject-object relation is abandoned to the disposition and comportment of self-likeness. However, in its rationalisation, mimesis transforms into the defensive mode of mimicry, a vicious cycle by which the fear of objective forces foments the principle of identification. This *real subsumption* of humanity's mimetic impulse as such clarifies a form of domination characterised by a process of commensurable identification of the nonidentical, a depreciated ability to differentiate characteristic of the projective identification of reducing particulars to abstract equivalents, that is, of the commodity form's qualitative incentive for the quantitative.

As likeness is contorted into equivalence, mimesis becomes the synchronisation of subjects to an alienated world, an identity between spectators and spectacle. As Debord argues in an April 1963 letter:

> The only point I dispute is the inevitability of the undifferentiation of human beings 'by their lack of originality and their sharp resemblance.' I think it's quite the opposite: a *system* makes people look alike by manufacturing the obligatory sameness of their gestures (from the small range of choices allowed) and the ways of feeling and reporting such gestures.[75]

For Debord, the spectacle is riddled with constant isomorphic solicitation, 'at once a faithful mirror held up to the production of things and a distorting objectification of the producers'. Making 'no secret of what it *is*',[76] the spectacle assumes a mirror structure which, rather than misrepresenting reality, accurately reflects a reality already mangled and perverted by the fetish-forms of the autonomous economy developing for itself. In short, the spectacle has advanced the rationalisation of mimesis as a development of the commodity economy.

The capitalist mode of production contorts the mimetic faculty into the form of mimicry. The rationalisation of mimesis can be described as a schema for both the labour process – as an adaptation to external mechanisations or dead labour – and the exchange process – as an adaptation to sacrifice for self-preservation. Just as money was for Marx the *becoming visible* of commodity relations in their totality, the spectacle is for Debord the *becoming visible* of capital as a totality. In other words, the spectacle is the *becoming visible* of the unity of appearances, that is, the mode of appearance of society unified under capital. Here, '[s]ociety in its length and breadth becomes capital's faithful portrait'.[77] The social form of the commodity is 'shown for *what it is*'. 'Not only is the relation to the commodity visible but it is all one sees: the world one sees is its world.'[78]

Within the spectacle, social activity is made to appear, and in doing so, is embedded with mimetic import. This entails the organisation of human perception, defining *what* is to be seen with *how* it is apprehended, that is, through pathic identification. As a 'monopoly of appearance', the spectacle 'naturally finds vision to be the privileged human sense which the sense of touch was for other epochs'. The spectacle thereby 'says nothing more than "that which appears is good, that which is good appears"',[79] an optimal environment for mimetic identification.

We find a similar diagnostic within the work of Adorno, that is, a social whole that need only disclose itself to justify itself. Here, consistent with the society of the spectacle, the exposition of social conditions becomes a mystification of those very same social conditions, insofar as it cultivates and stimulates mimetic regression towards recognising the already familiar, authoritarian intolerance towards ambiguity and as the confirmation of a damaged subject's pathological projections. It is for this reason that Adorno can say: 'the surface of life, the immediacy it makes available to people, has become ideology.'[80] The critique of mimetic identification and its allurements remains part of Adorno's critical theory of society no less than the spectacle's organisation of appearances theorised by Debord. For both, the aggressive demand that the world bend to our barbarically diminished expectations is indexical of a barbarically diminished horizon of experience itself.

Eric-John Russell is a Marie Skłodowska-Curie Postdoctoral Fellow at the Institut für Philosophie, Universität Potsdam and the author of Spectacular Logic in Hegel and Debord: Why Everything is as it Seems *(2021).*

Notes

1. Theodor W. Adorno, *Aesthetics 1958/59*, trans. Wieland Hoban (Cambridge: Polity Press, 2018), 185. As Adorno summarises elsewhere: 'Prior to total administration, the subject who viewed, heard, or read a work was to lose himself, forget himself, extinguish himself in the work. The identification carried out by the subject was ideally not that of making the artwork like himself, but rather that of making himself like the artwork. This identification constituted aesthetic sublimation; Hegel named this comportment freedom to the object. He thus paid homage to the subject that becomes subject in spiritual experience through self-relinquishment, the opposite of the philistine demand that the artwork give him something.' Theodor W. Adorno, *Aesthetic Theory*, trans. Robert Hullot-Kentor (London: Continuum, 2002), 17.
2. For example, as Tom Bunyard makes commendably clear, *The Society of the Spectacle* is 'best understood as ... a book that describes a society that has become *detached* from its capacity to consciously shape and determine its own future'. Tom Bunyard, *Debord, Time and Spectacle: Hegelian Marxism and Situationist Theory* (Leiden: Brill, 2018), 4; emphasis added.
3. Guy Debord, *The Society of the Spectacle*, trans. Donald Nicholson-Smith (New York, NY: Zone Books, 1995), §26. Both Nicholson-Smith's and the early 1970 Black & Red translation of *The Society of the Spectacle* will be referenced in this essay. Each have their own respective merits depending on the context.
4. Guy Debord, *The Society of the Spectacle*, trans. Fredy Perlman and John Supak (Detroit: Black & Red, 1970), §10; emphasis added.
5. Debord, *The Society of the Spectacle* (1970), §25.
6. See Eric-John Russell, *Spectacular Logic in Hegel and Debord: Why Everything is as it Seems* (London: Bloomsbury, 2021). There it is argued that both Marx's critique of political economy and Hegel's speculative logic emerges within Debord's critical theory as a really existing rationality that gives structural coherence to the actuality of the society of the spectacle.
7. Debord, *The Society of the Spectacle* (1970), §30.
8. Internationale Situationniste, 'Les structures élémentaires de la réification', in *Internationale situationniste: Édition augmentee* (Paris: Librairie Arthème Fayard, 1997),

451, 450, 452.

9. Walter Benjamin, 'Doctrine of the Similar' in *Selected Writings Volume 2, Part 2, 1931-34*, trans. R. Livingstone et al., eds. M.W. Jennings, H. Eiland and G. Smith (Cambridge: Harvard University Press, 1999), 695.

10. For further examination into the significance of mimesis within the work of Adorno, see Karla L. Schultz, *Mimesis on the Move: Theodor W. Adorno's Concept of Imitation* (New York: Peter Lang, 1990); Gunter Gebauer and Christoph Wulf, 'Vital Experience (Adorno)', in *Mimesis: Culture – Art – Society*, trans. Don Reneau (Berkeley: University of California Press, 1995), 281-293; Pierre-François Noppen, 'Adorno on Mimetic Rationality: Three Puzzles', *Adorno Studies* 1:1 (2017).

11. Theodor W. Adorno and Max Horkheimer, *Dialectic of Enlightenment: Philosophical Fragments*, trans. Edmund Jephcott (Stanford: Stanford University Press, 2004), 146.

12. Adorno and Horkheimer, *Dialectic of Enlightenment*, 5.

13. A nearly identical analysis can be found in the work of Debord's fellow Situationist International member Raoul Vaneigem. See Raoul Vaneigem, *The Revolution of Everyday Life*, trans. Donald Nicholson-Smith (Oakland: PM Press, 2012), 60-64, 91 and 118-119.

14. Adorno and Horkheimer, *Dialectic of Enlightenment*, 166.

15. Adorno and Horkheimer, *Dialectic of Enlightenment*, 150.

16. Caillois' examples, among others, include the Trochilium butterfly, which assumes the appearance of a wasp, the Choerocampa Elpenor caterpillar that contorts its body in the form of a snake when alarmed, as well as the Caligo butterfly, which spreads its wings to resemble the plumage of an owl.

17. Roger Caillois, 'Mimicry and Legendary Psychasthenia', trans. John Shepley, *October* 31 (Winter 1984), 28.

18. Caillois, 'Mimicry', 28.

19. See Debord, *The Society of the Spectacle* (1995), §28 and §192.

20. Georg Lukács, *History and Class Consciousness: Studies in Marxist Dialectics*, trans. Rodney Livingstone (Cambridge: MIT Press, 1971), 90.

21. Debord, *The Society of the Spectacle* (1995), §161, §170.

22. Caillois, 'Mimicry', 30.

23. Adorno and Horkheimer, *Dialectic of Enlightenment*, 148.

24. Within the Guy Debord archive at the Bibliothèque Nationale de France in Paris, all of Debord's notes on Gabel's book are marked with either 'SduS très important' or 'import. pour SduS'. Bibliothèque nationale de France. Département des Manuscrits. NAF 28603. Fonds Guy Debord. Fiches rassemblées sous l'intitulé: 'Philosophie, sociologie' 156 f. Gabel, Joseph 5 f.210 x 135, 155 x 70 et 20 x 90 mm and Gabel, Joseph 8 f.125 x 75 et 75 x 125 mm.

25. There are a number of specific themes within Gabel's work that Debord utilises for *The Society of the Spectacle*, most glaringly with the latter's description of the spectacle as the organisation of abstract, irreversible and essentially spatialised temporality under a 'perpetual present' (Debord, *The Society of the Spectacle* (1995), §108, §126). As Gabel echoes Debord's comments, specifically within chapter six of *The Society of the Spectacle*, 'the maniac lives in an eternal present. His personal time is a succession of present time without memory of the past and without plans for the future. ... Therefore, the eternal – and eternally renewed – present of the maniac corresponds to a sort of spatialization of duration.' See Joseph Gabel, *False Consciousness: An Essay on Reification*, trans. Margaret A. Thompson (Oxford: Basil Blackwell, 1975), 185.

26. Eugène Minkowski, *La schizophrénie. Psychopathologie des schizoïdes et des schizophrènes* (Paris: Payot, 1927), 198.

27. Gabel, *False Consciousness*, xxi.

28. Gabel, *False Consciousness*, 4.

29. Gabel, *False Consciousness*, 21.

30. Gabel, *False Consciousness*, 93.

31. Gabel, *False Consciousness*, 294-295.

32. Here, both 'stifling proximity and hopeless distance' oscillate within a world of paranoia that knows 'neither real distance nor real proximity'. Gabel, *False Consciousness*, 259, 272.

33. Debord, *The Society of the Spectacle* (1995), §212.

34. Debord, *The Society of the Spectacle* (1995), §219.

35. Gabel, *False Consciousness*, 124.

36. Notably, 'as a tendency to *make one see* the world by means of various specialized mediations (it can no longer be grasped directly), [the spectacle] naturally finds vision to be the privileged human sense which the sense of touch was for other epochs' (Debord, *The Society of the Spectacle* (1970), §18), which corresponds to Gabel's observation that while paranoid hallucinations are mainly acoustic, deranged perceptions are predominantly visual (Gabel, *False Consciousness*, 280).

37. Bibliothèque nationale de France. Département des Manuscrits. NAF 28603. Fonds Guy Debord. Fiches rassemblées sous l'intitulé : "Philosophie, sociologie" 156 f. Gabel, Joseph 5 f.210 x 135, 155 x 70 et 20 x 90 mm and Gabel, Joseph 8 f.125 x 75 et 75 x 125 mm.

38. Guy Debord, *Correspondance Volume 4: Janvier 1969 - Décembre 1972* (Paris: Librairie Arthème Fayard, 2004),

80.

39. For the Situationist International's position on psychoanalysis generally, see 'Les adventures du résultat parcellaire' in the tenth 1966 issue of *Internationale situationniste* wherein it is said that, '[t]he discoveries of psychoanalysis, like the thought of Freud, are at the end of the day unacceptable to the dominant social order.' Internationale Situationniste, 'Les adventures du résultat parcellaire', in *Internationale situationniste: Édition augmentee* (Paris: Librairie Arthème Fayard, 1997), 475.

40. Of course it can be said that neither Adorno nor Debord successfully resolve the larger question of how one relates problems of individual psychoanalysis to broader social tendencies, that is to the theoretical difficulties of sociologising psychoanalysis. See Alexandra Ivanova, 'Psychologizing Sociology?' in *Cured Quail Vol. 2* (2020), 217–228 and Frank Grohmann, 'Le nouveau parochialisme et la vielle critique des exigences tronquées de la pratique', *Palim Psao* (Feb. 2022), available at http://www.palim-psao.fr/2022/02/le-nouveau-parochialisme-et-la-vieille-critique-des-exigences-tronquees-de-la-pratique-par-frank-grohmann.html. Yet it remains the case that Adorno at least was aware of the challenges. (See Theodor W. Adorno, 'Revisionist Psychoanalysis', *Philosophy & Social Criticism* 40:3 (2014), 326–338.) Debord's diagnostic target is of course not clinical in nature nor an individual pathological agent, but society at large. In this way, his usage of psychoanalytic characterisation wields pronouncedly less commitment to the discourse of psychoanalysis itself, and ought to be grasped as part of his stylistic *détournements*, appropriations of language utilised without fidelity to their original context for altogether different purposes. Debord's concept of the society of the spectacle by no means requires psychoanalytic categories for its own internal coherence, even if they add to that concept's vivacity.

41. Bibliothèque nationale de France. Département des Manuscrits. NAF 28603. Fonds Guy Debord. Fiches rassemblées sous l'intitulé : "Philosophie, sociologie" 156 f. Gabel, Joseph 5 f.210 x 135, 155 x 70 et 20 x 90 mm and Gabel, Joseph 8 f.125 x 75 et 75 x 125 mm.

42. Debord, *The Society of the Spectacle* (1995), §219. For Gabel, 'an increased need for compensatory representation' and 'for imitation' characterises the pathology of hysterical pantomime. 'The abnormal need for representation here makes up for a torturing feeling of being on the edge of existence … hysterical imitation, like the *Identitätszwang* of schizophrenics, is a structural element of this inauthenticity which occurs on this side of the voluntary-involuntary alternative.' Gabel, *False Consciousness*, 199–200.

43. Gabel, *False Consciousness*, 200, 201.

44. Debord, *The Society of the Spectacle* (1995), §218. Debord derives the category of autism from Gabel's reference to Ignace Meyerson and Marinette Dambuyant's article 'Un type de raisonnement de justification', *Journal de Psychologie* (Oct. 1946), 387–404. Although beyond the scope of this essay, further investigation into the relation between the spectacle and autism would do well to consider Thomas Ogden's 'autistic-contiguous' position, which is constitutive of the experience of bounded *surfaces*. See Thomas H. Ogden, *The Primitive Edge of Experience* (London: Karnac, 1989).

45. Debord, *The Society of the Spectacle*, 1995, §219

46. Guy Debord, *Correspondance Volume 0: Septembre 1951 – Juillet 1957* (Paris: Librairie Arthème Fayard, 2010), 329.

47. Guy Debord, 'Préface à la 4ᵉ edition italienne de *La Société du spectacle*', in *Œuvres* (Paris: Éditions Gallimard, 2006), 1463.

48. Theodor W. Adorno, *Minima Moralia: Reflections from Damaged Life*, trans. Edmund F.N. Jephcott (London: Verso, 2005), 15, 147.

49. See Anselm Jappe, *Guy Debord*, trans. Donald Nicholson-Smith (Berkeley: University of California Press 1999), 103; Anselm Jappe, 'The Spectacle and the Culture Industry, the Transcendence of Art and the Autonomy of Art: Some Parallels between Theodor Adorno's and Guy Debord's Critical Concepts', in *The Sage Handbook of Frankfurt School Critical Theory, Volume 1*, eds. Beverley Best, Werner Bonefeld and Chris O'Kane, trans. Donald Nicholson-Smith (London: Sage, 2018), 1285–1301.

50. Debord, *The Society of the Spectacle* (1995), §30.

51. Adorno and Horkheimer, *Dialectic of Enlightenment*, 119.

52. Theodor W. Adorno, 'Television as Ideology', in *Critical Models: Interventions and Catchwords*, trans. Henry W. Pickford (New York: Columbia University Press, 1998), 62.

53. Adorno and Horkheimer, *Dialectic of Enlightenment*, 101, 118, 133, 119.

54. Debord, *The Society of the Spectacle* (1995), §213.

55. Internationale Situationniste, 'L'absence et ses habilleurs', in *Internationale situationniste: Édition augmentee* (Paris: Librairie Arthème Fayard, 1997), 374; emphasis added.

56. Adorno and Horkheimer, *Dialectic of Enlightenment*, 154.

57. Adorno and Horkheimer, *Dialectic of Enlightenment*, 156.

58. Debord, *The Society of the Spectacle* (1970), §23.

59. Raoul Vaneigem, 'Basic Banalities (Part 2)', in *Situationist International Anthology: Revised and Expanded Edition*, ed. and trans. Ken Knabb (Berkeley: Bureau of Public Secrets, 2006), 158.

60. Adorno and Horkheimer, *Dialectic of Enlightenment*, 140.

61. There is a common albeit erroneous tendency within the literature to characterise both Adorno's critique of the culture industry and Debord's critique of the spectacle as inculcating a standpoint of 'passivity', as if the objectivity of forces of abstract domination were not themselves ultimately the result of subjective activity. Here it should be recalled that Adorno's critique of *Aktionismus*, that is, 'action that overdoes and aggravates itself for the sake of its own publicity, without admitting to itself to what extent it serves as a substitute satisfaction, elevating itself into an end itself', is hardly reducible to passivity, even if one wanted to allot a certain 'pseudo' prefix to its practice. See Theodor W. Adorno, 'Resignation', in *Critical Models: Interventions and Catchwords*, trans. Henry W. Pickford (New York: Columbia University Press, 2005), 291; see also Theodor W. Adorno and Gerhard Richter, 'Who's Afraid of the Ivory Tower? A Conversation with Theodor W. Adorno', *Monatshefte* 94:1 (2002), 10–23. Additionally reductive would be to qualify Debord's spectators as simply 'passive'. While 'contemplation' as a register of reification is a term frequently employed by Debord, much as it is by Lukács, within the theory of the spectacle it is not tantamount to a passive disposition of an alienated subjectivity. As Debord writes in his notes comparing the work of *Socialisme ou Barbarie* to the theory of the spectacle, '[i]t is too simple to say that capitalism both requires and prevents participation …. Capitalism organises 'participation' as spectacle – in the spectacle…. It is wrong to say that <capitalism> prevents participation where in fact it is at the same time dependent on participation.' Laurence Le Bras and Emmanuel Guy, eds., *Lire Debord: Avec des notes inédites de Guy Debord* (Paris: Éditions L'Échappée, 2016), 29. The essential point here is that varied phenomenological oscillation between 'passive' and 'active' poles can be found within a critical diagnostic of mimetic behaviour, not the absolutisation of one pole over another.

62. As Adorno makes clear in *Aesthetic Theory*: 'Philistines are those whose relation to artworks is ruled by whether and to what degree they can, for example, put themselves in the place of the actors as they come forth; this is what all parts of the culture industry are based on and they foster it insistently in their customers.' Adorno, *Aesthetic Theory*, 346.

63. Lukács, *History and Class Consciousness*, 168.

64. Axel Honneth, *Reification: A New Look at an Old Idea* (Oxford: Oxford University Press, 2008), 40f.

65. See Raymond Geuss, 'Philosophical Anthropology and Social Criticism', in Honneth, *Reification*, 127. For an analysis of the ways in which ignorance and recognition work *in concert*, not with any form of misrecognition or non-recognition, see Mari Mikkola, 'Ideal Theory, Epistemologies of Ignorance, and (Mis)Recognition', in *Epistemic Injustice and the Philosophy of Recognition*, eds. Paul Giladi and Nicola McMillan (New York: Routledge, 2022).

66. Adorno and Horkheimer, *Dialectic of Enlightenment*, 103.

67. Theodor W. Adorno, 'On Popular Music', in *Current of Music: Elements of a Radio Theory*, trans. Robert Hullot-Kentor (Cambridge: Polity Press, 2009), 299.

68. Adorno, 'On Popular Music', 307.

69. Adorno, 'On Popular Music', 311.

70. Adorno, 'On Popular Music', 300.

71. Adorno, *Minima Moralia*, 202.

72. Christopher Lasch, *The Culture of Narcissism: American Life in An Age of Diminishing Expectations* (New York: W.W. Norton, 1979), 88–89.

73. Theodor W. Adorno, 'Theory of Pseudo-Culture', *Telos* 95 (1993), 33.

74. Adorno, *Aesthetic Theory*, 329.

75. Guy Debord, *Correspondance, Volume 2: Septembre 1960 – Décembre 1964* (Paris: Librairie Arthème Fayard, 2001), 221.

76. Debord, *The Society of the Spectacle* (1995), §16, §25.

77. Debord, *The Society of the Spectacle* (1995), §50. '[D]o not let the term "visibility" suggest that the spectacle is a concept, again, primarily concerned with literal visual imagery or is reducible to an environment oversaturated with advertisements or consumerism. Visibility here refers back to the riddle of the money-fetish – to the inverted world become, in Marx's words, "dazzling to our eyes"' (Russell, *Spectacular Logic*, 104).

78. Debord, *The Society of the Spectacle* (1970), §37, §42

79. Debord, *The Society of the Spectacle* (1970), §12, §18.

80. Adorno, *Aesthetic Theory*, 336.

History and revolution in Debord's *The Society of the Spectacle*

Tom Bunyard

The Society of the Spectacle was written, as Guy Debord once put it, 'with the deliberate intention of doing harm to spectacular society'.[1] Following the book's publication in 1967, he and the Situationist International (SI) declared that it sought 'nothing other than to overthrow the existing relation of forces in the factories and the streets', and that it 'makes no attempt to hide its *a priori* engagement' in revolutionary social change.[2] Its intended audience were all 'those who are enemies of the existing order and who act efficaciously, starting from this position',[3] not the academics and cultural commentators who would later come to adopt it. Debord reserved particular contempt for such 'specialists of the semblance of discussions', especially when they claimed to find value in *The Society of the Spectacle* whilst shying away from its formidable militancy. 'Of all those who have quoted from this book in order to acknowledge some importance in it', he wrote in 1979, 'I have not seen one up till now who took the risk to say, even briefly, what it was about'.[4]

The situation is not vastly different today: *The Society of the Spectacle* is often valued as a description of certain aspects of modern society, rather than as an attempt to articulate that society's transformation. This is not to deny that the book can be employed as a useful tool or reference point in such descriptions. Debord himself acknowledged this, albeit disparagingly: 'The critical concept of spectacle', he wrote, 'can undoubtedly ... be vulgarised into a commonplace hollow formula of sociologico-political rhetoric to explain and abstractly denounce everything, and thus serve as a defence of the spectacular system'.[5] Yet the book was meant to do more than this. It was intended to function not just as an interpretation of modern society, but in a manner more akin to a work of strategy, that is, as an intellectual component of a practical, concrete and decidedly combative project of social change.

Debord once stated that he was 'not a philosopher', but rather 'a strategist'.[6] This stance became more prominent in his work during the 1970s, when he became increasingly preoccupied with theorising the patterns of intrigue, surveillance and manoeuvre that followed the uprisings of 1968.[7] He was, however, fascinated by strategy and military history throughout his life, and a 'strategic' approach to the role of radical theory can be discerned in his work from at least the late 1950s onwards. He became increasingly invested in Hegelian Marxism and the theme of praxis at that time, and by the early 1960s, he had come to the view that the SI needed to produce theory capable of identifying, clarifying and facilitating such praxis in the revolutionary pursuit of a new form of social life. In many respects, these efforts culminated in *The Society of the Spectacle*. Like a work of strategy, that book attempted to set out the nature, stakes and challenges of an impending social conflict; and, like any piece of strategy, its value, for Debord, could only be ascertained practically.

This means that one of the ways in which this book might be assessed today is by treating it on its own terms and considering just how efficacious its analyses really were. I shall touch on this below. My primary aim, however, is preliminary to such an assessment: I want to demonstrate that *The Society of the Spectacle* was indeed meant to function as a contribution towards a project of social transformation, rather than as a mere work of 'sociologico-political rhetoric'. This will require reconstructing the ideas that underpin its uncompromising drive towards praxis. Doing so will lead to the view that

Debord may have been rather more of a philosopher than he wanted to admit, insofar as his 'strategic' book rests upon a set of philosophical ideas about time, history and social life.

'Historical life'

Debord's theory of 'spectacle' is centred around a broadly young-Marxian view of social life, according to which the latter is an ongoing, mutable construction. On this view, the history of human society is a process of constant social change and conflict, in which the norms and practices that articulate social activity are steadily generated, employed, contested and revised. This is a self-constitutive process, for Debord; history is not governed or steered by anything other than human action. It is not always conducted in a fully self-determining manner, however, because the structures that emerge within it can frame their inhabitants' understanding of their own collective agency in flawed, partial and socially divided ways.

For Debord, modern society had afforded the possibility of making this process a free, collective and fully self-determining affair. He and the SI held that this society's tremendous capacity to shape its environment and to mould lived experience evidenced the possibility of a new and more self-conscious form of 'historical life'[8] (his term for forms of social existence marked by an awareness of historical mutability). Because practically every aspect of social life had become shaped and constructed by human agency, modern society was held to harbour the potential for a new mode of life in which that process of historical construction could become enriched, ludic and collectively self-determining. Yet the phenomena that evidenced this possibility also kept it in check. Society's new powers to shape life operated through a set of economically derived structures that had taken on a degree of autonomy from their producers. Modern society had thus become subordinated to a set of alienated instantiations of its own collective power to shape itself in time.

Debord maintained that this predicament was due, primarily, to the 'colonisation of everyday life' by the commodity.[9] The latter had entailed the articulation of social life by fixed models and templates for behaviour, interaction and subjective identity. These reified norms, or 'images' of life, were held to govern life's practical conduct in ways that suited the needs of an effectively 'autonomous economy'.[10] Debord's theory thus describes a social context in which such subjects act and interact in response to the options and incentives presented to them but which they do not fully *control*; a world in which they have become alienated 'performers' within a kind of collective 'show' – an alternative translation of the French *spectacle*. Spectacular society is thus a society marked by stifled potential: by the separation of social individuals from their collective capacity to shape their own lived time, and by the consequent denigration of their ability to govern their own collective future.

This is why the book is so concerned with temporality. *The Society of the Spectacle* contains two entire chapters on time, and references to time and history occur throughout its pages. It casts modern society as having become characterised by a merely 'contemplative' relation to its own historical existence. In response, *The Society of the Spectacle* – which Debord claimed to be 'communist if it is anything'[11] – frames the modern revolution not solely as a demand to take collective control of the means of production, as in classical conceptions of communism, but rather as an attempt to lay claim to the available means of producing and shaping lived experience in time. Indeed, 'the spectre haunting modern society' for Debord was 'history itself'.¹² The aim was not to establish a perfect and static social formation, but rather to create a more fluid and mobile condition, in which collective social existence would 'at last be able to surrender itself joyously to the true divisions and never-ending confrontations of historical life'.¹³

Debord's theory, then, is not just an account of that which is 'contemplated' (a society shaped by the commodity, or the latter's cultural derivatives). Rather, it was meant to capture the predicament and arrested possibilities that such 'contemplation' entails, and thereby both the stakes and the aims of a revolutionary project that would respond to that predicament. His book thus addresses 'the historical moment in which we are caught'¹⁴ not just by describing some of the primary features of that moment, but rather by trying to identify, express and contribute towards resolving the very condition of being 'caught' in history.

Totality

The manner in which the theory does this relies on an attempt to think society as a totality. 'Methodologically', Debord wrote in a letter of 1964, 'the centre of revolutionary dialectical thought is the concept of the *totality*'.¹⁵ Revolutionary theory needs to understand the dynamics and tensions within a social whole, in order to engage with them and steer its transformation. A notion of totality as a mutable whole, and the 'dialectical thought' that could conceive the latter, were thus seen to be integral to any genuinely radical theory. His personal notes on strategy even state that it is 'the *same thing* to think dialectically and to think strategically', insofar as '*both denote the totality*'; both are 'aspects of the thought of praxis, which must act'.¹⁶ Thinking 'dialectically' allowed one to theorise a totality; theorising society as a totality enabled strategic engagement with the moving forces and shifting terrains of struggle within it.

The concept of spectacle enabled just such a conception of the social whole. It served to 'unify and explain a wide range of apparently disparate phenomena'¹⁷ as aspects of one general problematic. And because that problematic concerned the failures, struggles and possibilities of an entire social formation, it enabled conceiving modern society 'in its totality'¹⁸ from an explicitly revolutionary perspective, that is, from a perspective able to express the shared desires, and to focus the resultant demands and frustrations, of a specific historical moment. '[O]nly the revolutionary point of view', he maintained, 'can possess the *meaning* [*sens*, or orientation] of this ensemble of phenomena'.¹⁹

In its grandest, most overtly Hegelian and hubristic sense, Debord's efforts to do this amounted to an attempt to give conscious, theoretical voice to the movement of history itself. His aim was to facilitate a condition in which the historical movement of a social whole could become a self-conscious and collectively self-determining process. The hubris is tempered by the sense in which a theory that purported to afford such a perspective could only ever do so *provisionally*. It could be 'only "the maximum of possible consciousness at this moment in society"',²⁰ because only the unfolding of history could prove it right. And this, to reiterate, is why Debord's theory had to be employed, like a work of strategy, in concrete praxis. If it was not recognised, adopted and used fruitfully by those whose conditions it meant to express, it would be a failure, and could be deemed false or at least flawed. Hence: 'the critical theory of the spectacle can only be true by uniting with the practical current of negation in society'.²¹ As Debord put it in a letter of 1971:

> ... if the concept of spectacle is an error, the whole damn book falls apart. However, as far as I am aware, there is no *better* [book] on the subject that concerns us; a point that takes us back to the fundamental question of consciousness in history, and of what it does in it. For example, [Marx's] *Capital* is evidently true and false: essentially, it is true, because the proletariat recognized it, although quite badly (and thus also let its errors pass).²²

I shall return to those alleged 'errors' later. But we should note that the ideas sketched here inform the SI's contention, quoted earlier, that *The Society of the Spectacle*'s analyses were marked from the very outset by an '*a priori* engagement'. The book was meant to articulate, and assist, a 'practical current of negation in society' that was already present, albeit lacking in clarity and focus.

The subject-object of history

We can take a further step towards characterising Debord's position by noting that *The Society of the Spectacle* owes a great deal to Georg Lukács' *History and Class Consciousness* – an influence evidenced by the sheer number of quotations from Hegel and Marx that Debord appears to have taken from Lukács' pages. This is perhaps unsurprising. Sections of that book started to appear in French from the late 1950s onwards, at the time Debord was developing his mature theoretical ideas. By the early 1960s Lukács' book had acquired a degree of notoriety that no doubt appealed to Debord, and its emphasis on transformative, self-constitutive action accorded with the ambience of French existentialism, twentieth-century French Hegelianism and the legacies of Surrealism that informed Debord's developing views.

There is a striking resemblance between Lukács' own seminal account of 'contemplative' detachment and Debord's account of 'spectatorship'. In both cases, human subjects find themselves confronted by, and situated in a passive relationship towards, a seemingly immutable and independent objective world; in both cases, this condition is held to stem from the ubiquity of commodity relations; and in both cases, this predicament is to be overcome through revolutionary praxis, whereby those alienated subjects are to take conscious, collective control of their own objective existence. Moreover, although they framed this in different ways, both Debord and Lukács appear to have conceived revolutionary praxis as a condition of subject-object unity.

Debord seems close, broadly speaking, to a rather traditional reading of *History and Class Consciousness*. On such a reading, Lukács re-cast Hegel's account of 'Spirit's' ascent towards 'Absolute Knowing' as the emergence of a self-conscious and self-determining revolutionary proletariat. The latter, as subject, must come to recognise that the seemingly independent and immutable objective social world that confronts it is really the result of its own activity. In so doing, the proletariat can begin to comprehend and consciously employ its own transformative agency, shaping its world and itself freely and self-consciously as a subject-object unity. Communism is construed as the actualisation of this condition through collectively self-determining historical praxis.

The Society of the Spectacle owes a great deal to these ideas. Compare, for example, the following lines. Firstly, here is Lukács: 'the proletariat', he writes, must 'become the identical subject-object of history whose praxis will change reality'.[23] And now here is Debord: 'As for the *subject* of history, it can only be the self-production of the living: the living becoming master and possessor of its world – that is, of history – and coming to exist as *consciousness of its own activity [conscience de son jeu]*.' 'The history shaped by this subject', Debord writes, would have 'no goal [*n'a pas d'objet*] other than the effects it works upon itself.'[24] In both cases, the goal of revolution is to allow human subjects to take conscious charge of their own objective existence; and in both cases, this is framed via an emphasis on history, or rather on the temporal and social dimensions of the objective existence of those human subjects.

The finer details of the distinctions between Debord's ideas and those advanced in *History and Class Consciousness* cannot be addressed here,[25] but we should at least note his distance from Lukács' views on political organisation. This brings us to the connection between the concept of spectacle and the SI's fierce anti-authoritarianism.

Spectacle and authority

The concept of spectacle concerns the separation of the power to shape and direct lived time from that power's producers. Such separation occurs when that power becomes fetishistically located within constructions that emerge from the conduct of social life, and which come to ensnare and restrict it within fixed patterns of activity. Debord's chief concern in this regard was with a society that had become structured and spellbound by commodity relations. Yet the commodity was viewed as only example of this very general problem: he and the SI were opposed to *any* instance in which social groups locate their collective powers and agency within reified social structures. This informs the SI's opposition to dogma, ideology and religion, but also their rejection of hierarchical structures, political leaders and revolutionary figureheads. All were treated with hostility, and so too were all forms of representational social power liable to grow detached from their base ('wherever there is independent representation the spectacle reconstitutes itself').[26] Hence Debord and the SI's cautious enthusiasm for anarchism,[27] their wariness towards Leninism, and their efforts to avoid becoming figureheads themselves ('pro-situs' were condemned as 'enthusiastic spectators of the SI');[28] and hence also Debord's deep distaste for Lukács' enthusiastic visions of the Party.

Despite *The Society of the Spectacle*'s debts to Lukács,

the book's only direct references to him are an epigraph and a single set of damning remarks. Debord writes that Lukács' 'endless self-repudiations', conducted in response to the Russian bureaucracy, proved him to be a prime example of the 'despicable' nature of the intellectuals of his century. Lukács had shown himself to be 'an ideologue speaking in the name of the power most grossly external to the proletarian movement'; 'a power that disowns and suppresses its lackeys', and which amounted to the very 'opposite' of 'what he [Lukács] had supported in *History and Class Consciousness*.'[29] A genuine condition of subject-object unity, Debord held, could not involve any reliance on such an 'externality'. It could only take the form of social life governing and shaping itself *directly*.

Federated workers' councils were viewed as the best available means of achieving such a condition. Debord did not view such councils as a perfect or permanent solution to the problem of social organisation, and his enthusiasm for councilism did not stem from an uncritical view of labour.[30] The councils were only viewed as the best available initial means of managing a complex post-revolutionary society whilst minimising hierarchy and representative political power. Nonetheless, *The Society of the Spectacle* contains eulogistic statements such as the following:

> In the power of the Councils, which must internationally supplant all other power, the proletarian movement is its own product and this product is the producer himself. He is to himself his own goal. Only there is the spectacular negation of life negated in its turn.[31]

Or again: 'the power of the Councils' can 'be effective only if it transforms existing conditions in their entirety', and it 'cannot assign itself a smaller task if it wants to be recognized and to recognise itself in its world'.[32] Through such forms of organisation, a mode of social life could be established that would be 'inseparable from a coherent intervention in history'.[33]

Hegel and Marx

I have proposed that *The Society of the Spectacle* should be understood as a work of 'dialectical, strategic thought';[34] that it was written with the intention that its ideas should be actualised in praxis; and that the political project that it sought to articulate was that of rendering 'historical life' a self-conscious and self-determinate affair through the practical instantiation of a condition of subject-object unity. It is perhaps no wonder, then, that Debord once remarked that 'one cannot fully comprehend [*The Society of the Spectacle*] without Marx, and especially Hegel'.[35]

Hegel is 'especially' significant because Debord understood him as having made a huge contribution towards articulating 'the thought of history', that is, towards clarifying and setting out a mode of thought capable of grasping the conflictual dynamics of historical change. Yet Debord's Hegel fell short of casting that mode of thought as a means of actually *making* history. For Debord, Hegel presented human history as directed by a 'supreme external agent',[36] and as having reached a conclusion in the society of his own day; and despite setting out an inherently mobile mode of thought, well suited to thinking the world's transformation, he had locked it within a purportedly final and static metaphysical system. (Debord's reading of Hegel is, of course, highly questionable.) Marx's extraction of a 'rational kernel' from the 'mystical shell'[37] of Hegel's work was thus viewed as the removal of that dynamic mode of thought from the fixity and conservatism of the Hegelian system; a removal that allowed the 'realisation' of philosophy in concrete praxis, and thus that of dialectical thought as practical *strategic* thought. The famed Marxian 'inversion' of Hegel was thereby understood as a reversal of perspective, insofar as Hegel's retrospective vision of a completed past was replaced with an attempt to make the future. That attempt, for Debord, constituted the real core and lasting significance of Marx's entire *oeuvre*. 'Marx's project', for Debord, was 'the project of a conscious history'.[38]

Many of these ideas are encapsulated in the following claims, which are taken from a letter of 1969, and which draw heavily on Marx's final thesis on Feuerbach. 'The philosophers', before Marx, Debord writes, 'had interpreted the world as a given block'. Hegel, however, made a significant advance: he 'interpreted concrete change, the world constituting itself in its own history'. Yet Hegel remained at the level of 'philosophy', and thus of 'interpretation', because he 'reduced' that process of transformation to the 'project of the Spirit', and so 'remained a philosopher' confronted by 'an external history'. Or, in other words: Hegel, for Debord, fell short of the very subject-object unity that his own work had espoused, because he had failed to grasp that the real locus of that unity could not lie in a metaphysical construct, but only in the self-constitution of collective social life. Marx had contributed towards remedying this by indicating that the 'critique of Hegelianism' should lead directly towards recognising the need 'to take an active part in history'.[39]

It may be useful to place the foregoing in relation to the current interest in reading Debord's theory as echoing aspects of contemporary Marxist value theory.[40] These readings often focus on the German *Neue Marx-Lektüre* and *Wertkritik* schools, which developed roughly around the same time as Debord's theory. There is no direct line of influence between the SI and this material, but there are certainly echoes and resemblances.[41] This has fostered a growing interest in treating *The Society of the Spectacle* as a description of a world shaped by the commodity relations theorised in *Capital*, and that in turn has encouraged attempts to understand Debord's Hegelian Marxism in ways that centre around Marx's use of Hegel's *Logic* in *Capital*.[42] This kind of approach can be very fruitful indeed, not least because it can point towards ways of developing Debord's ideas beyond his own rather schematic formulations on the topic. Yet although this offers an excellent means of identifying what is important in Debord's work today, it seems to differ somewhat from what Debord himself felt to be of primary importance.[43]

Capital's account of the fetishistic subordination of human subjects to their own objective creations is certainly crucial to *The Society of the Spectacle*, and it merits serious study; but as Debord himself pointed out, practically all of his book's references to Marx are taken from earlier texts, produced between 1843 and 1846.[44] His use of Hegel is similar. As his archived reading notes show, he did indeed engage with Hegel's mature *Logic*, but in a rather cursory fashion, and he appears to have been far more concerned with the romantic themes of dynamism, movement and collective 'life' set out in Hegel's *Phenomenology* and earlier writings.[45] When viewed from what I take to be Debord's perspective, prioritising *The Society of the Spectacle*'s account of capitalist value would run the risk of prioritising its claims *about* modern society, potentially at the cost of his own emphasis on strategic intervention.

This brings us to the primary errors that Debord ascribed to Marx's work, and to elements of Marxism: namely, that of privileging economic analysis over the theorisation of revolutionary action. In chapter four of *The Society of the Spectacle*, Debord argues that the failure of the 1848 revolutions sent Marx in search of a 'scientific' and lawlike account of the capitalist present and its immanent end. This laid a basis for a focus on the determination of historical events by the economy; a focus that 'obscured his [Marx's] historical thought',[46] and which marred his 'theoretical legacy to the workers' movement'.[47] Subsequent Marxist theorists could then 'patiently study economic development' and thus adopt a 'contemplative' approach to a history purportedly made and ruled by the economy. The 'advent of the subject of history was consequently set back even further', whilst 'revolutionary practice ... tended to be thrust out of theory's field of vision altogether'.[48] This effectively replicated the very problem that needed to be resolved: the governance of social and historical life by its own constructions.[49]

So, for Debord, and despite their great contributions, both Hegel and Marx could be criticised for retaining a 'contemplative' approach to history, insofar as aspects of their work reflected and naturalised history's determination by forces other than human agency (Spirit on the one hand, the economy on the other). Nonetheless, he also held that their work contained vital resources for thinking the movement and conduct of social life.

This can be illustrated by Debord's personal reading notes on Hyppolite's *Studies on Marx and Hegel*, which include the following quotation:

> In the [early] *Logic* of Jena, Hegel thinks of infinity as a dialectical relation of the one and the many, but we can recognise in this logical dialectic the very idea of life. Reciprocally, life is this dialectic itself, and life forces the Spirit to think dialectically.[50]

Significantly, Debord wrote in the margin of this note '*a contrario* la non vie'.[51] A 'living', dynamic 'dialectical relation of the one and the many' contrasts with the condition of generalised 'non-life' described in *The Society of the Spectacle*: a condition of fragmentation, isolation and submission to reified norms, engendered by the articulation of social life through commodity relations. Two points can be made here. First, the quotation accords with Debord's indications that 'historical life' is somehow dialectical in nature. '[H]istory is dialectic', he wrote, and a 'dialectician ... possesses the intelligence of the real'.[52] Second, it is not just the experience of the conduct of social life itself that 'forces the Spirit [i.e. collective social life] to think dialectically', and to thereby come to know its own movement; *a contrario*, this is prompted within modern society by the existential *deficiencies* engendered by the 'autonomous movement of the non-living'.[53]

These ideas, I would suggest, inform Debord's claim that the experience of modern life obliges 'workers' to 'become dialecticians'.[54] If they were to respond to its existential poverty and govern their own collective lives in the absence of spectacular representation, they would need take up 'dialectical, strategic thought' in order to comprehend and direct the history that their own social agency creates. Modern life, it seems, was held to have both enabled and prompted such a perspective, due to the degree to which it had not only foregrounded society's vast capacities to shape lived experience, and to mould historical events, but because it had also separated its populace from the ability to consciously and collectively employ those capacities. Hence his *détournement* of *The Communist Manifesto*: because 'human beings have ... been thrust into history', they 'find themselves obliged to view their relationships in a clear-eyed manner',[55] and to thereby adopt the same 'dialectical' and 'strategic' perspective on historical life that Debord's book sought to articulate. This then brings us to the book's ambitious account of its own conditions of possibility.

Time and spectacle

The Society of the Spectacle rests on a philosophical anthropology that was influenced by Hegel, Marx and existentialism.[56] It treats human beings as historical, social and self-authoring creatures. We are held to shape ourselves and our world through the social actions and experiences that we conduct and undergo in time. But the book also holds that this capability for historical self-determination has been instantiated and understood in more or less adequate ways in differing socio-historical circumstances. The 'temporalisation of man [*sic*]', Debord claimed, is 'effected through the mediation of a society'.[57] Our experience of our own existence and agency in time, in other words, is shaped by the social structures that we inhabit.

This appears to rest on the following premises. First: social power – that is, the power available to the inhabitants of a given social structure – is predicated upon the activity and organisation of a society. Second: such power is, therefore, in some sense *collective*. And third: this power is, ultimately, the power to shape history. After all, the power available to a society, or to individuals within it, is the power to govern what happens in time, and to shape how events, actions and possibilities are understood. This is why Debord writes that 'To reflect on history is, inseparably, *to reflect on power* [*pouvoir*].'[58] His point seems to be that history – in the sense of human awareness of actions and events in time – is always made and told in ways that are articulated by the operation of social power.

The very possibility of this book – a book that attempts to articulate the revolutionary demands of its moment by framing 'historical time' as both 'the milieu and goal of the proletarian revolution'[59] – seems to be premised on the view that modern society's revolutionary dilemma had clearly revealed this ontological condition, showing it in a light that was unavailable in the past. This is presented via an extraordinarily bold philosophy of history that casts the radical demands of Debord's present as revealing the buried core of all previous social struggles.

Much of this is set out in the book's fifth chapter, which describes the differing conceptions of time enabled by a series of different socio-economic formations, and which casts them as developmental steps towards a full awareness of humanity's self-constitutive and historical nature afforded by Debord's present. The chapter's narrative begins with the 'cyclical' time of the very earliest human societies, in which the experience of temporal change is governed by the seasons, and in which, due to the absence of writing, memory lasts no longer than the memory of the present generation. Into this simple perpetual present, the division of labour, fostered by agriculture and surplus, introduces new possibilities for social change and a more complex sense of temporality. Significantly, Debord introduces class at this point: a distinction is drawn between those who enable the life of a community and those who direct this life.[60] The central idea here appears to be that the division of labour affords historical change in a manner that had previously been unavailable, but that it also entails the separation of an increasingly mutable history from those whose social activity enables its existence. This separation is then traced throughout the rest of the chapter's narrative, which takes in Ancient China, Greece, medieval and renaissance societies, the rise of the bourgeoisie and the temporality of capitalist society.

Capitalism is described as dispersing a new sense of historically differentiated time throughout society. Industry, technology and commerce inaugurate an increased sense of humanity's capacity to shape its world. That capacity still remains removed from its producers, however, because the 'qualitative use of life' becomes increasingly shaped by the quantitative abstractions of labour time.[61] Historical time thus becomes more obvious and universal, but only via the subordination of lived interactions to the demands of an autonomous economy. So, whilst historical change becomes more prominent, it also becomes more removed from conscious control. As Debord puts it: 'the bourgeoisie unveiled irreversible historical time and imposed it on society only to deprive society of its *use*'.[62] This, I would suggest, is why the book's celebrated fourth chapter, which discusses the history of the workers' movement, begins in the immediate *aftermath* of the bourgeois revolutions.[63] The modern revolutionary project, for Debord, is essentially aimed at grasping the new historical time afforded by the social, cultural and technological capacities of capitalist society.

As noted earlier, Debord indicates that the articulation of social life through commodity relations in his own present had demonstrated, explicitly, that modern society possessed a tremendous capacity to shape and structure lived social experience; but, by the same token, it also meant the extreme separation of that power from the direct control of its producers. He thus writes that 'though separated from his product, man [sic] is more and more, and ever more powerfully, the producer of every detail of his world', and yet 'the closer his life comes to being his own creation, the more drastically he is cut off from that life'.[64] Modern capitalist culture had thus foregrounded the problem that lay, *in nuce*, within the very first division of labour: namely, the separation of historical change from its producers.

This then means that the predicament posed by modern society was held to have revealed a problem that could now be identified, retrospectively, throughout the past. There is textual evidence to support this. Debord consistently located the emergence of spectacular society in the early decades of the twentieth century, but he seems to have understood this as a clearer, fuller, expression of something much older. He states in *The Society of the Spectacle* that 'all separate power has been spectacular';[65] that 'at the root of the spectacle lies the oldest of all social specialisations, the specialisation of power';[66] and that 'power draped itself in the outward garb of a mythical order from the very beginning'.[67] A letter of 1971 even states that the spectacle has its roots in antiquity, and that it appeared in its '*completed* form' (my emphasis) around '1914–20'.[68]

The 'new' proletariat

This purported clarification of the stakes of revolutionary struggle enabled by Debord's context also entailed a new characterisation of the revolutionary class. In *Capital*, Marx indicates that capitalist social relations render the inhabitants of society subordinate to the dictates of their own economic system. Although he clearly held that 'the capitalist is just as enslaved by the relationships of capitalism as is his opposite pole, the worker', insofar as both are required to play the roles assigned to them by this economic system, Marx stressed that these roles involve private ownership of the means of production, and that the worker and the capitalist thus experienced this enslavement 'in a quite different manner'.⁶⁹ For Marx, the proletariat are all those who have been separated from the possibility of producing their own means of subsistence independently, and who must perform wage-labour to maintain their existence. This then means that the general problem of fetishism – the subordination of society as a whole to the demands of its economy – is addressed in a manner that centres around the miseries of the proletariat and their impetus towards overcoming capitalist social relations.

Debord and the SI, however, were located within a version of capitalism that had seemingly remedied the nineteenth-century poverty that exercised Marx. More accurately, it had transported that poverty overseas. This relative affluence prompted questions concerning the motivation for revolt. The SI's answer was to contend that, within the advanced capitalist societies, a new, more existential form of poverty had come to the fore; one that foregrounded the sense in which the general problem of fetishism pertains to all. The 'new' proletariat, they claimed, were not just all those who had been separated from the means of *maintaining* their lives, but rather all those who had been separated from the means of *directing* their lives. This new, effectively class-less proletariat was vast – Debord writes of 'the proletarianisation of the world'⁷⁰ – because it was held to be composed of all those who, 'regardless of variation in their degree of affluence', have 'no possibility of altering the social space-time that society allots to them'.⁷¹ The nature of the new proletariat therefore corresponded to the changed stakes of the new revolution: access to history, not just to material goods.

This new poverty had foregrounded and clarified the basically temporal nature of the stakes of *all* social struggle. It seems that, in Debord's view, *every* demand for greater liberty, the amelioration of poverty and free time had essentially been a demand for increased self-determination, however those demands may have been construed in the past; and in consequence, *all* prior revolutionary efforts contained, implicit within them, a 'simple, unforgettable core' that had finally been revealed by the commodified malaise of Debord's own moment. This 'unforgettable core' was now expressed in the new proletariat's demand 'to *live* the historical time that it creates'.⁷² The true face of the temporal class division that emerges, in Debord's historical narrative, from the very first social division of labour was now in full view; hence his claim that the predicament posed by spectacular society 'leads the revolutionary project to become *visibly* what it always was *essentially*'.⁷³

This carries a significant corollary. If the problem thus revealed is not reducible to capitalist social relations, then the destruction of capitalism would not guarantee its final resolution. Spectacle – or some other version of the problem of separated social power – could reoccur in the future. This would happen if the revolutionary project pursued or established anything other than fluid, revisable and non-hierarchical forms of social organisation, and indeed if it employed such forms of organisation within revolutionary struggle. Debord's historical moment, and the failures of the past, had revealed a central insight: revolutionaries, as he put it, 'can no longer combat alienation with alienated forms of struggle'.⁷⁴

Theory in the war of time

The Society of the Spectacle's analysis of its own present is predicated on an ontology that is in turn supported by a philosophy of history. It sets out a view *of* history that had been made possible by a particular moment *in* history; a moment, moreover, in which the need to *make* history had become a particularly pressing concern. Yet as we saw earlier, the validity of its claims, and thus that of its visions of its past and present, could only be ascertained through its application in praxis. To put that more bluntly: the entire intellectual edifice outlined here was constructed as a means of framing the predicament posed by Debord's present, and its validity depends entirely on its success in that regard.

The Society of the Spectacle was intended to give theoretical voice to the revolutionary struggle of its own day. It was not intended to do so from a position *outside* and 'external' to that political movement. If it remained in such a position, it could hope to be no more than a description of that movement, or a set of didactic instructions directed towards it, rather than that movement's own immanent theoretical expression. Rather like the role of the party for Lukács, the role of theory for Debord is to mediate the relation between those whose social activity enables historical life, and the self-determinate conduct of that life. But it can assume no prior authority: its merits can only be established practically, through the extent to which it is recognised and employed fruitfully by those whose situation it endeavours to explain. If this does not take place, the theory must be as flawed as any faulty battle plan; and if it stands at one remove from concrete action, lays claim to some sort of timeless validity, or imposes dictates and putatively 'correct' ideas, it can only be a 'contemplative' and false representation of the revolutionary movement of its time.

These ideas entail that *The Society of the Spectacle*'s analyses must be specific to its own historical moment. This is usually overlooked. The temptation to use the book as a critical sociological description of modern society fosters an understandable desire to claim that the book's relevance has only increased since its publication in 1967. But such claims sit rather uncomfortably alongside statements such as this:

> The petty people of the present age seem to believe that I have approached things by way of theory, that I am a builder of theory – a sort of sagely architecture which they imagine they need only move in to as soon as they know its address, and which, ten years later, they might even modify a little by shuffling a few sheets of paper, so as to achieve the definitive perfection of the theory that will effectuate their salvation. But theories are only made to die in the war of time. Like military units, they must be sent into battle at the right moment; and whatever their merits or insufficiencies, we can only use those that are available in the time that they are needed. They have to be replaced because they are continually being worn out – by their decisive victories even more than by their partial defeats.[75]

No instance of radical theory, for Debord, can ever hope to remain true beyond the moment in which it is meant to intervene. Celebrating and preserving a theory, and imposing it upon subsequent moments, would only render it a reified image of the agency that it purported to articulate.

Moreover, *The Society of the Spectacle* could now be judged to be 'false', given that it heralded a revolution that never came. Debord denied this, and in the years that followed the book's publication, he declared that history had only continued to prove him right. In 1979, he wrote of 'the confirmation all my [book's] theses encounter',[76] and in 1992, he stated that 'the continued unfolding of our epoch has merely confirmed and further illustrated the theory of the spectacle'.[77] But this position was maintained by focussing on the extent to which he had correctly predicted trends in the development of capitalist society, rather than revolutionary praxis, and as the revolutionary potential of May 1968 retreated into the past, a growing sense of lost possibility entered Debord's work. This informs his *Comments on the Society of the Spectacle* of 1988: a book that argued that the contradictions identified in 1967 had deepened, but in ways that rendered social change more difficult.

One of the ways in which we might now approach this material is to address it in this vein. Once the 'strategic' notion of praxis that subtends the book is reconstructed, it could be read critically on its own terms: a political and historical study could then relate the theory's development and articulation to the social contexts in which it sought to intervene, and questions could be asked about its adoption and use by those whose struggles it sought to facilitate.[78] But I do not think that this is the only option. Once that reconstruction has been conducted, it also becomes possible to treat the model thus produced as an object of critical enquiry in its own right, that is, to view these ideas about temporality, social life and normativity independently from Debord's own ambitions. This would entail drawing out and addressing the 'philosophical' foundations that the purportedly 'strategic' dimensions of his theory rest upon.

Those ideas merit criticism regardless of their efficacy in praxis. The historical narrative described above is concerned with social power and domination, but it has almost nothing to say about the history of slavery, and it is completely silent about race and gender. It is also profoundly Eurocentric; an issue sharpened by Debord's insistence on the significance of 'Hegel, Marx [and] Feuerbach' and the dilemmas raised in 'modern Western poetry and art' for a global revolution.[79] In addition, Debord's conception of revolution *qua* subject-object unity can, at times, resemble a secularised but nonetheless furious holy war: an utterly uncompromising campaign dedicated to eradicating *all* forms of separated power, wherever they might arise.[80] Perhaps the theory's opposition to flawed normative structures and its openness to critical revision provides grounds for addressing such omissions and concerns. And perhaps, moreover, it contains resources that could be drawn out of Debord's work and developed independently. At the very least, the difficult ontological questions posed by his conception of praxis deserve further consideration and discussion, and that inevitably means drawing the 'philosopher' out of the 'strategist' to some degree. Regardless of whether or not such avenues are or indeed should be pursued, the intent of the reading set out here has been to go at least some way towards placing Debord's commitment to revolution at the centre of his theory, and thereby towards justifying his cherished 'bad reputation'.[81]

Tom Bunyard teaches at the University of Brighton. He is the author of Debord, Time and Spectacle: Hegelian Marxism and Situationist Theory *(2017).*

Notes

1. Guy Debord, 'Preface to the Fourth Italian Edition of *The Society of the Spectacle*', trans. Michel Prigent and Lucy Forsyth (Chronos Publications: London, 1979), available at https://libcom.org/library/preface-fourth-italian-edition-society-spectacle-guy-debord#_ednref6, 1979; *Oeuvres* (Paris: Gallimard, 2006), 1794. This is a revised and expanded version of my 'Histoire et révolution dans *La Société du spectacle* de Guy Debord' in *Revue Française d'histoire des idées politiques* 55 (2022), 91–118. I am grateful to Bertrand Cochard, Robb Dunphy, John McHale, Anthony Hayes, Stewart Martin, Eric-John Russell and Ross Sparkes for helpful comments on earlier versions of this text.
2. Situationist International, *Situationist International Anthology*, trans. and ed. Ken Knabb (Berkeley, CA: Bureau of Public Secrets, 2006), 340–1; Situationist International, *Internationale situationniste* (Paris: Librairie Arthème Fayard, 1997), 615.
3. Debord, 'Preface to the Fourth Italian Edition'.
4. Debord, 'Preface to the Fourth Italian Edition'.
5. Guy Debord, *The Society of the Spectacle*, trans. Donald Nicholson-Smith (New York: Zone Books, 1995), 143, translation altered; *Oeuvres*, 852.
6. This is an anecdote relayed by Giorgio Agamben in his 'Difference and Repetition: On Guy Debord's Films', trans. Brian Holmes, in *Guy Debord and the Situationist International: Texts and Documents*, ed. Tom McDonough (London: October Books/MIT Press, 2004), 313.
7. As he put it in a letter of 1974: 'The principal work that it appears to me should be envisaged now – as the complementary contrary to *The Society of the Spectacle*, which described frozen alienation (and the negation that was implicit within it) – is the theory of historical action. This means to bring forth, in its moment, which has come, strategic theory'. Guy Debord, *Correspondance Volume 5: Janvier 1973 – Décembre 1978* (Paris: Librairie Arthème Fayard, 2005), 127.
8. Debord, *The Society of the Spectacle*, 57 translation altered; *Oeuvres*, 799.
9. Debord, *The Society of the Spectacle*, 29.
10. Debord *The Society of the Spectacle*, 34.
11. Guy Debord, *Correspondance Volume 4: Janvier 1969 – Décembre 1972* (Paris: Librairie Arthème Fayard, 2004), 457.
12. Debord, *The Society of the Spectacle*, 141.
13. Debord, 'Preface to the Fourth Italian Edition'.
14. Debord, *The Society of the Spectacle*, 15, translation altered; *Oeuvres*, 768.
15. Guy Debord, *Correspondance Volume 2: Janvier 1960 – Décembre 1964* (Paris: Librairie Arthème Fayard, 2001), 304.
16. Guy Debord, *Stratégie*, ed. Laurence Le Bras (Paris: Éditions l'échappée, 2018), 430, emphasis in the original.
17. Debord, *The Society of the Spectacle*, 14, translation altered; *Oeuvres*, 768.
18. Debord, *The Society of the Spectacle*, 13.
19. Debord, *Correspondance 4*, 455, emphasis in the original.
20. Debord, *Correspondance 4*, 456.
21. Debord, *The Society of the Spectacle*, 143.
22. Debord, *Correspondance 4*, 457. I am grateful to John McHale and Denis Chevrier-Bousseau for help with this translation.
23. Georg Lukács, *History and Class Consciousness: Studies in Marxist Dialectics*, trans. Rodney Livingstone (London: Merlin, 1971), 197.
24. Debord, *The Society of the Spectacle*, 48, translation altered; *Oeuvres*, 792.
25. *History and Class Consciousness* was published at the same time as Korsch's *Marxism and Philosophy* (another work to which Debord was indebted, and indeed one that greatly informed his critique of 'economism' outlined below). Both books were criticised by the Party, but where Korsch refused to capitulate, Lukács eventually distanced himself from his book. In 1967 he wrote a new and critical preface to it, where he criticised the book's vision of subject-object unity, contending that he had presented alienation in a manner that could not account for the necessary objectification of subjective agency in action: all such objectification, he claimed, had been blurred with alienation, and thus the call for subject-object unity was really a call for a condition of tranquil perfection that amounted to an attempt to 'out-Hegel Hegel' (Lukács, *History*, xxiii). We can assume that Debord did not read this preface before its publication (it was not translated into French until 1974; *The Society of the Spectacle* was published in 1967, but Debord started writing it in 1965). He may,

however, have read a short statement that Lukács published in *Arguments* following the French translation of *History and Class Consciousness* in 1960. The statement warned readers away from *History and Class Consciousness*, and I suspect that it would only have reinforced Debord's view that Lukács had simply capitulated to his critics. The question still stands, however, as to whether Lukács' criticisms pertain to *The Society of the Spectacle*'s own vision of subject-object unity. I would suggest the following response. Lukács states in his 1967 preface that he came to realise his errors after reading Marx's *Economic and Philosophical Manuscripts of 1844* in 1930. Debord drew heavily on the *Manuscripts* when writing *The Society of the Spectacle*, and the ontology that underlies its claims is greatly informed by Marx's early work. Admittedly, the textual evidence is limited, but I would propose that his ostensible understanding of human existence in time goes some way towards avoiding the problem of confusing objectification with alienation, and of thereby mistakenly implying the need for objectification's erasure. Referencing Hegel, Debord writes that 'time ... is a *necessary* alienation, the milieu in which the subject realises himself whist losing himself, becomes other in order to become truly himself. The opposite obtains in the case of the alienation that now holds sway'. Debord, *The Society of the Spectacle*, 115-6, translation altered; *Oeuvres*, 835, emphasis in the original. Jappe makes the same point in Anselm Jappe, *Guy Debord*, trans. Donald Nicholson-Smith (Berkeley, CA: University of California Press, 1999), 26.

26. Debord, *The Society of the Spectacle*, 17, translation altered; *Oeuvres*, 770.

27. Debord criticises anarchism in theses 91–4 of *The Society of the Spectacle*, chiefly for lacking a theory of history, but praises the Spanish anarchists of the 1930s as 'the most advanced model of proletarian power ever realised'. Debord, *The Society of the Spectacle*, 64.

28. Situationist International, *The Real Split in the International*, trans. John McHale (London: Pluto Press, 2003), 32.

29. Debord, *The Society of the Spectacle*, 81.

30. In a letter of 1972, in which he discussed the councils, he stressed the 'necessity of abolishing work', and stated that their organisation should 'not be a question of the self-management of the existing productive process'. Debord, *Correspondance 4*, 617.

31. Debord, *The Society of the Spectacle*, 87, translation altered; *Oeuvres*, 818.

32. Debord, *The Society of the Spectacle*, 127.

33. Debord, *The Society of the Spectacle*, 87.

34. Guy Debord, *Correspondance Volume 7: Janvier 1988 – Novembre 1994* (Paris: Librairie Arthème Fayard), 78.

35. Debord, *Correspondance 4*, 454.

36. Debord, *The Society of the Spectacle*, 51.

37. Karl Marx, *Capital, Volume 1*, trans. Ben Fowkes (London: Penguin, 1990), 103.

38. Debord, *The Society of the Spectacle*, 52.

39. Debord, *Correspondance 4*, 94–5

40. This approach can be traced back to Anselm Jappe's seminal *Guy Debord* (first published in Italian in 1992). This was the first substantial work to address Debord's Hegelian Marxism seriously, and it is significant in this regard that Debord described it as 'the best-informed book about me' (Debord, *Correspondance 7*, 453). Its claims concerning the contemporary relevance of Debord's theory have also proved influential: its contemporary salience, he held, lies in its account of commodified social relations, rather than in the notions of alienated agency and praxis that subtend it, and its emphasis on class struggle remains too close to an outdated classical Marxism. For Jappe, the relevance of Debord's theory thus lay in its proximity to new readings of 'the Marxian theory of value'. Jappe, *Debord*, 18.

41. As in Debord, the idea of fetishism is typically foregrounded by these readings of Marx, and emphasis is placed on the ways in which value functions as a mode of abstract, impersonal domination. In *Wertkritik*, with which Jappe is associated, one also finds a scepticism towards traditional Marxism's prioritisation of class that accords with the SI's vexed moves away from traditional class analysis (discussed below).

42. Eric-John Russell's impressive *Spectacular Logic in Hegel and Debord: Why Everything is as it Seems* (London: Bloomsbury, 2021) affords the most extensive discussion of the relation between Debord and Marx's mature value-theory that I am aware of. It identifies homologies between Debord's discussion of spectacle, Hegel's *Logic* and Marx's mature account of commodities and capitalist value.

43. I am indebted to Eric-John Russell for this formulation.

44. Debord, *Correspondance 4*, 140.

45. Debord's archived notes, which consist almost entirely of quotations that he copied and kept for reference, are now being published. His notes on the Hegel's *Logic* are extremely sparse. All but one are taken from that book's prefaces; there is almost nothing from the text itself, save for a set of lines quoted from the Doctrine of Essence. The publishers of the notes have pointed out that these lines don't match the French translation of the *Logic* that Debord seems to have used, or indeed other available French translations (Debord, *Marx Hegel*, 508). It thus seems that he found the lines elsewhere; and if that is so, the evidence that Debord conducted a serious reading of the *Logic* looks thin. It is significant, moreover, that these lines present contradiction as the 'source of all movement and life'. See Debord, *Marx Hegel*, 387; the quoted lines can be found in G.W.F. Hegel, *The Science of Logic*, trans. George Di Giovanni, (Cambridge: Cambridge University Press, 2015), 381–2. Once again, one gets the impression that Hegel is significant for Debord because his philosophy provided a means of thinking change, movement and conflict in the conduct of historical life. These same lines were used in a letter of 1970 (Debord, *Correspondance 4*, 317). If they were used at that time because Debord had recently encountered them, then that encounter would have happened *after* he wrote *The Society of the Spectacle*.

46. Debord, *The Society of the Spectacle*, 56, translation altered; *Oeuvres*, 798.
47. Debord, *The Society of the Spectacle*, 54.
48. Debord, *The Society of the Society*, 54–5.
49. Debord's views here are very close to, and seem informed by, Korsch's *Marxism and Philosophy*.
50. Debord, *Marx Hegel*, 148. Hyppolite also used these lines in his *Introduction to Hegel's Philosophy of History*, trans. Bond Harris and Jacqueline Spurlock (Gainesville, FL: University Press of Florida), 43, and Debord copied them from that text too, clearly finding them important (*Marx Hegel*, 418). The translation used here has been taken from Hyppolite's *Introduction*, as it is slightly clearer.
51. Debord, *Marx Hegel*, 148n.
52. Debord, *Correspondance 4*, 60, 609.
53. Debord, *The Society of the Spectacle*, 12, translation altered; *Oeuvres*, 766.
54. Debord, *The Society of the Spectacle*, 89.
55. Debord, *The Society of the Spectacle*, 48. See Karl Marx and Friedrich Engels, *The Communist Manifesto*, trans. Samuel Moore (London: Penguin, 1985), 83.
56. This combination of influences is evidenced in *The Society of the Spectacle*'s claim, made via a quotation form Hegel, that 'Man – that "negative being who *is* to the extent that he abolishes being" – is one with time'. Debord, *The Society of the Spectacle*, 92.
57. Debord, *The Society of the Spectacle*, 92.
58. Debord, *The Society of the Spectacle*, 98.
59. Debord, *Correspondance 4*, 79.
60. See thesis 128 of Debord, *The Society of the Spectacle*, 93–4, and *passim*.
61. Debord, *The Society of the Spectacle*, 105.
62. Debord, *The Society of the Spectacle*, 105.
63. *The Society of the Spectacle*'s chapter on the history of the workers' movement opens with a critique of Hegel. This accords with Debord's claim that the bourgeois order inaugurated a world shaped by a sense of history, but which seemed to move of its own accord. As indicated above, Debord viewed Hegel's philosophy as echoing this problem, and the 'economistic' aspects of Marxism as echoing it further.
64. Debord, *The Society of the Spectacle*, 24.
65. Debord *The Society of the Spectacle*, 20.
66. Debord, *The Society of the Spectacle*, 18.
67. Debord, *The Society of the Spectacle*, 20.
68. Debord, *Correspondance 4*, 455–6.
69. Marx, *Capital*, Volume 1, 990.
70. Debord, *The Society of the Spectacle*, 21.
71. SI, *Situationist International Anthology*, 141.
72. Debord, *The Society of the Spectacle*, 106.
73. Debord, *The Society of the Spectacle*, 89–90.
74. Debord, *The Society of the Spectacle*, 89; *Oeuvres*, 819. These issues shaped the SI's fraught efforts to balance both 'real accord on a central basis *and* individual autonomy'. Debord, *Correspondance 4*, 53; see also thesis 121 of *The Society of the Spectacle*, 88. They sought to achieve that balance through dialogue and debate between equals, but the result was a tendency to expel individuals whose positions did not meet with the emergent consensus.
75. Debord, *Complete Cinematic Works*, 150–1, translation altered; *Oeuvres*, 1353–4.
76. Debord, 'Preface to the Fourth Italian Edition'.
77. Debord, *The Society of the Spectacle*, 7.
78. For the SI's own views on the ways in which their ideas related to the political issues and events of their day, see for example their essays: 'The Decline and Fall of the Spectacle-Commodity Economy', which addresses the Watts riots of 1965; 'Address to Revolutionaries of Algeria and of All Countries'; their 1966 contribution to student politics, 'On the Poverty of Student Life'; 'Our Goals and Methods in the Strasbourg Scandal'; their 1969 reflection on the events of the preceding May, 'The Beginning of an Era'. Debord's correspondence is also full of variously supportive and condemnatory letters to groups and agents around the world.
79. SI, *Situationist International Anthology*, 190.
80. I am indebted here to Daniel Lopez' interpretation of Lukács in his *Lukács, Praxis and the Absolute* (Leiden: Brill, 2019), and to some of the ex-Situationist T.J. Clark's reflections on the SI.
81. Guy Debord, *Cette mauvaise réputation* (Paris: Gallimard, 1993).

The toxic ideology of longtermism
Alice Crary

The intellectual movement that calls itself longtermism is an outgrowth of Effective Altruism (EA), a utilitarianism-inspired philanthropic programme founded just over a decade ago by Oxford philosophers Toby Ord and William MacAskill. EA, which claims to guide charitable giving to do the 'most good' per expenditure of time or money, originally focused on mitigating the effects of poverty in the global South and the treatment of animals in factory farms.[1] This initially modestly-funded, Oxford-based enterprise soon had satellites in the UK, US and elsewhere in the world, several of which became multi-million-dollar organisations, while the amount of money directed by EA-affiliated groups swelled to over four hundred million dollars annually, with pledges in the tens of billions.[2] During this period, Ord and MacAskill starting using the term 'longtermism' to mark a view championed by members of a conspicuous subset of effective altruists, many affiliated with Oxford University's Future of Humanity Institute. The view is that humanity is at a crossroads at which we may either self-destruct or realise a glorious future, and that we should prioritise responding to threats to the continued existence of human civilisation. The 'existential risks' – to use the term introduced by Oxford philosopher and Future of Humanity Institute founder Nick Bostrom[3] – that longtermists rank as most probable are AI unaligned with liberal values and deadly engineered pathogens. They urge us to combat these risks to make it likelier that humans (or our digitally intelligent descendants) will live on for millions, billions or even trillions of years, surviving until long after the sun has vaporised the earth, by colonising exoplanets.

Ord published a monograph defending a longtermist stance in early 2020, and MacAskill followed suit in the summer of 2022.[4] Ord's book received plaudits in high-profile venues,[5] and MacAskill's was a best-seller that came with a blitz of largely positive media attention, including a *New Yorker* profile, a review featured on the cover of *Time*, and an appearance on *The Daily Show*, as well as an endorsement from Elon Musk.[6] This was the coming out party for a tradition that, despite its notable influence in Silicon Valley and elite universities, had previously flown mostly under the radar.

The public mood changed in mid November of 2022, when one of the movement's biggest funders, the crypto exchange FTX, declared bankruptcy. It was then known that MacAskill and FTX's CEO Sam Bankman-Fried had been acquainted since 2012, when MacAskill advised Bankman-Fried, at the time an MIT undergraduate, to channel his altruistic zeal into 'earning to give'.[7] It was also known that, with a group of Oxford-affiliated longtermists, MacAskill had been an advisor to FTX's charitable Future Fund, and that the Future Fund had committed large sums to building EA's own institutions, including fourteen million dollars to MacAskill's main organisation, the Centre for Effective Altruism, fifteen million to Longview Philanthropy, for which MacAskill is an advisor, and another roughly seven million to fellowships, prizes and the like at these and other organisations with which MacAskill is affiliated.[8] Such institutional ties have been mentioned, alongside facts about how prominent tech multi-millionaires and billionaires support longtermist projects,[9] in a journalistic narrative that faults longtermism in moral terms for enriching itself by indulging the self-aggrandising, techno-utopian fantasies of its donors while ignoring questions about the sources of their wealth.

This critique of longtermism is correct as far as it goes. It is also desperately incomplete. One thing it fails to capture is that an uncritical attitude toward existing political and economic institutions is part of longtermism's philosophical DNA. The point of departure for longtermism is EA, and, like other utilitarianism-inspired doctrines, EA veers towards forms of welfarism that are unthreatening to the status quo. This posture increasingly exposed EA to corruption during its growth into a broad-scale philanthropic movement. EA shares the tendency of large charitable foundations to undemocratically organise entire realms of public engagement, diverting money and other resources from movements for liberating social change. And it owes its ability to secure the funding requisite for this role to its affinity with political and economic systems generative of the suffering it claims to address.[10]

Longtermism's sins are different and more ominous, but there are points of convergence. Longtermism deflects from EA's wonted attention to current human and animal suffering. It defends in its place a concern for the wellbeing of the potentially trillions of humans who will live in the long-term future, and, taking the sheer number of prospective people to drown out current moral problems, exhorts us to regard threats to humanity's continuation as a moral priority, if not *the* moral priority.[11] This makes longtermists shockingly dismissive of 'non-existential' hazards that may result in the suffering and death of huge numbers in the short term if, as they see it, there is a reasonable probability that the hazards are consistent with the possibility of a far greater number of humans going on to flourish in the long term.

When longtermists turn to existential hazards, they discuss wholly natural threats (such as large asteroids hurtling toward the earth, super-volcanic eruptions and stellar explosions) while focusing on human-caused risks, which they regard as more likely to rise to extinction-level. Alongside value-divergent AI and human-produced pathogens, they consider climate change, other forms of environmental degradation, and all-out nuclear war, and they set out to calculate the probability that these different anthropogenic threats will instigate existential disasters. This accent on existential dangers is theoretically unjustified and morally damaging, but even stripped of it, longtermism is a poor guide to solicitude for prospective humans.

Longtermism calls on us to safeguard humanity's future in a manner that both diverts attention from current misery and leaves harmful socioeconomic structures critically unexamined. As a movement, it has enjoyed stunning financial success and clout. But its success is not due to the quality of its conception of morality, which builds questionably on EA's. Rather, it is due to longtermism's compatibility with the very socioeconomic arrangements that have led us to the brink of the kinds of catastrophes it claims to be staving off. At issue is not only an especially dangerous, future-facing variation on ideologies, like EA, that thwart struggles for liberating change with suggestions of the cure-all properties of existing economic tools. It is a variation lacking any plausible rationale, since many of these struggles have long contributed to the area longtermism wrongly represents as its innovation – fighting for a just and livable future.

The longtermist enterprise has been publicly thrashed for its ties to FTX, but it remains well-funded and well-positioned to repair its reputation and go on enlisting earnest individuals to energetically support and spread it. There is a pressing need to criticise its theoretical weaknesses and forcefully bring out its material harms, exposing it as the toxic ideology it is.

Longtermist moral logic

The ethical core of longtermism is a set of commitments, shared with EA, from the moral tradition of consequentialism. For consequentialists, the mark of right action is producing outcomes that are best in the sense of containing the greatest amount of value. That leaves open what is of value, and, although longtermists often insist on respect for uncertainty about the correctness of any one moral theory, they still incline toward versions of consequentialism that identify value with wellbeing and so fall under the heading of utilitarianism. In making these theoretical moves, longtermists help themselves to a methodological assumption that is itself morally significant. Together with effective altruists and many others partial to utilitarian stances, they assume that wellbeing is discernible from a dispassionate and abstract 'point of view of the universe'.[12] That is morally significant because it is what seems to make it possible to use wellbeing as a measure for comparing outcomes anywhere – not only across space to the global poor and across species to non-human animals but also across time to those living in the far distant future.

Longtermism proper emerges from within a set of contemporary ethical discussions, typically described as composing the field of 'population ethics', in which utilitarianism-tinged modes of thought are applied to prospective humans.[13] Debates among population ethicists pivot around questions about whether our moral assessments appeal to total aggregate wellbeing, average wellbeing, or wellbeing above a certain critical level, as well as around questions about whether moral assessments reflect equal versus unequal distributions of wellbeing. A signature gesture of these moral theorists is insisting that their research programme is extremely difficult, presenting participants with nearly intractably vexing problems.[14] But the issues that trouble population ethicists presuppose their methodologically abstract, calculative approach to people and circumstances. Their conundrums don't arise for moral thinkers who reject this method as unsuited to the subject matter.

What distinguishes longtermism from other positions within population ethics is a pair of related claims, one empirical and the other ethical. The empirical claim is that we live 'at a time uniquely important to humanity's future' in which 'major transitions in human history have enhanced our power and enabled us to make extraordinary progress' while also putting us at risk of self-annihilation.[15] The ethical claim has to do with what population ethicists call 'the intuition of neutrality', that is, the intuition that what matters morally is the quality of peoples' lives, not how many people there are. Thinkers who incline toward neutrality hold that whether a greater or smaller number of people live at a given time is in itself morally neutral. Longtermists in contrast reject this notion of neutrality, maintaining that any additional person who lives makes the world better, as long as the person enjoys adequate wellbeing.

This is the ethical backdrop against which longtermists' empirical claim about humanity standing at a historical 'precipice', a time both of great promise and of increased risk of auto-extinction, seems momentous. Now it appears that a circumstance in which human beings die out in a few thousand years is worse, by many orders of magnitude, than one in which trillions of humans live on to flourish in the distant future. It appears that it would be a massive moral achievement to improve the prospect of avoiding extinction by even a fraction of a percentage. The endeavour would be so important that it would justify almost any means, however seemingly callous or appalling, including steps that resulted in the near-term suffering and death of millions.[16] Not that all longtermists explicitly contemplate extreme or violent actions to avoid existential disasters.[17] Even those who actively oppose such measures, however, offer frighteningly few safeguards to keep their moral calculations from echoing the reasoning of murderous dictators and sci-fi villains.

Empty ethical equations

Longtermists' turn to existential risk marks a dramatic shift from the concern with present and near-term suffering that is the hallmark of their effective altruist progenitors. Unsurprisingly, some advocates of EA are fiercely critical of longtermism. That includes Peter Singer, whose contributions to utilitarian ethics were EA's original inspiration. Singer is skeptical about whether humanity is indeed at a uniquely portentous moment in history, and he de-emphasises existential risk in a manner that indicates impatience with longtermists' commitment to the posture they call non-neutrality. His aim is to redirect attention back to EA's accent on suffering now and in the short-term. 'If we are at the hinge of history', he writes, 'enabling people to escape poverty and get an education is as likely to move things in the right direction as almost anything else we might do; and if we are not at that critical point, it will have been a good thing to do anyway'.[18]

Singer proposes to strip longtermism of the claims that differentiate it from EA, leaving a future-oriented outlook that might be described as a generic position within population ethics. Such a future-directed EA would, he suggests, be an authoritative guide to doing good for human beings to come. But this suggestion reflects a fundamentally limited diagnosis of what ails longtermism. Even without the claims that lead its advocates to wrongly represent existential risks as swamping other moral concerns, the tradition is incapable of furnishing an understanding of our social circumstances that could responsibly inform future-oriented action.

The grounds for this more negative appraisal of longtermism can be found in one of the most well-known critiques of EA. Since EA's inception, critics have noted that its emphasis has been on assessing single action-types (e.g., medical, public health or educational interventions) in terms of the sort of wellbeing grasped by the metrics of welfare economics. They have observed that EA's slant toward welfarism is at the same time a slant away from questions of justice, and they have revisited in reference to EA a classic charge against utilitarianism. The charge's thrust is that EA is politically corrosive because it neglects the structural roots of global misery and so weakens political bodies capable of challenging those structures, ensuring the regular reproduction of suffering.[19]

Some effective altruists respond to this critique by arguing that, even if EA has in practice veered toward welfarism, there is in principle nothing to keep it from evaluating social movements' coordinated efforts to fight for more just social arrangements and also nothing to prevent it from using the kinds of qualitative metrics that we find in disciplines in the social sciences, such as sociology and political theory.[20] But this rejoinder falls flat. It is undercut by effective altruists' reliance on the god's eye moral method that seems to enable them to quantify values across space and species and arrive at aggregative judgments of 'most good'.

This methodological stance disqualifies anyone who adopts it from discerning the systematic injustices targeted by social justice movements. When participants in anti-racist, feminist and Indigenous rights movements protest sustained physical, psychological and political violence against specific oppressed human groups, they are moved by structural obstacles to flourishing and the absence of reparations. It is not possible to adequately grasp the nature of such wrongs without an appreciation of the history and function of the social mechanisms that reproduce them. Attempts to understand these injustices, when approached in the abstract and aperspectival manner characteristic of EA, uninformed by pertinent historical, cultural and political considerations, are bound to misfire. They also risk strengthening the oppressive structures in question because one way in which these structures function is by obscuring the historically and socially specific suffering of the oppressed. This, then, is why EA is unable to slough off the allegation that it has a politically conservative, welfarist bent. It lacks the immanent resources necessary for illuminating systematic injustice and envisioning appropriate remedies to it.[21]

Longtermism is tainted by the same lack. Population ethics, the original home of longtermism, is premised on the assumption that, appropriately specified, an abstract account of an action's effects on the lifetime wellbeing of prospective populations equips us to answer questions about the action's rightness. This assumption is false. Instead of making it possible to determine what counts as right action, a detached approach obscures from view just and unjust relationships that are part of these determinations' lifeblood. Because the calculative enterprise in which population ethicists are engaged is based on false presuppositions, the technical headaches with which it presents them are at bottom self-inflicted injuries. The correct attitude to their disciplinary puzzles is to dissolve not solve them, and this applies to the debate, central for those population ethicists who self-denominate as longtermist, about whether to affirm an 'intuition of neutrality'. The debate's conceit is that there is a coherent abstract question about whether creating more happy people is a moral gain. But longtermists' assertion of non-neutrality is nothing more than an empty gesture. The emptiness extends to the non-neutrality-based computations that seem to support longtermism's insistence on regarding existential risk as a great or even overwhelming moral priority. Longtermists' distinctive moral math simply falls apart.[22]

Exploiting existential angst

This isn't yet an adequate inventory of longtermism's major weaknesses. Once we set aside the morally free-floating calculations on which longtermists build their case for an extreme prioritising of existential risks, it might seem that we retain the makings of a helpfully future-oriented practical programme. That is the gist of Singer's proposal for exchanging longtermism's fixation on historical precipices with a forward-looking, utilitarian-themed project that recentres longtermism's origins in EA. But this is a non-starter. It fails to register that EA itself is incapable of shedding light on unjust and harmful social structures or assessing efforts to resist them. Even shorn of its wrong-headed stress on existential hazards, longtermism is a treacherous guide to acting responsibly towards those who will come after us.

This emerges concretely in MacAskill's and Ord's treatments, in their respective recent books, of climate change and other forms of anthropogenic environmental destruction. Both discussions are distorted by a disturb-

ing interest in existential risk that makes it seem pertinent to investigate whether global heating will lead to human extinction or whether it will 'only' kill billions of humans and trillions of animals and devastate ecosystems, while still permitting the survival and ultimate flourishing of small human groups.[23] This misguided preoccupation with existential dangers is closely tied to other outrages, such as MacAskill's selective and highly contentious appeal to climate science in support of his chillingly casual 'best guess' that some human beings would survive 'fifteen degrees of warming'.[24] But, even apart from their morally disastrous hang-ups with human extinction, MacAskill's and Ord's reflections on the environmental crisis are ruinously wrong-headed. When they consider strategies for reducing greenhouse gas emissions to combat the devastation of climate change, they limit themselves to strategies that can be pursued within existing socioeconomic arrangements. This includes technological innovations such as 'clean' or low-carbon energy sources and different forms of geoengineering.[25] It also includes policies such as internationally coordinated emission-reduction schemes.[26] MacAskill at one juncture mentions youth activism admiringly, but his point about it is simply that it can increase public support for climate pledges.[27] Nowhere in Ord's or MacAskill's remarks is there any real acknowledgment of the reality, repugnant to members of the billionaire class they assiduously and successfully cultivate, that meaningful environmental action will need to involve new values and substantial social change.[28]

Still more striking, perhaps, is that MacAskill and Ord try to diminish our sense of the urgency of environmental issues, arguing that we should regard renegade AI and human-developed pathogens as more critical because likelier to trigger human extinction. This line of argument, common among longtermists, is a further expression of the warping moral effects of a fascination with extinction risks, which seems to speak for downgrading the exigency of things that don't extinguish human life altogether, and so supports treating as relatively morally insignificant the terrible fact that huge numbers of people are already dying, being uprooted from their communities, and suffering other great hardships because of climate change.[29] Yet, even within the context of MacAskill's and Ord's extinction-focused programme, it is not clear why the environment fails to loom larger. Ord argues that environmental degradation is relatively unlikely to directly produce an extinction event and more likely to generate forms of political instability that indirectly lead to one, providing the conditions for other anthropogenic dangers.[30] It's not clear why that should make it less imperative to attend to environmental factors, or why a deviant robot takeover should be a bigger priority, unless it's just that, considered in isolation, deviant AI appears be a hazard addressable with the kinds of instruments that Ord and other longtermists have at their disposal. Here the drive to downplay the seriousness of environmental crisis plainly outruns the grounds for doing so.

Longtermism is marred not only, therefore, by a misjudged positioning in population ethics that swings it toward existential risk but also by methodological presuppositions that prevent it from recognising that movements for social change, such as the environmental movement in its interplay with anti-racist and other social justice movements, have long been engaged in the kind of future-facing social enterprise it preposterously credits itself with inaugurating.[31]

These objections are not at base about the troubling fact that the tradition is the brainchild of a group of white men at an elite university, some of whom have records of racist statements.[32] More fateful is a dimension of longtermism's signature theories of existential risk. These theories treat as less urgent those anthropogenic hazards that won't snuff out humanity altogether, and the theories' adherents place the currently intensifying human-caused climate crisis squarely in this category, encouraging us to regard as morally less important the suffering and death it is occasioning. The harms in question are falling in dramatically lopsided fashion on racialised and Indigenous groups the world over, groups whose very vulnerability to these harms is a product of long histories of injustice. Such theory-induced callousness to losses and damages visited grossly unequally on racialised people licenses talk of a racist strain in longtermist thinking, and individual longtermists deepen this strain in specific ways. A well-placed young longtermist once argued that inhabitants of rich countries are generally more 'innovative' and 'economically productive' and that saving their lives is hence substantially more important for humanity's future than saving lives in poor countries.[33] Today some of the tradition's most prominent champions advocate projects of bio-enhancement, reminiscent of twentieth-century eugenics, aimed at developing a transhuman species that is better equipped for survival in the long-term.[34] These sorts of reinforcements of longtermism's racist streak are only strengthened by the tradition's inability to grasp, and consequent proclivity to make invisible, contributions to revolutionary anti-racist struggle.[35]

Mega-philanthropic delusions

The story of longtermism is not just a tale of a no good, very bad moral theory. As the coffers of longtermism's institutes and related charities have swelled, it has begun to enact its priorities, funding research on misaligned AI and anthropogenic pathogens and supporting institution-building, with research grants as well as grants to EA's and longtermism's institutes.[36] Its arrival as a philanthropic player exposes it to concerns about having an unmerited sway on social issues. Like other wealthy private foundations, longtermist organisations are able to specify what counts as good and shape civic life without real public answerability. In the US and elsewhere, tax exemptions of well-funded private charities take from the public till huge sums that voters could otherwise have directly determined how to spend, and, apart from relatively insignificant tax obligations and reporting duties, there is little accountability. This is a money-fuelled arrangement involving 'the exercise of wealth-derived power in the public sphere with minimal democratic controls and civic obligations'.[37] With its growth into a movement, longtermism has joined this undemocratic commandeering of the public realm, using its financial heft to promote its dangerous obsession with existential risk.

Longtermism's moral case for accenting such risk deflects from present suffering in a manner that simultaneously absolves harmful socioeconomic mechanisms from criticism and hastens the sorts of hazards it is supposed to head off. Yet it has been singularly successful at attracting rich backers to its project. In treating the economic arena to which these individuals owe their wealth as critically off limits, it positions them to look upon themselves, not as complicit in the arena's injustices, but as singled out by their success in it to be world saviours.[38] A deceitful narrative of selfless heroes riding to humanity's rescue has proven ideologically effective, and it seems clear that many longtermists – students, researchers and members of the public, as well as donors – are sincerely committed to what they take to be a uniquely important moral enterprise. But their sincerity is no argument against the corruption of a movement that uses a bankrupt morality to justify profiting from the systems most threatening to the future it claims to secure.

The fact that some major supporters of longtermism, such as Bankman-Fried, have been suspected of financial fraud is a sideshow to the main event. Longtermism's corruption is inseparable from the way in which its core ideas are put into practice, and the baseness is still there when its programmes are pursued with rigorous legality. A critique of longtermism that enabled its adherents to see it in this harshly revealing light would be a welcome step towards envisioning and enacting a just and livable future.[39]

Alice Crary is a philosopher and writer based at The New School who divides her time between New York, Oxford, and Berlin. Her most recent book, co-edited with Carol Adams and Lori Gruen, is The Good it Promises, The Harm it Does: Critical Essays on Effective Altruism *(2023).*

Notes

1. In a previous article for this journal, I criticised EA with particular reference to its tendency to work against its own commitment to the cause of non-human animals. See 'Against 'Effective Altruism', *Radical Philosophy* 2.10 (Summer 2021), 33–43.
2. Benjamin Todd, co-founder of the EA-affiliate 80,000 hours, estimated in summer 2021 that total pledges to EA had reached forty-six billion dollars. See 'Is effective altruism growing? An update on the stock of funding versus people', July 21, 2021, at https://80000hours.org/2021/07/effective-altruism-growing/. In a post in the EA Forum on May 9, 2022, MacAskill gave a more conservative estimate of thirty billion. See https://forum.effectivealtruism.org/posts/cfdnJ3sDbCSkShiSZ/ea-and-the-current-funding-situation#fnaavi420x9rk.
3. See Nick Bostrom, 'Existential Risks: Analyzing Human Extinction Scenarios and Related Hazards', *Journal of Evolution and Technology* 9:1 (2002).
4. Toby Ord, *The Precipice: Existential Risk and the Future of Humanity* (New York: Hachette Books, 2020); and William MacAskill *What We Owe the Future* (New York: Basic Books 2022).
5. See, for example, Jim Holt, 'The Power of Catastrophic Thinking', *The New York Review* (February 25, 2021); and also the mention of Ord's book in the 'Briefly Noted' section of *The New Yorker* (April 5, 2020).
6. See Gideo Lewis-Kraus, 'The Reluctant Prophet of Effective Altruism', *The New Yorker* (August 8, 2022), https://www.newyorker.com/magazine/2022/08/15/the-reluctant-prophet-of-effective-altruism; and Naina Bajekal, 'Want to do More Good? This Movement Might Have the Answer', *Time Magazine* (August 10, 2022). MacAskill appeared on *The Daily Show with Trevor Noah* on September 27, 2022, https://www.cc.com/video/8fl6g9/the-daily-show-with-trevor-noah-william-macaskill\-what-we-owe-the-future; and on August 2, 2022, Musk retweeted MacAskill's book announcement to his own more than 120 million followers, commenting: 'Worth reading. This is a close match for my philosophy', https://twitter.com/elonmusk/status/1554335028313718784.
7. For one of the most detailed accounts of MacAskill's acquaintance with Bankman-Fried, see Adam Fisher, 'Sam Bankman-Fried has a Savior Complex – and Maybe You Should Too', *Sequoia* (September 22, 2022), https://web.archive.org/web/20221027180943/https://www.sequoiacap.com/article/sam-bankman-fried-spotlight/.
8. For these figures, see John Hyatt, 'Sam Bankman-Fried's Donations to Effective Altruism Nonprofits Tied to an Oxford Professor are at Risk of Being Clawed Back', *Forbes* (November 17, 2022), https://www.forbes.com/sites/johnhyatt/2022/11/17/disgraced-crypto-trader-sam-bankman-fried-was-a-big\-backer-of-effective-altruism-now-that-movement-has\-a-big\-black-eye/?sh=6c346564ce78. Although, together with four other EA-affiliated advisors to FTX's Future Fund, MacAskill stepped down from his role the day before FTX's bankruptcy filing (see https://forum.effectivealtruism.org/posts/xafpj3on76uRDoBja/the-ftx-future-fund-team-has-resigned-1), it seems clear that alarms about Bankman-Fried's conduct were raised by effective altruists not days but years before the FTX debacle. See Reed Albergotti and Louise Matsakis, 'Effective Altruism Group Debated Sam Bankman-Fried's Ethics in 2018', *Semafor* (November 18, 2022), https://www.semafor.com/article/11/18/2022/effective-altruism-group-debated-sam-bankman-frieds\

-ethics-in-2018.

9. This includes, for example, both Facebook co-founder Dustin Moskovitz, who co-founded the grantmaking foundation Open Philanthropy that takes longtermism as one of its main cause areas and Skype founder Jaan Tallinn, who co-founded Cambridge University's longtermism-oriented Centre for the Study of Existential Risk.

10. For development of these charges against EA, see Carol Adams, Alice Crary and Lori Gruen, eds., *The Good It Promises, The Harm It Does: Critical Essays on Effective Altruism* (Oxford: Oxford University Press, 2023).

11. Longtermists distinguish weak versions of their creed, which treat existential risk as *a* moral priority, from strong versions, which treat it as *the* moral priority. Some, such as MacAskill, defend the weaker doctrine in public-facing work (e.g., *What We Owe the Future*) while championing the stronger one in scholarly writing (e.g., 'The Case for Strong Longtermism', co-authored with Hilary Greaves, https://globalprioritiesinstitute.org/wp-content/uploads/The-Case-for-Strong-Longtermism-GPI-Working-Paper\-June\-2021-2-2.pdf.) The argument of the current article does not distinguish weak and strong longtermism and bears on both.

12. This phrase was introduced by nineteenth-century utilitarian Henry Sidgwick and adopted by contemporary utilitarian Peter Singer, whose work, discussed below, is foundational for EA. See Singer and Katarzyna de Lazari-Radek, *The Point of View of the Universe: Sidgwick and Contemporary Ethics* (Oxford, Oxford University Press, 2014). Not all effective altruists and longtermists use this nomenclature, but all make moves in value theory that treat moral thought as coming from an Archimedean point.

13. The idea of population ethics (although not the label) comes from Derek Parfit's *Reasons and Persons* (Oxford, Oxford University Press, 1984).

14. For MacAskill's version of this gesture, see *What We Owe the Future*, 169–170.

15. The inset quote is from Ord, *The Precipice*, 11.

16. One of the most vocal critics of longtermism, Émile Torres, has helpfully stressed this aspect of the tradition's moral logic. See 'Against Longtermism', *Aeon* (October 19, 2021), https://aeon.co/essays/why-longtermism-is-the-worlds-most-dangerous-secular\-credo.

17. But see Nick Bostrom, 'The Vulnerable World Hypothesis', *Global Policy* 10:4 (2019), 455–476.

18. Singer, 'The Hinge of History', *Project Syndicate* (October 8, 2021), https://www.project-syndicate.org/commentary/ethical-implications-of-focusing-on\-extinction-risk-by-peter\-singer-2021-10?barrier=accesspaylog.

19. Some of the earliest versions of this criticism of EA, later dubbed 'the institutional critique' of EA, were presented as responses to a 2015 forum in the *Boston Review* on Peter Singer's 'The Logic of Effective Altruism', https://www.bostonreview.net/forum/peter-singer-logic-effective-altruism/. See especially the responses by Angus Deaton (https://www.bostonreview.net/forum_response/response-angus-deaton/) and Iason Gabriel (https://www.bostonreview.net/forum_response/response\-iason-gabriel/).

20. For a clear defense of EA along these lines, see Jeff Sebo and Peter Singer, 'Activism', in Lori Gruen, ed., *Critical Terms in Animal Studies* (Chicago: University of Chicago Press, 2018), 33–46.

21. This paragragh rehearses in compact form the main – 'composite' – critique of EA that I develop in 'Against "Effective Altruism"'.

22. I owe the ideal of 'longtermist moral math' to Kieran Setiya's critique of MacAskill in 'The New Moral Mathematics', *The Boston Review* (August 15, 2022), http://www.bostonreview.net/articles/the-new-moral-mathemathics/. Setiya's critique, one of the best to date, is insightful, though not critical enough. It falls short in treating MacAskill's longtermist theory as a mere set of ideas as opposed to a materially significant ideology.

23. See Ord, *The Precipice*, Chapter 4, and MacAskill, *What We Owe the Future*, Chapter 6.

24. MacAskill, ibid., 137. See also Ord's claim, in *The Precipice*, 110, that thirteen degrees of warming would be 'a global calamity of an unprecedented scale' but not an existential catastrophe.

25. See Ord, *The Precipice*, 112–113, and MacAskill, *What We Owe the Future*, 135.

26. MacAskill, 135.

27. Ibid.

28. Late in his book, MacAskill surprises by saying he advocates 'systemic change'. 'In order to solve climate change', he writes, 'what we actually need' is not 'personal consumption decisions' but for 'companies like Shell to go out of business' (ibid., 232). For this, he recommends donations to 'effective' non-profits, presenting his 2016 book *Doing Good Better* (London: Penguin, 2016) as a guide. This recommendation undermines his avowed system-changing aims, since *Doing Good Better* is a welfarism-oriented EA manifesto with a conservative bent that lacks any serious critical engagement with anthropogenic global heating. (See Rupert Read, 'Must Do Better', *Radical Philosophy* 2.01 (February 2018).) MackAskill's talk of systemic change in *What We Owe the Future* is empty rhetoric, disconnected from his practical proposals and commitments. That hasn't stopped it from fooling some commentators. In 'An Effective Altruist? A philosopher's guide to the long-term threats to humanity', *Times Literary Supplement* (September 9, 2022), 9–11, Regina Rini breezily, and wrongly, cites this passage as evidence that MacAskill is 'no corporate shill' (9).

29. There is almost no acknowledgement of these harms in MacAskill's and Ord's recent books. On page 136 of *What We Owe the Future*, MacAskill does consider the prospect of global heating doing great damage to poorer, agrarian countries in the tropics 'that have contributed the least to climate change'. But he represents this 'colossal injustice' as something that may happen in the future and simply sets aside the question of how to respond to it.

30. Ord summarises his ranking of existential risks in Table 6.1 of *The Precipice*. MacAskill's similar ranking is reflected in the order of treatment of risks in *What We Owe the Future*.

31. For MacAskill's farcical suggestion that longtermism introduces a long-neglected future-orientation to social thought, see *What We Owe the Future*, 9, where he describes 'previous social justice movements, such as those for civil rights and women's suffrage' that have 'sought to give greater recognition and influence to disempowered members of society', adding that he sees longtermism, with its concern with future people, 'as an extension of these ideals'.

32. On January 9 2023, Future of Humanity Institute founder and longtermist Nick Bostrom posted online about an explicitly anti-Black email he wrote in the mid 1990s, apologising for the email but doing so in a manner that is itself racist. (His easily findable post is intentionally not included here.)

33. Nick Beckstead, currently a research fellow at the Future of Humanity Institute, defends this view in his 2013 PhD thesis, 'On the Overwhelming Importance of Shaping the Far Future'. Beckstead has appended a note to the relevant passage of his thesis (see page 11 of https://drive.google.com/file/d/0B8P94pg6WYClc0lXSUVYS1BnMkE/view?resourcekey=0-nk6wM1QIPl0qWVh2z9FG4Q), denying that he thinks 'lives in rich countries are intrinsically more valuable' and insisting that 'it is generally best for public health to prioritize worse-off countries'. But he hasn't disavowed the longtermist reasoning that led him to his startling early view.

34. Bostrom is among the high-profile longtermists who hold that a 'transformative change of human biological nature' may be key to avoiding existential catastrophe ('Existential Risk as a Global Priority', *Global Policy* 4:1 (2013), 15–31). Ord sympathises with this view. See, e.g., his claim that 'forever preserving humanity as it is now may ... squander our legacy' (*The Precipice*, 239).

35. Longtermism suffers from serious defects beyond those discussed in this article. Its account of how non-human animals figure in future-oriented moral thought is particularly objectionable. For a compact treatment of this topic, see Carol Adams, Alice Crary and Lori Gruen, 'Coda – Effective Altruism and Future Humans' in Adams, Crary and Gruen, eds., *The Good It Promises, The Harm It Does*.

36. Online reports of the 2022 grants of, e.g., Longview Philanthropy, the FTX Future Fund (pre-collapse), and the longtermism-wing of Open Philanthropy reveal general alignment with the longtermist agenda of MacAskill's and Ord's books, as described in this article.

37. Joanne Barkan, 'Plutocrats at Work: How Big Philanthropy Undermines Democracy', *Dissent* (Fall 2013), https://www.dissentmagazine.org/article/plutocrats-at-work-how-big-philanthropy-undermines\-democracy. Barkan's critique of mega-philanthropy belongs to a small and valuable corpus that is reprising, with reference to the Gates Foundation and today's other biggest charitable organisations, themes of a twentieth-century debate about damaging political effects of the Ford, Rockefeller and Carnegie foundations.

38. For a virtuoso filmic expression of this false but alluring trope of the mega-wealthy individual as guardian of humanity, see the billionaire businessman and inventor Peter Isherwell in Adam McKay's 2021 film *Don't Look Up*.

39. While writing this article, I benefitted from helpful correspondence with Carol Adams, Jay Bernstein, Victoria Browne, David Cunningham, Lori Gruen, Émile P. Torres and Nathaniel Hupert.

Antagonisms between bourgeois and coalitional formations

Roderick Ferguson

A speech that the singer, activist and historian Bernice Johnson Reagon gave at the 1981 West Coast Women's Music Festival was published two years later in the classic anthology *Home Girls: A Black Feminist Anthology*, edited by the Black lesbian feminist Barbara Smith. The speech is entitled 'Coalition Politics: Turning the Century', and in it, Reagon argues that coalitional work must be foundational for late twentieth century organising.* Here Reagon – a former member of the Student Nonviolent Coordinating Committee and the founder of the Black women's leftist singing ensemble Sweet Honey in the Rock – was referring to coalitions among leftist activists and social movements rather than coalitions between nation-states. In particular, she was speaking during a time in which the women's movement was struggling over how to come together amid differences of race, ethnicity, sexuality and class. Reflecting on the importance of the speech for that moment and for *Home Girls*, Smith said over thirty years later: 'I always tell people, the reason "Coalition Politics: Turning the Century" is the last piece in the book is because that's what I wanted people to leave the book with: the idea of working together across differences … The only way that we can survive is by working with each other, and not seeing each other as enemies'.[1]

I begin with Reagon's speech and the memory of it because I believe that coalitions among progressive forces are very much at stake in our present day. In addition, I am interested in the formations that try to prevent them. As such, I'd like to concentrate on bourgeois formations and their emergence in neocolonial and neoliberal contexts as principal antagonists to progressive coalitions. More specifically, neocolonialism and neoliberalism have represented the conditions for the emergence of bourgeois formations that have withered the insurgent demands and possibilities of various radical coalitions. In this essay, I'll refer to several bourgeois formations (Western, Black, and briefly LGBTQ+), but I focus quite a bit in this essay on the Black bourgeoisie because of its longstanding history and the opportunities that it provides for observing an early model minority.

As a result, I am not simply addressing the bourgeoisie in the classic Marxist sense – as a class that owns the means of production and exploits labour. The bourgeois formations that I discuss – ones made up of minoritised subjects – have an uneven relationship to property and labour. Sometimes they possess productive and labour forces. Sometimes they don't. They do, however, aspire to the normative status of the archetypical bourgeois subject (i.e. Western, white, heteropatriarchal) and thus try to socially reproduce the regulatory norms, practices and infrastructures of dominant institutions (i.e. the state, the family, capital, the academy, etc.). They understand their social differences as sometimes obstacles to, and at other times catalysts for, that reproduction. And in the effort to reproduce dominant institutions, the lower classes and non-normative subjects among and near them become resources for discipline and exploitation.

The contexts of neocolonialism and neoliberalism provide unique windows into these aspects of bourgeois formations among the minoritised. The first thing that

---

* This article, and that of Gail Lewis which follows in the issue, were given as public lectures at the University of British Columbia, located on the unceded and ancestral lands of the Musqueam First Nation, in October 2022. As Visiting Professors at Green College, Roderick Ferguson and Gail Lewis convened an interdisciplinary workshop and delivered lectures on the theme of 'Coalitional Possibilities'.

we might say is that both neocolonialism and neoliberalism emerge out of the contexts of formal emancipation – that is, out of the discourse of rights. As such they both bear the trappings of independence but also resuscitate the inequalities of their antecedents and produce new types of inequalities.

In 'On the Jewish Question', Marx identified formal emancipation this way: 'The limits of political emancipation appear at once in the fact that the state can liberate itself from a constraint without man himself being really liberated; that a state may be a free state without man himself being a free man'.[2] Here Marx identifies emancipation on the state's terms as a faux emancipation. Neocolonial and neoliberal regimes arise out of this contradiction of formal emancipation – that is, the state's presumed liberation from social constraints and the population's continued subjugation through those constraints.

Consider, for instance, Kwame Nkrumah's definition of neocolonialism as a response to anti-colonial militancy in the global south in *Neo-colonialism: The Last Stage of Imperialism*. In it he writes: 'Faced with the militant peoples of the ex-colonial territories in Asia, Africa, the Caribbean, and Latin America, imperialism simply switches tactics'. Dispensing with its paraphernalia and its representatives, former colonial powers would surrender their authority, give independence to former subjects and follow that surrender with aid and development. With flags and officials gone, the colonial apparatus would begin to 'devise innumerable ways to accomplish objectives formerly achieved by naked colonialism'. Neocolonialism – or the 'modern [attempt] to perpetuate colonialism while at the same time talking about "freedom"' – would be born as global capital's answer to insurgent movements.[3]

Six years before Nkrumah's book, Aimé Césaire touched on the essence of neocolonialism in his lecture at the 1959 Congress of Negro Writers and Artists in Paris. There he said, 'One too often sees perpetuated or reconstituted within the societies constituted by nations

which have been liberated from the colonial yoke, structures which are in truth colonial or colonialist'.[4] For Césaire, the repetition of colonial structures under the ruse of independence produced the conditions for the emergence of the native-born and neocolonial bourgeoisie. As he said, 'Inside imperfectly decolonized nations, there is a danger that typically colonialist phenomenon of recurrence will be seen to emerge at any moment, utilized no longer by a colonialist or imperialist, but by a group of men or a class of men, who from that moment, inside the liberated nation, take on the role of the Epigoni of colonialism and use the instruments invented by colonialism'.[5] In this context, the native and neocolonial bourgeoisie emerges as the offspring not of decolonisation but of its incompletion. In Marx's terms, bourgeois formations have arisen out of the ethos of formal rather than real emancipation. They are thus the representatives of an incomplete emancipation.

Neoliberalism in liberal democratic states arises out of a formal emancipation that seemingly responds to social protest as well. For instance, in her definition of neoliberalism, historian and theorist Lisa Duggan writes: 'The culture wars strategy allowed emerging neoliberal forces to attack and isolate the cultures of downward redistribution located within social movements since the 1960s. The flip side of this strategy was the nurturing of forms of "identity politics" recruitable for policies of upward redistribution ... Neoliberalism's emergent strategy for the new millennium: A new "equality" politics compatible with a corporate world order'.[6] In our article, 'The Sexual and Racial Contradictions of Neoliberalism', Grace Hong and I argue for an extension of the definition of neoliberalism 'as the current stage of racial capital that emerged after the worldwide liberation movements of the mid-twentieth century, what Elizabeth Povinelli (2011) describes as "the governance of social difference in the wake of anticolonial movements and the emergence of new social movements"'.[7]

Similar to neocolonialism, neoliberalism represents a cannibalistic response to insurgent struggles. As I argued in *The Reorder of Things*,

> National liberation, civil rights, and neocolonialism should be understood as part of a larger social context that proclaimed the command of a new mode of power, a mode that was composed of power's new techniques of management, especially around internationalism and minority difference, as well as its insinuation into political agency.[8]

Neoliberalism and neocolonialism would thus become mechanisms for resuscitating and regenerating colonial and liberal inequalities rather than annihilating them.

As neocolonialism and neoliberalism have expressed themselves by claiming certain articulations of insurgent struggles and minority difference – articulations reconciled to the needs of global capital – they have revealed how flexible local and minority differences are, that they can – in a paraphrase of Stuart Hall's classic essay 'The Local and the Global' – 'live with', be overcome by, and incorporated through global capitalism.[9] That flexibility also brought the question of what form of emancipation will yield real and broad emancipation into stark relief. In a 1959 address, Aimé Césaire got at this question through the competing forms of decolonisation at work in the anti-colonial and post-colonial contexts. He wrote,

> But in the end I say, and I maintain, that inside decolonization itself there are degrees, that all forms of decolonization are not equal, and if a 'good decolonization' can only be defined by a contrast with a 'less good decolonization' I would say that the latter is one which within the framework of independence, only thinks of utilizing the old colonial structures by adapting them to the new realities, whereas the true decolonization is the one which realizes it is its duty to shatter the colonial structures in definitive fashion.[10]

In the passage, we can see that Césaire attempts to parse the forms of decolonisation in ways not dissimilar to Marx's parsing of emancipation in 'On the Jewish Question'. There's a 'good decolonization' versus a 'less good decolonization' for Césaire and a human emancipation versus a political emancipation for Marx.

Ironically, one of the places where this kind of decolonisation took place in the US was not only in the Black Power movement but also the civil rights movement. When Martin Luther King gave his 'Trumpet of Conscience' speech against the Vietnam War in 1967, he critiqued the political ideology of bourgeois moderation. He said,

> It is difficult to exaggerate the creative contributions of young Negroes. They took nonviolent resistance, first employed in Montgomery, Alabama in mass dimensions,

and developed original forms of application – sit-ins, freedom rides, and wade-ins. To accomplish these, they first transformed themselves. Young negroes had traditionally imitated whites in dress, conduct, and thought in a rigid, middle-class pattern. Gunnar Myrdal described them as exaggerated Americans. Now they ceased imitating and began initiating. Leadership passed into the hands of Negroes, and their white allies began learning from them. This was a revolutionary and wholesome development for both. It is ironic that today so many educators and sociologists are seeking to instill middle-class values in Negro youth as the ideal in social development. It was precisely when young Negroes threw off their middle-class values that they made an historic social contribution.[11]

For King, bourgeois ideology – whether by the white bourgeoisie or the Black one – was a commitment to the status quo. The moment that young Black people – en masse – rejected it is the moment that they ushered in historic change. This is a searing critique of respectability politics and of the bourgeois classes; King is in fact saying that the civil rights movement was a historic repudiation of respectability politics as well as bourgeois ideals and that there would have been no movement had that not been the case. The implication here is that the Black bourgeoisie can in no way be the author and finisher of Black freedom struggles.

In his classic book *The Golden Age of Black Nationalism, 1820-1925*, Wilson Jeremiah Moses also touched on the Black bourgeoisie as an agentive formation, one whose agency was part of its entrenchment in social reproduction. Of those nineteenth-century formations, he argued,

> The middle class Negroes would remain victims of prejudice, so long as the masses remained untutored, impoverished, and demoralized. The goal of uplifting freedmen was similar to the goal of uplifting Africa, and was to be carried on for the same purposes as the old antebellum African civilizationism. The building of Afro-American culture would demonstrate to all the world that blacks were able and willing to make a contribution to American life, and were, therefore, fit to be United States citizens. As the masses were elevated, the bourgeoisie would rise correspondingly.[12]

Here Moses makes clear that the African American bourgeoisie was an agent of social reproduction but not just the reproduction of a national order pertaining to the U.S. but a civilisational order concerning the status of the colonial project in Africa.

W.E.B. Du Bois's notion of the talented tenth expressed a belief in the agency of the Black bourgeoisie. As he wrote,

> The Negro race, like all races, is going to be saved by its exceptional men. The problem of education, then, among Negroes must first of all deal with the Talented Tenth; it is the problem of developing the Best of this race that they may guide the Mass away from the contamination and death of the Worst, in their own and other races.[13]

By the 1930s, Du Bois had begun to reconsider his beliefs about the Black bourgeoisie. Referring to Du Bois's Rosenwald lecture of 1933, Cedric Robinson argued: 'Du Bois was addressing himself directly to the problem of the alienation of the black elite from the black masses'. In Du Bois, we find someone who began with a faith in the coalitional impulses of the Black elite toward the Black poor but who ended in disillusionment about both those impulses.[14]

Feminist and queer components of the Black radical tradition have powerfully demonstrated the failure of the Black bourgeoisie to coalesce with their poor and working-class counterparts across class as well as gender, nation and sexuality. Consider, for instance, M. Jacqui Alexander's contention in her classic 1997 chapter 'Erotic Autonomy as a Politics of Decolonization: An Anatomy of Feminist and State Practice in the Bahamas Tourist Economy' in the book that she co-edited with Chandra Mohanty – *Feminist Genealogies, Colonial Legacies and Democratic Futures*. In it, Alexander identified heteropatriarchal law as a carry-over from the colonial period, writing, 'there are certain functions of heteropatriarchy which supersede the sexual or marking of sexual difference. At this historical moment, for instance, heteropatriarchy is useful in continuing to perpetuate a colonial inheritance ... and in enabling the political and economic processes of recolonization'.[15] We can read Alexander's essay as an extension of Césaire's argument that all decolonisations are not created equal. For instance, as she argued,

> While the Black Nationalist Party (The People's Liberal Party) wrested power from an elite group of white powers in 1972, which was formerly influential in the colonial legislature, it seized ownership of some of the more popular symbols of Black working-class political struggle, like the Burma Road Rebellion, and claimed the right of women to vote (initiated in 1962) as its own benevolent achievement. This would mark its first attempt to erase the memory of popular struggle. It narrowed its own vision of popular nationalism, turning the mobilization of women, youth, trade unions and churches on which it relied for support into a constitutional convention, organized in Britain, in which the Queen was retained as head of State.[16]

The Black Nationalist Party, which would become The People's Liberal Party, would narrow the visions of grassroots and feminist movements to fit within the ideals of the new postcolonial state. In doing so, The Black Nationalist Party would attempt to close the political universes imagined by grassroots and feminist movements and adopt the postures of political versus human emancipation.

Cedric Robinson described the Black bourgeoisie in *Black Marxism* as 'a broker stratum seemingly secured from above by a ruling class that proffered them increments of privilege while ruthlessly repressing mass black mobilization'.[17] We may read Alexander's observations as an adjustment of Robinson's in that ruthlessly repressing mass Black mobilisation was concomitant with the repression of gender and sexual freedom. Even as national liberation movements contested the racial and class exploitations of liberal capitalist states, those movements would retreat from the ways in which those exploitations depended upon gender and sexual regulations. This proved devastating in a moment in which global capital during the 1970s and onwards was producing the conditions for transgressions and regulations along the lines of gender, sexuality and race as seen in the feminisation of immigrant and service labour as well as the reassertion of heteropatriarchal controls through the state. More pointedly, minority bourgeoisies would emerge as the supervisors of gender and sexual normativity in that historical context, making bourgeois privilege a proxy for gender and sexual normativity. These processes could be seen in a variety of contexts – through the emergence of neocolonial bourgeoises in the Caribbean, managing forms of sexuality in the context of Western tourism; or through the rise of an African American bourgeoisie, supervising healthcare for poor, drug-addicted, and HIV-positive Black people; or through the emergence of diasporic communities from the global south, managing cultural events to exclude LGBTQ+ people from those same diasporic communities.[18]

A historical, comparative and transnational approach to bourgeois formations means assessing the ways that they claim to fulfil the terms of emancipation while fulfilling the existing social order, doing so across racial, gender, sexual and national identities. It is also a means linking the rise and regulation of social movements across global terrains to one another. Moreover, it also means developing modes of scrutiny that can distinguish between different forms of emancipation and their relationships to state and capital.

Part of that geopolitical task means unpacking bourgeois formations then and now. I have always been intrigued by the seductions that have coaxed Black bourgeois formations into being – seductions that offer not just personal distinctions, but exclusive forms of agency withheld from everyday Black people. For Alexander, it's the capacity of Black bourgeois formations in the Caribbean to express gender and sexual normativity. It's also the ability to shape and often wither the meanings of Black popular and working-class struggles to buttress the nation state. Another signature capacity has been the assumption of a comprador role between the nation state and the minoritised.

The emergence of an LGBTQ bourgeoisie represents a similar moment of danger where insurgent and coalitional struggles are concerned. In an essay entitled

'Stonewall was a Riot. Now we Need a Revolution', the Asian American activist and writer Merle Woo takes sharp aim at that bourgeoisie. Discussing gay moderate responses to the anti-gay crusades of Anita Bryant, Woo writes,

> Gay moderates had tried to counter the hysteria of Bryant's crusade with public information campaigns that emphasized privacy rights, downplayed or didn't even mention homosexuality, and ignored the far right's ongoing mobilization against all civil rights gains. These timid reformists scorned alliances with other oppressed groups and insisted that outspoken opposition to anti-gay initiative campaigns would spark a backlash. They betrayed gay rights, as they have betrayed people of color, workers and women – as if there are no gays among these groups.
>
> In the mid-'80s, one gay San Francisco Supervisor refused to fight for immigrant rights while he campaigned for gay rights legislation, saying, 'I don't want to hitch my wagon to a losing star'. As if there are no queer immigrants. Last year, the Human Rights Commission refused to add transgender rights ('gender identity') to the Employment Non-Discrimination Act (ENDA) because we're supposed to accept liberation in stages.[19]

Woo addresses how a gay bourgeoisie narrowed an LGBTQ political platform into a single-issue politics and in doing so undermined a coalitional politics that would have supported other minoritised groups. Woo's caution resonates with Reagon's admonitions. In her speech, she argued: 'The thing that must survive you is not the record of your practice, but the principles that are the basis of your practice'.[20] Coalitions, she said, are ways of holding those principles in awareness. Coalitions, also mean striving to be something other than the inheritors of the bourgeois legacies that capital, the state and the academy intend for us.

Roderick A. Ferguson is Professor of Women's, Gender and Sexuality Studies at Yale University.

Notes

1. Keeanga-Yamahtta Taylor, ed., *How We Get Free: Black Feminism and the Combahee River Collective* (Chicago: Haymarket Books, 2017), 62.
2. Karl Marx, 'On the Jewish Question', in *The Marx-Engels Reader*, ed. Robert C. Tucker (New York: W.W. Norton and Company, 1978), 32.
3. Kwame Nkrumah, *Neocolonialism* (Bedford: Panaf Books, 1970) 239.
4. Aimé Césaire, 'The Man of Culture and His Responsibilities', *Présence Africaine: Cultural Journal of the Negro World* 24-25 (1959), 128.
5. Ibid.
6. Lisa Duggan, *The Twilight of Equality? Neoliberalism, Cultural Politics, and the Attack on Democracy* (Boston: Beacon Press, 2003), 42.
7. Roderick A. Ferguson and Grace Hong, 'The Sexual and Racial Contradictions of Neoliberalism', *Journal of Homosexuality* 59:7, 1057.
8. Roderick A. Ferguson, *The Reorder of Things: The University and its Pedagogies of Minority Difference* (Minneapolis: University of Minnesota Press, 2012), 25.
9. Stuart Hall, 'The Local and the Global', in *Dangerous Liaisons: Gender, Nation, and Postcolonial Perspectives*, eds. Anne McClintock, Aamir Mufti and Ella Shohat (Minneapolis: University of Minnesota Press, 1997), 183.
10. Césaire, 'The Man of Culture', 128.
11. Martin Luther King, Jr., 'Trumpet of Conscience', in James M. Washington, ed., *The Essential Writings and Speeches of Martin Luther King, Jr.* (New York: Harper Collins, 1986), 645.
12. Wilson Jeremiah Moses, *The Golden Age of Black Nationalism, 1850-1925* (Oxford: Oxford University Press, 1978), 71.
13. See https://glc.yale.edu/talented-tenth-excerpts.
14. Indeed, we can read Du Bois's 1935 text *Black Reconstruction in America, 1860-1880* as an expression of this shift towards appreciating the Black poor as historical agents.
15. M. Jacqui Alexander, *Pedagogies of Crossing: Meditations on Feminism, Sexual Politics, Memory and the Sacred* (Durham, NC: Duke University Press, 2005), 24.
16. Ibid, 25.
17. Cedric J. Robinson, *Black Marxism: The Making of the Black Radical Tradition* (Chapel Hill: University of North Carolina Press, 2000), 191.
18. For further discussion, see the conclusion to *Aberrations in Black: Toward a Queer of Color Critique* (Minneapolis: University of Minnesota Press, 2004).
19. Merle Woo, 'Stonewall was a Riot – Now We Need a Revolution', in Tommi Avicolli Mecca, ed., *Smash the Church, Smash the State! The Early Years of Gay Liberation* (San Francisco: City Lights Books, 2009), 287.
20. Bernice Johnson Reagon, 'Coalition Politics: Turning the Century', in Barbara Smith, ed., *Home Girls: A Black Feminist Anthology* (New York: Kitchen Table, 1983), 366.

Whose movement is it anyway?
Intergenerationality and the problem of political alliance

Gail Lewis

Your children are not your children;
They are the sons and daughters of
Life's longing for itself.
They come through you
But are not from you
And though they are with you
They belong not to you.
You may give them your love
But not your thoughts,
They have their own thoughts.
You can house their bodies but not their souls,
For their souls dwell in a place of tomorrow,
Which you cannot visit,
Not even in your dreams.
You can strive to be like them,
But you cannot make them just like you.
Strive to be like them
But you cannot make them just like you.

The Black feminist acapella ensemble, *Sweet Honey in the Rock*, first launched their version of Lebanese poet, visual artist and philosopher Khalil Gibran's 1923 poem, *On Children*, into the world of justice politics in 1988. A tender, loving and powerful statement that disrupts the assumptions and terms of the heteronormative family and the hierarchy of generational authority and power it inscribes and reproduces, whether these words are engaged visually through the eye as text, or sonically through the ear as song, the profundity of its injunction summons the reader/listener to attention as it poses surprising questions about an aspect of life that often goes unthought and unremarked. That this is so is in many ways astounding since the terrain it disrupts is one that is central to many areas of social movement activism, including queer critique of heteronormativity and the coloniality of cis-gender normativity as the pivot of technologies of social and biological reproduction of the human.

And yet, despite *On Children* being a manifesto – or ethical directive – about social relations of generation, the issue of the intergenerational (familial-political-cultural) as a complex nexus of the distribution of heritage and obligation, gift and responsibility, seems strangely muted in the landscape of social critique and reimagining futures, at least as it plays out in the UK, the place from which I write, live, think, experience.[1] Some sense of why the call to attention signalled in *On Children* could be inferred from the provenance of the poem/song: the Arab world in the inter-war years; and Black feminist cultural production in the post-Civil Rights/Black Power years of the USA.

That these would have been, and remain, sites for the emergence of simultaneous critique *and* envisioning of possible futures relevant universally, i.e. beyond their immediate constituencies of production, was and remains unthinkable in the western critical canon. By extension, this is why (I might hazard) the lived alternative modes of relation across generations that are part of, for example, Indigenous sociality, and the cosmological models these might offer those wishing to disrupt heteropatriarchal conceptions of kin and kinship, are unseen, ethnically particularised and/or occluded by the self-referentiality of so much critical praxis organised under the logics of western modernity and its framing of contestatory politics.

Located in a self-reflexive consideration of intergenerationality in the social movement activism of Black feminism in Britain, I want to take seriously the provocation of *On Children* and ask: what is the relationship between a preceding generation of activist/scholars and those of the subsequent generations who take up the baton, if not one of proprietorial birthing and authority? How can this relation be conceived and practiced outside of the unquestioned logics of heteropatriarchal kinship? What is the intergenerational ethical relation between and for both the 'parents' and the 'children'?

Two central questions arise for me. First, if each generation has its own thoughts, how can a temporal frame that is always 'now', and also one that simply repeats, be avoided? The now/repeat dilemma poses profound issues of vision and strategy. Struggles for social transformation in pursuit of justice and freedom always raise the challenge of how to draw from history whilst avoiding being constrained by it (a dilemma embodied in intergenerational dynamics). Analysis involves being able to chart and understand changes and how they occurred and locating moments of struggle in their time/space specificity. If always 'now' such analysis is occluded. A temporal frame of perpetual 'now' also erases the gains and impacts of prior movements for justice and freedom – for example, the ways in which current attacks on women's autonomy and bodily integrity are, at least in part, linked to the backlash for gains won by feminist organisation since the 1970s. By extension, this also forecloses analysis of the various ways in which power has responded – e.g. by a strategy of assimilation, marginalisation, pathologising or criminalisation, or a mix of all these. Somewhat paradoxically, a permanent 'now' also erases the particularities of perspective, political methodology and objectives of different generations in a particular conjunctural moment. In short, the specificities, continuities, discontinuities and entanglements between and across generations are lost and the danger of endless repetition, as opposed to development and/or refinement of praxis, becomes more pronounced.

This leads to a second question, one that I am devoid of even a provisional response, yet believe is pressing – i.e. how can movements of coalition and solidarity be sustained across difference, including the difference of generation, and enabled to work ceaselessly toward freedom?

In accepting the challenge of disruption to the proprietoriality of lineage transmission, I propose that this involves a rejection of seeing Black feminist movement as a project of sameness, as if its development was a project of cloning, and instead requires re-casting of the intergenerational as a terrain of potential, ongoing coalition. At the same time, this poses the challenge of how to develop ways of working, building and imagining together, across constituencies and spaces of specificity *without* surrendering the 'inter-am' of all life forms, so brilliantly articulated and theorised by Lata Mani in her recent book *Myriad Intimacies*.[2]

Against this background, my offering is focused on a moment of Black feminism in the UK linked to the Organisation of Women of African and Asian Descent (hereafter OWAAD) and Brixton Black Women's Group (hereafter BBWG). OWAAD was a national umbrella network of women's groups from across the racially minoritised population – predominantly African, Caribbean, and South Asian; but also Arab, South East Asian, and Latin American. Toward the end of the piece and in less detail, I consider a small, dynamic community-based organisation of Muslims who work in ways that queer gender, sexuality, identity.[3] In considering what these illustrate about the demands and possibilities of coalitional formations, I conceive the construction of spaces of coalition in the sense offered by Audre Lorde in her work on difference:

> Difference must be not merely tolerated but seen as a fund of necessary polarities between which our creativity can spark like a dialectic. Only then does the necessity for interdependency become unthreatening. Only within that interdependency of different strengths, acknowledged and equal, can the power to seek new ways of being in the world generate, as well as the courage and sustenance to act where there are no charters ... Difference is that raw and powerful connection from which our personal power is forged.... Without community there is no liberation, only the most vulnerable and temporary armistice between an individual and her oppression. But community must not mean a shedding of our differences, nor the pathetic pretense that differences do not exist.[4]

I cite this to indicate that I share with Lorde the idea that it is through difference that we come to form the most meaningful coalitions and 'otherwise' modes of relationality. And I share the understanding that this takes work and love and care, particularly given the current context of neoliberal multiculturalist modes of governmentality, in which 'recognition' of cultural or ethnic identity is the ground of subjection in which racialised groups submit to their 'othering'. In such circumstances, the aim of coalition must exceed the call for 'recognition' by the state – recognition only made possible through modes of colonial/anti-Black/heteronormative intelligibility. It also exceeds the kind of 'respectful but ultimately disregarding listening' (so characteristic of EDI[5] processes in institutions) and asks is there something more – '*Somethin Else*', as Cannonball Adderley might phrase it,[6] that has the potential to disrupt whiteness in its guises as raced, gendered, sexual, classed and ableist normativities. This is something that requires us to respond to the haunting in the sense conceived by Avery Gordon and implement the 'something that remains to be done';[7] that resurrects and deploys the modes of world-sense, to invoke Oyèrónké Oyěwùmí,[8] that so many of us have forgotten we know and use it in our otherwise world making; something that hears and feels the kinetic vibrations in the sense of something 'set off' because it 'lands' viscerally and emotionally, sounding the otherwise knowing that vibes in the excesses of the flesh, to herald Hortense Spillers, via Ashon Crawley, into this space with us now.[9]

I should make it clear that if the above is the framing, more specifically/concretely, I am thinking of 'coalition' in a kind of double move. First, is that my query unfolds via the description of two kinds of coalitional practice: on the one hand, the more familiar kind that is linked to the generation of a feminism through the creation of organisations (or a movement) of various constituencies differentially racialised as minority, each with specificities of gendering, sexualisation and classed locations. OWAAD was one such organisation constituted in this mode. On the other, is the coalition generated from the work of people of different age-based groups (in a mirroring of parents/offspring) from within one faith-based constituency (itself characterised by its 'multi-raciality') to address questions of belonging, identification and community in the context of queer life.

I am concerned about these two modes because I wonder how it might be possible to think them in relation to one another as both structured by a kind of intergenerational membership and whose practice raises questions of intergenerational relation, explicitly or implicitly. Finally, there is my concern to respond to the provocation of *On Children* that I referred to earlier – this is the issue of ethical responsibility between 'elders' and 'children' outside a logic of heteropatriarchal ownership and authority. To begin to disentangle from such a structure requires a practice of self-reflection and self-reflexivity if a capacity to see/imagine oneself in *relation* is to develop at both the individual and collective level and which is an irreducible precursor to impactful critique, as Lorraine O'Grady, African-American-Jamaican visual artist and theorist, tells us: 'self-expression is not a stage that can be by-passed. It is a discrete moment that must precede or occur simultaneously with the deconstructive act'.[10]

O'Grady is proposing the need for subjugated constituencies and subjects to bring themselves fully into the frame of visibility and analysis (for her, of visual arts practice). I am suggesting the double move of self-reflection and self-reflexivity as both adopting a stance of observation of self/constituency in situated positionality and relation; and a stance of reflexive consideration of the values, modes of relating that characterise self/-

constituency. I suggest this is a necessary prelude to deciphering the intersectional constellations of historical and contemporary social relations and practices, which would include their psychic and affective inscriptions, within which we are all embedded and which structure our relations. Such reflection/reflexivity augments structural analysis by opening a lens on the multiplicity of life forms with whom we are in relation, not only in structures of power and domination, but also in visions of future commons working to the logics of care, and from which movement towards living consciously as 'inter-am' can proceed.[11] Such creative construction of 'me-not me-always in relation' then becomes the generative, 'erotic' space that channels the deconstructive acts into a mode of creative pursuit of justice and freedom.[12]

When read alongside the earlier quote from Audre Lorde, *On Children* can be read as a teaching (and perhaps warning) as to the tasks that emerge in formations of coalition: the need to generate an image of the self out of a collective process of reflexive consideration as to what and who that is; the need to hold the partners to coalition as near, yet still separate from the self; the need to 'know' who each other are – the conditions of existence, narratives and visions of those 'not me' – and be open to what each offers; understand and hold in ethical responsibility practices of care and nurture outside existing hierarchies of value, authority and proprietorial relation; and the need to take seriously the concept of the 'generative' as a potentiality between generations. This latter has a direct relevance to political formations that are (by accident or design) constituted by cross-generational memberships, but the others are equally important.

So, this paper is an exploratory piece aimed at stimulating conversation about and development of a way of thinking about intergenerationality as a form of coalition. And since coalition work is demanding, requiring energy, the capacity for pause, and a willingness to look inwards to engage outwards – it requires a capacity for thinking, in order to foster the kind of collaborative transformation the pursuit of freedom demands.

My conception of 'thinking' is heavily influenced by two theorists, on the surface at opposing ends of the political/theoretical spectrum, but whom I read as echoing each other across the canyons of socially constituted, psychically lived hierarchical difference and disciplinary boundaries in regard to conceptualisations of 'thinking'. The two are Black, lesbian, feminist, mother, anti-imperialist poet Audre Lorde, and white, English, upper class, raised for his first eight years in India (under imperial rule) by an ayah, psychoanalyst Wilfred Bion.[13] Both conceived 'thinking' as an apparatus developed to allow humans to process emotional experience and develop 'thoughts' from this 'thinking'. The root of 'thoughts' (channelled through 'thinking') is emotional experience – thoughts that come as emotions (feeling states) which themselves contain knowledge about the world (and the suffering the world imposes) but need to be processed and transformed into meaning. These emotions (vibrations) must be 'met' and engaged and made intelligible in ways that foster understanding and freedom. Since emotions contained[14] by a mind capable of 'thinking' have this potential, they offer a way to know the world and its potentialities, prohibitions. As linked to the work of coalition, the issue is to constantly ask (oneself and one's co-conspirators), what are the experiences that need to be rendered intelligible and harnessed to the pursuit of justice and freedom? In other words, the 'thinking apparatus' needs to be deployed in this direction when considering coalitional politics.

With this in mind, let me come back to the arena of coalition building that is my concern here: the question of *intergenerational conversation, activism, theory-building*.

Why has this presented itself as an issue for me? There are probably two reasons (though since one never entirely 'knows' one's mind it is likely more overdetermined than that). We can begin with my age, since this is one reason why the issue of intergenerationality as a mode of coalition has become a concern for me. I am now an elder and despite the fact that, in being hailed as such, I often find myself looking round to find the elder being hailed, I now occupy a particular position within Black feminist political formations in London that require me to be one of the holders/transmitters of our history and use this to offer direction to younger ones. Though at one level an effect of individual life course, autobiographical history – which is never 'just' that, since all ways of storying lives signal the condensation of wider social, cultural, political and emotional patterns – and/or their contestation, this itself signals the challenge of coalition: how is it possible to speak with/walk with those that are me/not me in ways that foster movement towards freedom? That is, the very tasks of reconceptualisation signalled by *On Children*, as noted above. And to these we might add that thinking through the similarities and differences embodied in the various generations within Black feminist formation also helps to avoid a collapse of time into an ever present 'now' (as if nothing has changed or needs to change in the character or visions of the formation), and avoids producing a vision of Black feminism in Britain as an ossified formation, in some mirroring of the teleology of multiculturalist versions of contemporary British history. Rather, it articulates a need to evaluate shifts in visions and priorities in the light of complex intertwining of ideological, material, psychic, local, national and global conditions.

The second reason pivots around the link between personal and political formation as made material in the Black feminist, diasporic formation of which OWAAD and BBWG were representative and of which I was part. As a member, I helped build these, but more significantly they 'built' me; they enabled a differently embodied personhood outside of the subjectivities constituted by the multicultural coloniality of British governmentality and outside of the heteropatriarchal logics of authority and proprietoriality. As a consequence, it helped reformulate my thinking apparatus as it offered a way to live in the heart of a declined but still kicking colonial centre of racial capitalism and its settler colonialist / imperialist / multicultural practices.

Development of my thinking apparatus in this way was, and must be understood as, an effect of collective organising and struggle, and not as an act of a sovereign individual in the image of neoliberal constructions of subjectivity. Following Lorde, it instantiates the fundamentally collective and relational roots of individual psychic development even under the pressures and violences of intersectional practices of power and subjugation.[15] Following both Lorde and Bion, and located in the activism of OWAAD and BBWG, it also becomes clear that capacity for thinking – i.e. processing experience into meaning and thereby thought – is an ongoing, iterative process. Nevertheless, it could perhaps be assumed that I was well positioned for the pursuit of intergenerational political relation not premised on precisely the heteropatriarchal logics of authority and proprietoriality that I critique.

Haha! If only, and here the need for continuous practice of self-reflection and self-reflexivity is illustrated by a way of thinking that I have which could precisely open a disjunction between my theoretical claims and my political analysis of Black feminism in Britain as an intergenerational formation of me/not me. This is my tendency to think of our movement as a *continuous* project of *space-making and place holding*, i.e. that this remains an unchanged characteristic of Black feminist practice in Britain not just as a continuity of struggle but also because of a continuity of inheritance, in the sense that the 'children' do exactly as the 'parents' did. In the former, any quality of continuity is less vulnerable to prior generational authority or 'truth' about what is common to different generations in struggle. In the latter, an unreflexive assumption as to the aims, claims and effects of struggle (e.g. space making) as an unchanging feature, is more available to the logics of the very authoritarian and proprietorial practices I critique. And I can hold this view despite knowing that it is not necessarily true at all.[16]

Attempts to avoid such unreflexivity require openness and clear exposition of one's ideas and approaches, here in relation to the idea of space-making. By space-making / place-holding, I gesture to the disruptions to the orthodoxies through which racialised people have been named and made intelligible in the logics of governance and regulation by state institutions and media alike. This disruption also opened space for other modes and practices of personhood – ways of living Blackness and brownness in excess of the subject positions offered in terms such as 'coloured immigrant', 'ethnic minorities', 'settled communities' and 'BAME' (Black and minority ethnic) communities. Black feminist praxis was central to the processes of disruption and it was a profoundly coalitional movement – bringing together a variety of constituencies, and this was its place-based originality and power.

But: even if it is continuous, understanding how Black feminist practice moved, and deciphering and tracing when and where its punctuation marks[17] occurred within and between specific generations remains a central question. And from there one might analyse whether, how and with what effects it is a continuity between an earlier moment linked to OWAAD and BBWG and contemporary organisations such as Sisters Uncut or Not Nowhere. If all four of these organisations are about space-making and place-holding, is this as a tactical manoeuvre en route to some broader objective shared across the generations, or has this larger horizon changed? If so, in what ways; what challenges do they pose and to whom? Centrally, does my sense of continuity invoke a kind of assimilationist move that suffocates 'difference' (ethnic, sexual, classed, dis/abled and, crucially, age-based generational) and the capacity for thinking, and thus the potential for creative thinking? Or does adopting an analytical approach based on deep questions about what is continuous and how, open a space between generations that hold me/not me in ethical relation and capacity for generative creativity?

These are questions that haunt the landscape today, and though there is a great deal of looking back and archive building in the interests of knowing, documenting and learning from our history that is being undertaken, the driving temporal logic seems at times (to me) to be teleological, in the sense of working to a logic to chart 'progress' as opposed to understanding shifts in the registers and conceptualisations of what constitutes radical change and how it might be pursued. This, I think, makes clear another issue related to intergenerational coalition – how to know, name and reckon with shifts in project and vision that different generations bring to the table of coalitional formation. What, if any, are the shifts in key logics, aims, organisational form and practice associated with specific generations? Ultimately, assessment as to the character and implications of continuity and/or change in project must turn on whether the practice is in the mode of 'business as usual knowledge production / presence making' with a view to making space for inclusion in unchanged terms of citizenship and national belonging, or whether the activism is informed by a desire to trace the formation and praxes of 'otherwise' emergent personhoods and relations (then and now), made possible by the generation of a methodology that disrupts the colonial apparatus of knowledge formation and all the hierarchies of human value contained therein. Such a disruptive intervention would work through a different spatio-temporal imaginary consistent with the wider practice of Black feminist scholar-activists working to a radical, not assimilationist, agenda. The details of this may be beyond the scope of the concerns of this offering, but it does intertwine with my focus on the question of in what ways and with what implications are relations among cohorts of different age-determined generations *coalitional* formations; and what does it mean for how we understand and evaluate legacy and responsibility, and our desires for reimagining ourselves, our visions and relations.

And here, despite my own cautions, I remain concerned to think about this in relation to two issues: that of space-making in the sense of crafting a space of production of new personhoods (subjectivities) crafted outside the logics of colonialist / racist / multiculturalist citizen-subject making; *and* spaces *into* which these new personhoods could flow as agents demanding radical transformation as part of a diasporic and internationalist praxis. The Black feminism of OWAAD was consistent with the latter in that it was a field of practice located in a specific national formation but *not* belonging to that nation. It refused the racialised/gendered categories by which we were 'known'. It had the effect, then, of crafting new personhoods breathing and living in old spaces differently constellated so that the spaces themselves were reshaped and could become new spaces.

So, one challenge in the early part of the second decade of the twenty first century, is in what ways are these new personhoods/spaces continuing to be brought into being? Are they the same as, different from, or overlapping with the spaces/personhoods crafted in the 1980s and 1990s? Is this process of space-making an identifiable and core characteristic of Black feminist praxis in Britain across time? If so, where/why, and if not, does it matter? These may be the concerns of an 'elder', but perhaps, from the place from which I ponder, they resonate with the concerns of activists living and practicing in colonial-settler / anti-Black spaces in which similar racial logics of death, denial, expropriation, alienation and extraction structure relations of rule. But beyond this, and in attunement with other ways of knowing, being and relating, these concerns may open a pathway to learning from other cosmological frames and conceptualisations of heritage transmission, personhood and relationality (with all life-forms), enabling other ways of thinking and telling the story beyond any repetition or simple modification of the coloniality of authority, knowing, and relating.

But to shift back to the telling of my story from the vantage point of London, in the second decade of the twenty first century (by one modernist accounting of time), I want to address a second, related issue regarding intergenerational formation. This is how or what holds the formation that is Black feminism in London/Britain together now? At one time it was the sign 'Black' that did this work – not without error – but adequately enough to enable a vibrant coalitional formation of activism, radical analysis, rethinking, theory building and person-making. In this iteration 'Black' was a highly deracinated / historically-located naming of the present conditions of and alliances among numerous diasporic and migrant/exile constituencies who shared a common condition of British (and United States) colonial rule and its violences. As I have written elsewhere, building alliance and movement under the sign 'Black' meant that:

> in its multi-ethnicity and multi-nationality this Black feminism had already disrupted the national inscription of Black women's struggles and political visions. Thus, there was already a possibility that the modernist and colonialist logic of nation, as well as the modes of racist and sexual and gender subordination and exclusion connected with it, could be greeted as unintelligible, subject to critique and contestation from other, counter-discourses of belonging that had multi-sited trans-Atlantic and transnational provenance".[18]

The sign 'Black' held open a space for conversation and practice across Africa/African diaspora; South Asia/South Asian diaspora; Arab world/Arab diaspora; central/South America/and its diasporas and within that make coalition with those in the Irish struggle.

All this opened the possibility of thinking, knowing and becoming differently – outside of the colonial and multicultural normativities by which we were all (in our variety) named, known and governed by the racial capitalist state. Significantly what this held together were both the specificities of anti-Blackness/brownness *and* colonialist logics more generally. Anti-racism and anti-colonialism were not seen as separate but indivisibly tied together and this enabled a mode of cross-national thinking and connecting in tandem with diasporic thinking and connecting.

Yet, as a sign with the power to interpellate numerous constituencies, bringing them together under the sign 'Black', this contained both the potential and challenges of coalition work. This animating power was sustained for a long time but began to erode under the material and ideological pressure encompassed in state policies and 'namings' of minoritised communities (referred to earlier); practices of multiculturalism and increasing logics of neoliberalism, in which a politics of affect was as central as the logics of individual 'sovereignty', self-regulation, and something called 'ambition' (to succeed in and be recognised by the status quo). In these conditions, which included state-organised competition for funding and 'recognition', the sign 'Black' came under pressure as a way to articulate the struggles of various minoritised communities and struggles against racism in its gendered, heteronormative guises.

In other words, what was a profoundly coalitional field began to fracture under the effects of a shifting nominal categorisation of the logics of assembly, identification and belonging (kinship), but also in terms of the constellations around which political mobilisation was organised. This was a shift that in part mirrored the distribution of state funds and services aimed at 'ethnic minority' communities in which anthropological concepts rose to the fore as a way of 'knowing' and treating racialised populations. Here 'culture' became predominant, and it tapped into a need for 'cultural' expression such that coalitional alliances broke up. But so too did 'sexuality' – as an erstwhile sublated category of identification and 'knowing' within Black feminism itself, its unruliness burst out and led to a fracturing of various organisations, even as it fostered the formation of offshoot organisations and events, such as the Black lesbian group, or the Zami conferences. The latter shows that because we had made space all was not destroyed by the combined effects of suppression of difference within our movement and the rationalities and violences of state multiculturalism and modes of carcerality (immigration, deportation, mental health sectioning, CJS).

The space-making segued into place-making in different ways, one mode being the generation and practice of alternative onto-epistemological frames encoded in Black feminism. Modes in which what might be variously called 'affect', 'feeling', 'emotion' was a dynamic, albeit often unacknowledged as such. Drawing on Kara Keeling's foregrounding of 'affect' in her theorisation of the impossibility yet urgent necessity for alternative visions,[19] Grace Hong points to the place of affect in Black-/queer feminist disruptions to neoliberalism: '… affect is one of the forces that somehow manages to exceed the present-day conditions of possibility to gesture to a different epistemological, if not ontological and empirical regime'.[20] I take this to mean that 'feeling' could provide the fertile ground in which knowledge-production might proceed differently whilst drawing on the varieties of 'experience' faced by various constituencies rendered surplus, without value and fungible. And since 'experience' is always socially and psychically patterned, and thus material/structural, along with being felt at the level of subjectivity, 'feeling' is both located and exceeds the logics of oppression/social death. 'Feeling' as I call it, or affect as Keeling and Hong call it, also travels/flows, making links between constituencies and different life forms as it is a kind of vibration (think flowers that produce more pollen as they detect the vibrations of honey bees!). In this sense, the combination of oppressive material structures along with the legacies and transmission of structures of feeling (if invoking Raymond Williams here is not too uncanny[21]), Black feminism was expanding as one generation (OWAAD, etc.) aged and younger generations identified with and expanded the size and visions of Black feminist constituency and redefined its analytical approaches and practices. This meant there was an increasing involvement in 'intergenerational conversation'.

This was at once enriching – and exciting, certainly in the increased visibility of queer/non-normative sexualities within Black feminist constituency – *and* raised those pressing questions articulated in *On Children*:

- how to discern, plot and understand what was new / what was a repeat; what was a repeat but with a difference; how to identify where the analytical heat lay and what identified as the most pressing social/-political concerns; what was / should be the predominant mode of understanding the moment/present/-conjuncture;
- how to make visible varieties of Black feminist generational analytic in the present whilst holding the history, noting the change, and not privileging one generational side or the other; but instead, using it as motor of creative development analytically and practically;
- how to discern what our respective responsibilities as generational cohorts were/are and how to understand how these are or should be distributed in specific contexts.

These intertwined with other concerns, such as the issue of the state; the implication of shifting the naming 'Black' to that of 'Black and brown'; issues of the national, the postcolonial/decolonial, international; and the conceptual categories through and around which the current conjuncture was/is analysed and the understanding of contingent possibilities that this gave rise to. One might pose this tension as turning on how to address themes that foreground the suffering of systemic racisms, misogynies, class-based oppression, and exploitation, heteronormativities and ableism, *but not* to the exclusion of seeing and theorising possibility whilst generating modes of life-giving practice in Black and brown life. Thus, two things above all arise as central.

The first returns to my repeated refrain: how to conceive, build and sustain *intergenerational* coalition in ways that don't simply reproduce/collude with the coercions of colonial modernity that underpins modes of racialisation in social policy, immigration and border control, and overall practices of governance:[22] a conceptualisation of the intergenerational as a structure of hierarchy and linearity (succession) of authority and value. Second, and in more positive mode, this involves how to decolonise the conception of the intergenerational in ways that foster a profoundly 'otherwise' way of thinking relation across age-based generational segmentation and distribution of authorial value.

It is about space-making again – for otherwise personhoods, otherwise ways of understanding experience/wisdom/knowledge – cycles of life and relationality. A way to practice intergeneration that simultaneously has a profoundly different conception of kinship and what constitutes 'kin'; and allows for responsibility to the ancestors and spirit; enables the current generations to be good ancestors in the now/making; praise and take guidance from the ancestors and the grandchildren here and yet to come. Rephrasing this as a query as to how to do this in a way that contributes to the interruption of the spatio-temporal coordinates of colonial onto-epistemology – coordinates that Denise Ferreira da Silva identifies as 'separability, sequentiality, determinancy'[23] – shows how the question of intergenerationality is as much about the social relations of 'kin' as it is of politics and constituency.

I want to conceptualise the intergenerational as a process of making whereby a different constellation of elements signalled in the notion of 'a third', as yet *unknown*, is conjured through the interactions of different age cohorts. In this, age is understood as intensity of experiencing in specific times, in the arena of specific constellations of elements that structure and propel to the fore specific social/political urgencies. Then the emphasis in the word intergenerational is precisely on *generation* – with the emphasis on 'bring about', 'effect', 'prompt' as opposed to 'procreate'. What is generated in the process of cross-cohort relating and how does this object / these objects foster moves towards freedom – or not! And part of this move towards freedom will be the unsettling/disruption of colonial conceptions of generationality with its emphasis on linearity, hierarchal authority, heteronormative understandings of kinship. It will also be grounded in and propelled by 'feeling'/'affect' and this links back to my point earlier about how I conceptualise 'thinking' – for not only is 'feeling' / emotional experience the generating ground for the need for thinking, but it also foregrounds 'suspension' as central to a decolonial disruption – suspension of knowing, of future end point; abandonment of the phantasy that to be Human is to be in command of all that is, has been, will be.

Leanne Betasamosake Simpson tells us that the Michi Saagiig Nishnaabeg have a word – *kobade* – about which she writes:

> According to elder Edna Manitowabi, kobade is a word we use to refer to our great-grandparents and our great grandchildren. It means a link in a chain – a link in a chain between generations, between nations, between states of being, between individuals. I am a link in a chain. We are all links in a chain ... [So the] ... nation Kina Gchi Nishnaabeg-ogamig [is not only] the place where we all live and work together [but also] ... an ecology of intimacy.[24]

This is a beautiful, profoundly 'otherwise' way of conceiving the connection between generations, and it emanates out beyond the orbit of fore-parents and their offspring, thereby disrupting the temporal logics of linearity – and thus 'progress', 'improvement', 'modernising' (terms that have been central to the armoury of valorisation by which coloniality has ordered and governed the world). It offers a profoundly decolonial way into intergenerationality as it makes space for different linkages and personhoods/life-forms. If I use this to reframe my emphasis on the generating potential in intergenerationality, the centre of conceptual gravity shifts to *practising* intergenerationality as a gifted responsibility in which the before, the present and the future co-exist in a kind of spiral time, constellating ages, locatednesses, experiences, human-extra-human life forms in a mode of radical sharing, responsibility and hospitality – even within the context of a declined but still colonial state / national formation called the UK, where I work from, or Turtle Island in its manifestation as Canada, where Simpson works from.

And so enter the anonymous, non-profit queer / feminist / faith community-based organisation (with which I sometimes work) and which manifests something of a disruptive intervention in generative ways. Its membership is of radical Muslims who queer multiculturalist logics, heteronormative interpretations of the holy book, and gendered exclusions in prayer, and age-based hierarchies of authorial voice, whilst being respectful of the elders. The aspect of the work of this non-profit I am referring to aims to provide a space of care for:

- queer 'children' who practice faith and are grounded (or want to remain) in their communities, whilst not being excluded from collective prayer or their families;
- parents of these queer children who are struggling with their queerness and worrying that it is 'haram' and goes against the holy book, but who do not want to disown or coerce their children – want to find a way to reconcile their desire to hold with their fear;
- both parties need containing – in the sense of being held so that they can transform feelings into thoughts via a process of relational holding and thinking and refuse the disruptions to their connectedness resulting from the imposition of heteronormative, religious interpretation and the logics of neo-liberal multiculturalist governance;
- this 'thinking' (containment) is in communion with others in prayer and guided by both an imam (woman or man) and a 'secular' volunteer;
- content involves interpreting the book and word in other ways, also informed by an understanding of the social/cultural positionalities in place-based specificities;
- workshop format – which is collective and iterative, and operates as a 'thinking space' in which no generation, no gender, no caste has a privileged entitlement to speak/explore.

This is deeply challenging work, so the organisation calls on people 'outside' to help them bring into clearer view some of the dynamics (emotional and relational), and to process and understand them so that all participants may go again armed with the learning, support, gifting and receiving they have been offered. The intergenerational generates new modes of praxis and new challenges and circles out to build coalition 'within' and across constituencies.

This brief description of one aspect of this organisation's work shows how it is possible to disrupt the spatio-temporal logics of colonial modernity by mobilising the creative potential of intergenerational dialogue around queer desire and modes of living within the constraints of specific forms of cultural knowing and forms of racialisation. With the hope that I am not being too precocious, it enacts an ecology of intimacy as described by Simpson in her exposition of Nishnaabeg Brilliance:

The Seven Fires creation story sets the parameters for Nishnaabeg intelligence: the commingling of emotional and intellectual knowledge combined in motion or movement, and the making and remaking of the world in a generative fashion within Indigenous bodies that are engaged in accountable relationships with other beings. This is propelled by the diversity of Indigenous bodies of all ages, genders, races and abilities in attached correlations with all aspects of creation ....[This involves struggle] because this way of living necessarily continually gives birth to ancient *Indigenous* futures in the present.[25]

And as a link in the chain of feminisms emerging from Black, brown and other constituencies racialised as of colour from OWAAD and BBWG to today? Perhaps the micro-level, almost quotidian, practice of this small organisation re-frames but continues its inherited but not privileged agendas of space-making in the interstices of state devalorisation, surveillance, abjection; place-holding for new/different personhoods to emerge, that disrupt the prevailing logics of separation, sequentialism, determinacy; hold open and work with/to the generative potentials of difference, in the sense offered by Lorde. And in this, perhaps the nominal sign under which they convene and have identification with doesn't really matter, and is just the wistfulness of an aging Black feminist with a foot in the then and now of Black feminist coalition in London. And finally, in the here-and-now of this moment of engagement between reader's thoughts and mine as written ...? Let's keep talking.

Gail Lewis is a writer, psychotherapist, researcher and activist. She is Visiting Senior Fellow in the Department of Gender Studies at the London School of Economics, and Reader Emerita of Psychosocial Studies at Birkbeck.

Notes

1. I exclude from this statement the centrality accorded intergenerationality in scholarship and policy considering the impact of abuse of all kinds on family dynamics, such as in the psychodynamic and sociological study of trauma and/or domestic abuse. In addition, intergenerational relationships are of concern in the social policy, gerontology and geriatrics literature concerned with the distribution responsibilities between children and the state for the care of aged and/or disabled elders/parents. See, for example, A. Walker, 'The Politics of Intergenerationality', *Z Gerontol Geriat* 35:4 (2002), 297–303.

2. Lata Mani, *Myriad Intimacies* (Durham: Duke University Press, 2022).

3. The organisation will remain anonymous for reasons of confidentiality.

4. Audre Lorde, 'The Master's Tools Will Never Dismantle the Master's House', in *SisterOutsider* (New York: The Crossing Press Feminist Series, 1984), 111–112.

5. EDI is the acronym for Equality/Equity, Diversity and Inclusion commonly used within academic and corporate institutions in the UK at present.

6. Or 'sound it'. Cannonball Adderley, saxophonist, released his album *Somethin Else* in 1958 on Blue Note. Miles Davis plays trumpet on it; other musicians are Hank Jones, Sam Jones and Art Blakey. Just listen to how Adderley subtly disrupts in his renditions of 'Love for Sale' or 'Autumn Leaves'!

7. Avery Gordon, *Ghostly Matters: Haunting and the Sociological Imagination* (Minneapolis: University of Minnesota Press, 2008).

8. Oyẹ̀wùmí, Oyèrónké, *The Invention of Women: Making an African Sense of Western Gender Discourses* (Minneapolis: University of Minnesota Press, 2007).

9. Hortense Spillers, 'Mama's Baby, Papa's Maybe: An American Grammar Book' in *Black, White and In Color: Essays on American Literature and Culture* (Chicago: The University of Chicago Press, 2003/1987), 203–229; Ashon Crawley 'Stayed|Freedom|Hallelujah', in *Otherwise Worlds: Against Settler Colonialism and Anti-Blackness*, eds. Tiffany Lethabo King, Jenell Navarro and Andrea Smith (Durham, NC: Duke University Press, 2020), 27–37.

10. Lorraine O'Grady, 'Olympia's Maid: Reclaiming Black Female Subjectivity' in *Art, Activism and Oppositionality: Essays from Afterimage*, ed. Grant H. Kester (Durham, NC: Duke University Press, 1998), 272.

11. Mani, *Myriad Intimacies*, 2022.

12. Audre Lorde, 'Uses of the Erotic: The Erotic as Power' in *SisterOutsider* (New York: The Crossing Press Feminist Series, 1984), 53–59.

13. Lorde, 'Uses of the Erotic'; and 'Poetry is Not a Luxury' in *SisterOutsider*, 36–39; Wilfrid R. Bion, 'The Psycho-Analytic Study of Thinking' in *International Journal of Psychoanalysis* 43:4-5 (1962), 306–310.

14. Here I do not mean 'containing' in the sense of restriction, but I am using it in a way indebted to Bion's conceptualisation of 'containment'. Containment in this psychoanalytic theorisation is a live process between two minds (modelled on the relation between infant and maternal object) connected through unconscious communication. It involves the projection (psychic expulsion) of unbearable states of mind (often physically embodied) into the mind of another (the container) who has the capacity to receive, hold and process (make sense of) these states of mind. Then, when ready, the projection is given back to the projector in a way that can be tolerated by them. In this processed/held state the emotional experience that was unbearable is now intelligible and thus stripped of its terror-inducing force, making the experience amenable to 'thinking', made intelligible and can become a 'thought'. This capacity, for what Bion termed alpha function, becomes a feature of psychic life, though ongoing replenishment is required too as it is not established as a once and for all, lifetime achievement.

15. Lorde, 'Uses of the Erotic' and 'Poetry is not a Luxury'.

16. See Gail Lewis, 'Visions of Legacy: Legacies of Vision', in *Transatlantic Conversations: Feminism as Travelling Theory*, eds. Kathy Davis and Mary Evans (Farnham: Ashgate, 2011), 167–182.

17. Here I invoke David Armstrong, systems, psychodynamic theorist of organisational process and relatedness, who conceived institutional roles, statuses and the emotional meaning attached to them by the organisations' membership, as a kind of grammar in which interpersonal space was punctuated. See Armstrong, *Organization in the Mind: Psychoanalysis, Group relations, and Organisational Consultancy* (London: Karnac, 2005), 52.

18. Lewis, 'Visions of Legacy: Legacies of Vision', 176.

19. Kara Keeling, 'Looking for M–: Queer Temporality, Black Political Possibility, and Poetry from the Future', *GLQ: A Journal of Lesbian and Gay Studies* 15:4 (2009), 565–582.

20. Grace Kyungwon Hong, *Death Beyond Disavowal: The Impossible Politics of Difference* (Minneapolis: University of Minnesota Press, 2015), 15; citing Keeling, 'Looking for M–'.

21. Raymond Williams, 'Preface to Film' in Williams and Michael Orrom, *Preface to Film* (London: Film Drama Ltd, 1954).

22. Keguro Macharia, *Frottage: Frictions of Intimacy Across the Black Diaspora* (New York: New York University Press, 2019).

23. Denise Ferreira da Silva, 'On Difference Without Separability', *32nd Bienal De Sâo Paulo Art Biennial: Incerteza Viva*, (2016), 57–66, available at: *https://issuu.com/bienal/docs/32bsp-catalogo-web-en*.

24. Leanne Betasamosake Simpson, *As We Have Always Done: Indigenous Freedom Through Radical Resistance* (Minneapolis: University of Minnesota Press, 2017), 8.

25. Leanne Betasamosake Simpson, *As We Have Always Done*, 21.

Health without security?
An interview with Mark Neocleous
Mark Neocleous with Sam Kelly

Mark Neocleous is Professor of the Critique of Political Economy at Brunel University London. He is the author of numerous books including War Power, Police Power *(2014),* Critique of Security *(2008),* The Monstrous and the Dead: Burke, Marx, Fascism *(2005) and* A Critical Theory of Police Power *(2000). Most recently he has authored* The Politics of Immunity: Security and the Policing of Bodies *(Verso, 2022), in which he excavates the violent and repressive tendencies underlying the pervasive obsession with immunity in both medicine and politics. He was a member of the editorial collective of* Radical Philosophy *from 1998 to 2016.*

Sam Kelly: How did you become interested in the concept of security?

Mark Neocleous: It began when I was writing a book on the concept of police. I discovered this wonderful line of Marx in his essay on the Jewish question, where he says, 'Security is the supreme social concept of bourgeois society, the concept of police'.[1] He brought them together in a very direct and immediate way. I thought it was an insightful observation, which gets to the heart of how security underpins everything that is done in the name of police. By using the term police I'm not referring to the narrowest sense of the word, the uniformed, professionalised police services, but the whole range of ways in which the state polices civil society, which is what Marx was alluding to. So, my interest in security originally stems from a critical engagement with the police concept. Since then I have been trying to think them together – more recently, combined with the logic of war, again understood in the broadest sense to incorporate the social wars of capitalist modernity.

Of course, since first working on the idea of security a quarter of a century ago, that very concept has come to dominate political discourse. One sees this in the emergence of a range of ways in which security has been connected with everyday life: the notion of food security, for example, or water security, climate security, and so on. There are a lot of elisions that take place when the language of security gets foregrounded in these ways. Issues such as food, water, climate change, have long been the grounds for radical political struggles, campaigns and activism, but those took place without having to attach the notion of 'security' to them. From a critical perspective, attaching 'security' to them adds little and offers us nothing. However, it offers politicians and the ruling class a way of talking about this issue without addressing the issues which actually concern us. The talk of food security is not going to get more kids arriving at school with a full stomach, it's not going to feed more people, but what it does instead is it allows politicians to do other things, most obviously securing supply lines. In other words, what is being satisfied is not a human need, but the needs of capital in ensuring the security of its production and distribution.

In the book on police power, which was originally published in 2000,[2] a couple of chapters explore the ways in which policing takes place through the idea of order, on the one hand, in the sense that in the cry for 'law and order' it is 'order' that underpins the police logic, and security, on the other hand. I realised that there was more to say about security and so over the next few years I extended that argument, which became the basis for *Critique of Security*.[3] In that book, the critique of police power was ratcheted up to challenge the whole ideology of security. It is a book *against* security, and not simply a book within critical security studies, which purports to be critical but actually ends up as a rethinking of security rather than an actual critique of it. The question is then, what should we be doing instead? And the implication of the argument is that we need a different kind of language for radical politics in general and for critical theory in particular. In other words, I wanted to push the argument that critical theory must involve a critique of security.

SK: I want to come back in a moment to some of your comments about security, but can I first ask you when you began to consider how the question of security extended into medicine and public health?

MN: In the first articulation of my argument about police I discussed the long and fascinating history of what went by the name of medical police. Throughout the early modern period, the idea of medical police was one means through which the state could administer civil society through the lens of health, medicine and public health. It allowed for intervention into the bodies of people and the body of the people, or the 'social body', through medicine, management of contagious diseases or improvement of the drainage system to stop cholera, for example. This also had very obvious class dimensions. For example, Edwin Chadwick's attempt to improve London's sewers in the early nineteenth century was connected to his other role on the Health Board, and then to his role as police reformer, and these were bound up with his reform of the poor law and the need to police the working class through that law. This history has been obscured by the professionalisation of police forces and what we are encouraged to understand as 'police' in the narrow sense, but it has also been lost and replaced by other ways of thinking about how civil society is managed with regard to medicine, with other administrative terms such as public health or the national health service. I'm interested in what happens if we retain the idea of medical police, because we can then connect arguments around public health to a broader account of the ways in which the state administers civil society.

SK: In your most recent book you extend your argument about security and the logic of capitalist property relations to show how this shapes how we imagine our own relationships to our bodies.[4] Could you elaborate on that and explain how this emerges?

MN: The whole history of liberalism takes its cue from the idea of the property-owning individual. Specifically, that every individual is in some sense a property owner because at the very least they own their own body. As soon as you start thinking about your own body as a form of property you create the possibility of selling it as a commodity, or at least selling its power to labour. Here you have the grounds for wage labour and therefore accumulation and exploitation. But what also emerges is a set of ways of thinking about the body and its relationship to the self. As the individual as a property-owning body or a body as property emerges, so too does the development of certain ideas around selfhood, with concepts such as self-interest, self-regulation, self-governance and self-defense, all emerging around the same period. There's also self-destruction, which I touch on in this new book, and which opens the space for an argument gleaned from psychoanalysis and the death drive. The body is central to all of these and is also central to our ideas of property ownership.

SK: So why is immunity and the field of immunology so central to this conception of the body within liberal capitalism? What is it about immunity that interests you?

MN: I arrived at the question of immunity partly through the lens of security, but also through a very personal experience. In 2015 I was diagnosed with an autoimmune disease and this was very new to me, both as a concept and a process. Unsurprisingly, I started reading up on immunity to try and understand what was going on, mostly through reading popular books on immunity, but also some more advanced medical texts. I was immediately struck by how remarkably political these texts are. I started encountering discussions of Hobbes's *Leviathan*, Clausewitz's account of war and George Orwell's description of the totalitarian state. The imagery was consistent: if you want to understand your body, think of it as though it's a security state, of the kind described by Hobbes or Orwell, or as an entity at permanent war against dangerous others. These books were describing immunity through the lens of security, police, war. I suddenly found myself in a strange moment of trying to learn about what was going on in my body and being referred back to texts that I had been reading and teaching for years. In other words, I had for many years been developing a critique of security and then suddenly I was confronted with the idea of immunity as security. At the same time, debates within security politics were undergoing a remarkable immunitarian turn, using the idea of immunity to try and reinforce the drive towards security.

This was connected to a wider issue within the history of ideas. As soon as the body's immune process was discovered in the late nineteenth century, so the way in which the body politic is imagined could be transformed. No longer simply a mechanical body or a body with a nervous system, the body politic could now also be presented to us as either possessing an immune system or being an immune system. So once the idea of immunity was invented as a medical idea – I say medical idea because immunity as a legal idea has a much longer history, which I also discuss in the book – it could quickly come to oscillate back and forth between the physiological and political registers.

So, there was a general issue, concerning immunity and security, but what also concerned me was what this political connection meant for our understanding of the autoimmune disease. Then also, and at the same time, what the idea of an autoimmune disease might tell us about this politics of immunity. Because in the autoimmune disease, the immune system seeks to destroy the very body it is meant to secure.

SK: Can you say a bit more about that, especially given that immunity was already well-covered ground, appearing in the work of other thinkers?

MN: Absolutely. As you suggest, there was already a fair amount of philosophical work on immunity, and I was aware of it to varying degrees. I returned to the thinkers in question, and one thing that struck me was how the autoimmune disease was either ignored or poorly understood and badly integrated into the work. In the work of Luhmann, for example, probably the first writer to really push the idea of the social system as possessing an immune system, he is so taken by the idea of autopoiesis that he has to completely ignore the fact of the autoimmune disease. For Luhmann, the social system simply protects itself and secures itself in an autopoietic fashion against social infections such as protest and resistance, in a way that immunises the system against further threats. And because of this, the autoimmune disease simply cannot be addressed, so you end up with a social theory of immunity that has nothing to say about the immune process going wrong. In similar fashion, Sloterdijk's interest in architectures of immunity and what he calls spatialised immune systems also veers him away from the autoimmune disease.[5] He occasionally notes that the search for security sometimes drives the immune process into auto-immune pathologies, but he can't pursue that line of argument because it would thoroughly undermine his own account of immunological spheres of protection as a defensive basis for what he likes to call 'co-immunism'.

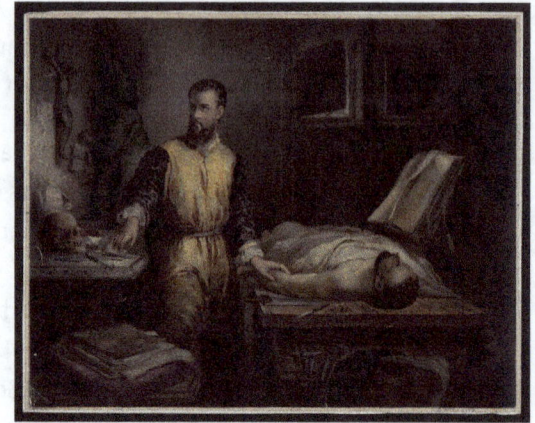

More complicated is the work of Esposito, who has really pushed the idea of using the idea of immunity to reimagine our concepts of community, arguing for a new philosophical paradigm of immunisation with the kind of conceptual weight previously attached to concepts such as secularisation or rationalisation.[6] Esposito does at least address the autoimmune disease, but his understanding of it is odd, to say the least. Because his interest lies in protection, he tends to focus on the border and when the body or body politic is penetrated. This question of borders allows him to reinforce the idea of immunisation as a process, to the point where he complicates the fundamental differences between immunisation and the autoimmune disease. For example, he talks about the autoimmune disease turning against itself as an immune system.

In reading these texts it struck me that they were so committed to a paradigm of immunity and immunisation that they could not recognise what seems to me to be a rather important political point about security: that if the immune process is the body's security system, then the autoimmune disease is the body's security system turning against the very thing it is meant to secure.

Derrida at least takes seriously the idea of autoimmunity, although somewhat problematically tends to conflate autoimmunity with autoimmune disease.[7] They are not the same thing. Autoimmunity is in fact a normal immune function to help maintain the body's optimal state. To put it bluntly, autoimmunity is a normal feature of the immune process without which one dies, whereas an autoimmune disease is a failure of the immune process which will eventually help kill you. This conflation undermines some of Derrida's insights about the terrifying features of autoimmunity, as it leads him to sometimes talk about the self being infected, and to sometimes treat the autoimmune disease as an attack on the body's immune system in a way that confuses autoimmune disorders with immunodeficiency disorders such as HIV/AIDS. That said, Derrida's work in this field at least alerts us to what he calls the terrifying idea of a threat within the body politic.

It is also the case that in the medical literature, no one has a real explanation for the autoimmune disease. Immunologists are as perplexed by the autoimmune disease as the philosophers. This is perhaps evident in the way that both the medical and the philosophical literature tend to use phrases such as 'civil war' or 'coup' to try and capture what is at stake in an autoimmune disease. But neither term really works. There is no civil war, in the sense of two sides fighting, and there is no coup, in the sense of the body being taken over. So, what I do in the book is pursue the idea of autoimmune disease as self-destruction and hence a manifestation of the death drive – in which case, imagined politically, the autoimmune disease can be understood as the suicidal self-destruction of the body politic in the name of security.

What the autoimmune disease does is alert us to a situation in which the body is damaged and destroyed from within by its own system of immunity-security, and a parallel in which the body politic is damaged and ultimately destroyed from within by its own security-immunity. What I try and do in the book, then, is to use the autoimmune disease to confront security's destructive power.

SK: How did the COVID-19 pandemic alter your research?

MN: I had already done the bulk of thinking and writing when COVID-19 hit. As you know, COVID-19 pushed the idea of immunity onto the front pages of every media outlet from that point onwards. Obviously, this was not about the autoimmune disease, but it foregrounded the connection between the immunity of the individual human body and the immunity of the system. In other words, it reinforced the idea of our bodies as part and parcel of the body politic and that the immunity of both go hand in hand. This is what was most obviously entailed by those early debates about 'herd immunity'. And the implication of this became clear, which is that the security of our bodies is wrapped up in the security of the body politic. This made explicit the role of securing the social system from utter collapse by securing our own individual bodies from this thing called COVID-19. We as individual subjects of the system are embedded within it, embodied within it, and are also the very thing that keeps it going. For this reason, the state was falling over itself to keep us alive, because otherwise the system was in genuine crisis. The system meaning the capitalist system.

SK: Do you really think the state was desperate to keep us all alive, because it didn't really feel like it?

MN: No, I don't. I think the biggest mistake we can ever make is to think that the state cares about us. It only cares about us as a resource. It cares about us as a resource used for the continuation of the system. That's what the state is interested in. As much as the politicians were talking about keeping people alive, what they were really focused on was keeping the health system going. They needed to keep the health system going, to keep people alive, yes, but because if the health system collapsed it would be an even bigger problem than COVID-19. Remember: 'protect the NHS'. This is one reason to think of it through the lens of medical police. But we can also think about this another way. As we speak, people are still dying in large numbers and people are still being hospitalised in large numbers, but the system now seems to be back largely on an even keel. The politicians have got the health service to a place where it's creaking but surviving, just, and for them 'just enough' is good enough because it is just enough in its role as a sub-system of The System as a whole. This explains why there was so much talk about COVID-19 becoming the new normal, as endemic rather than a pandemic. Herein lies the comparison that is always made with flu, and from a critical perspective we can draw out the implications of what is going on when we are encouraged to think of it this way. The point about COVID-19 becoming endemic in the way that flu is, is as follows. In the UK, there are around 8,000 deaths a year from flu, with a bad year seeing closer to 20,000 deaths. The system can cope with an average of 8,000 deaths, rising to 20,000 in a bad year. And it can especially cope given that those deaths are generally either of the older generation or have some kind of other illness which weakens them – like an autoimmune disease, for example. This is what we are moving to with COVID-19. The message is clear: x number of deaths per year will be normal, y number of deaths per year will be difficult but manageable, now stop worrying and get back to work. To return to your question: no, the state wasn't desperate to keep us alive, it was desperate to keep the system alive, but it needs enough of us alive to work the system.

SK: Returning to the pervasive nature of security, do you think the left (however we might describe it in its current formation) has developed a sufficient critique of security in its response to COVID-19?

MN: The left has always had a major philosophical political problem in thinking about the state. Despite an extended history of the critique of the state, the critique of political power and the relationship between state and capital, large parts of the left still tend to think of the state as the solution. In that context the concept of security is interesting because, to put it crudely, some forms of security are considered by the left to be ok and others not. For example, and again to put it crudely: national security bad, social security good. Yet it's difficult to separate these things out because, for the state, they operate on the same terrain. The concept of national security that emerged following the Second World War, for example, was modelled directly on the concept of social security that was developed between the two world wars, and for a very good reason: the earlier concept had shown what could be undertaken by the state in the name of security and, moreover, through the very same logic of emergency. Both social and national security are about policing the system. Secondly, it's very hard to concede ground to the logic of security in one area and then resist it in another, given the centrality of the state to the security industry and its ideology. Which returns us to my earlier point, about the pull of the notion of security, that it seemingly becomes irresistible.

We could look at this another way, through some of the most radical demands being made by different movements at the moment in the form of abolition politics. For example, in the US, the demands being made around police abolition are quite remarkable. The very slogan, never mind the struggles, is a stunning challenge to the state and the way it envisions social order, and it's a real shame that those demands are not being replicated elsewhere. However, one of the difficulties is precisely that instead of challenging the whole logic of security, they tend towards asking for other ways of imagining security. In other words, they're still on the terrain of security, only asking that it be 'reconceptualised'. What I'd really like to see is police abolition rolled up into a wider idea of security abolition. In a sense, what is at stake here is whether we are thinking about institutions or imaginations.

SK: Can you explain that a little more?

MN: Much of abolition politics focuses on an institution: police abolition, say, or prison abolition. These are incredibly radical demands, and ones we should be making, and it is even more radical to then think about other linked demands, such as debt abolition. But my desire is to see them rolled up into a broader program of security abolition because this asks broader questions about why those institutions exist in the first place. And that requires a broader argument about capital and the state. This is what the critique of security aims to do, which is why it mobilises a broader concept of police power, beyond the police institution and against police power in general. What this means is that instead of merely targeting an institution such as the police or the prison, security abolition demands something else from us. It demands a different way of imagining politics. It's not just about particular institutions. It's about the political imagination as a whole. Security abolition demands imagining politics beyond security.

SK: What might this look like in the sphere of health and medicine?

MN: As we said earlier, throughout the pandemic we've witnessed the advance of arguments about health security along with food security, water security, and so on. The concept of health security wasn't entirely new in 2020, but it's been pushed to the forefront by COVID-19. In the UK, we now have the Health Security Agency (HSA) which claims on its website that it aims to provide intellectual, scientific and operational leadership to secure the nation's health. It's significant that the HSA has a three-letter acronym that reminds us of the NSA: health security as mirror image of national security. Their organisational model and their response systems are designed explicitly to mirror the structures for responding to terrorist attacks. The first implication of what I'm saying is that we should be trying to think about health outside of the frame of security. We're not interested in health security; we're interested in health. Then again, perhaps it might be even more valuable to reconsider health itself as a concept. Because, to return to our earlier discussion, it's applied to us as a way of making us think about our own bodies as workers. We are to be made 'fit for work',

as the British medical system likes to describe us. Not fit for life, not fit for pleasure, but fit for work. This is 'the health unto death' to which Adorno alludes in the section with that title in *Minima Moralia*.[8] Critical theory needs to show the sickness of the system, not the sickness of the self. It needs to build on the idea that work makes us sick, that illness is itself a weapon against the system. We easily forget that the only reason the health system exists under capitalism is to keep us healthy for work. So beyond struggling against health security, maybe we need to be thinking beyond health as a category. Or at least, to resist a notion of health that is imposed on us by the state in the name of capital.

One way to think about this is through some of recent arguments about a politics of care. Modern capitalism wants to insist on the idea of health, and we instinctively feel that this makes sense, but what if we were to instead ask: 'health for what?'. Health tends to position us within what Foucault calls the doctor-patient couple. Alternately, or alongside that couple, it imposes upon us a notion of self-responsibility – eat your 5 a day, do your exercise, drink less. But what if we eschew health and ask instead about care? Health points us towards labour, on the one hand, or to cure, on the other hand, a key feature of the doctor-patient couple. One seeks a cure for whatever it is that is rendering one unable to labour. Donald Winnicott somewhere makes the point that cure and care were once intimately connected, but in modernity cure started to become medicalised, increasingly narrowing into a term for medical treatment. My sense is that the politics of care could pursue the idea of care over cure. But here's the thing that interests me as well, to go back to that problem of health security: security in its origins meant someone who was free from care, and this was a negative state. After all, who could want to be free from care? My own thinking is that within the critique of security there lies a critique of health and an argument for something like 'care not cure' as the grounds of sociability. And 'care not cure' might, in turn, help move us away from medical police.

SK: It can be difficult to consider how to manage a pandemic whilst maintaining a critique of security. Various groups are attempting this and some have arrived at very reactionary positions that valorise free market dynamics, demanding business as usual with no medical intervention from the state. What are your thoughts on that political current?

MN: There is to be sure a certain kind of madness to the anti-vax position in the degrees that some of the arguments go to suggest COVID-19 is completely fabricated. But I do think there is something interesting in the lower levels of suspicion that some people have, which shouldn't be disregarded simply because it's based on idiotic ideas about viruses and bodies. It's also important to remember that there is a long history of admirable campaigns by working-class communities against medical policing. The term 'conscientious objector' comes to us from the original working-class struggles against vaccination in their communities. Again, they may well have misunderstood the science, but they had a sense that there was something problematic about this. After all, why wouldn't we be suspicious of an officer of the state coming to penetrate our bodies and inject us with a chemical about which we know nothing?

What interests me most, however, is that one of the many strands of the anti-vax position is remarkably consistent with a major strand in liberal philosophy. I'm using liberal in the broadest sense here, but the liberal position (or neoliberal, if you'd prefer it, given the time of COVID-19), is that bodies are self-regulating or they should be left to be self-regulating. Let the system do what it's going to do. This aspect of anti-vax politics appear to us as slightly crazed, but it actually has deep roots in classical liberal thought, and it connects with the wider arguments made against lockdown. It involves a profound belief in laissez-faire as the highpoint of the myth of self-regulation. If you are consistent with the idea that society is self-regulating, that the social body and individual bodies will naturally find their balance, then they really should be left alone. Obviously, this strand of liberalism as it was articulated in relation to COVID-19 had a certain kind of madness about it, but it certainly taps into something that is worth thinking about in terms of how we imagine bodies, if only so we can better challenge it.

SK: This reminds me of the story you repeat in *The Politics of Immunity*, concerning Adam Smith's advice to David Hume, shortly before the latter's passing, which bears an uncanny resemblance to many of the right's responses to the pandemic.

MN: Absolutely, yes, and it was one reason for including it. In the middle of 1776 David Hume was very ill and mentioned to Smith that he was going to travel to Bath to sample the mineral waters as a way of managing his illness. Smith's advice to him was to the effect that a mineral water is as much a drug as any that comes out of the apothecaries and is likely to produce the same violent effects upon the body as a more drastic intervention, and might even produce an even worse disease. So, rather than intervening with something as mild as spa waters, never mind professionally 'doctoring' his body, Smith recommends Hume follows a more 'natural' or 'balanced' path, nothing more interventionist than a change of air and some moderate exercise. Ultimately, he says, Hume should simply let the power of nature do its job. Hume was talking about something as mild as taking some time in spa waters and Smith just says, no, that's way much too interference. A few weeks later Hume was dead. I included it in the book because it captures in part what was going on in the eighteenth century, when liberals such as Smith were talking about needing to avoid doctoring the system, out of which I was trying to get to the heart of how we imagine systems as bodies and bodies as systems. But I also included it because it takes us to the heart of some recent liberal responses to lockdown.

SK: On the question of systems, you dedicate a large part of your recent book to a discussion of systems. Is the system an inherently repressive concept or is there revolutionary potential there?

MN: That is a tricky question but also a good one. We're attached to the idea of systems and The System and, continuing from your previous question about classical liberalism, we are attached to the idea of systems that function. But of course, we are constantly confronted time and again with system failure, with systems that let us down or get jammed. We have a perpetual frustration with systems, which also extends to our bodies, which we are expected to imagine as a system of systems. We find ourselves daunted by the power of systems, lost in a world of systems. So then we are forced into confronting the question that I think is behind the one you ask: can you have a critical theory of society without the concept of system? And if we can't do without it, what are we going to do with it? Specifically, how can we employ it in ways that don't encourage us to think of ourselves as lost in them. Can we fight the system and are we able to control the system?

SK: That tension seems to coalesce around the question of closed systems versus open systems.

MN: The only interesting systems are open systems. Because that makes them changeable. Open systems have entry points and orifices. They're leaky and permeable. They have cracks.

SK: Does the changeable nature of open systems prevent them from becoming naturalised as easily? Meaning we might be less likely to subordinate ourselves to their demands?

MN: I think there are two ways in which the notion of naturalisation might play out in that instance. I'm not sure which of them you're getting at, but maybe it's both. One way is the belief we are encouraged to hold, that the system in which we live is natural – that this system is the natural way that human beings organise. We are naturally property owners by virtue of owning our body, to go back to our earlier conversation, and we are naturally geared towards seeking more wealth, more money, more property ownership. We are naturally individualists. That's why the capitalist system is so easily presented to us as natural. Then there's another way of considering the relationship between system and naturalisation, which is we are encouraged to think of our bodies as systems and as a system of systems. In other words, systems operate within us. We are a system. In both cases, we are encouraged to think of systems as natural. The outcome is that when we imagine the capitalist system, we are encouraged to imagine it as natural. This is what underpins what Adorno calls the frenzy of systems that runs through modernity.

The notion of system then gets compounded, and we find ourselves lost in this world of systems, despite the fact that we hold on to the idea of system a category for critique. And to return to a previous point, the question is then whether the system is self-regulating or can be managed. Is our immune system self-regulating or do we need to manage it and police it through various forms of intervention? Is the capitalist system generally self-regulating, as some claim, or is it being policed? In this way, the notion of system throws up the problematic question of human control.

SK: Yet it's not clear to me why you attribute the position that bodies should be left to self-regulate instead of receiving medical intervention to (neo-)liberalism. Isn't this the definition of ancient Hippocratic medicine? But also, is Smith really relevant to this, given that when self-regulation in a modern sense is discovered by Claude Bernard in the nineteenth century, it is not opposed to intervention? The active physiologist is considered essential in assisting the return of a pathological body to a normal homeostatic state. And when cybernetics reinvigorates this position in the twentieth century, it only does so to conceive of means to artificially extend the normal capacities of an organism, not at all to leave them be.

MN: Well, in relation to the Hippocratic tradition, the answer is yes, absolutely, though it was considered through the lens of balance rather than self-regulation. Moreover, the history of this, like all histories, is not straightforward. One of the predominant themes in modern biological thinking is the idea of war – a war on this or that disease, a constant battle in which are permanently defending ourselves against the world. The prevalence of this idea came to the fore once again during COVID-19. A few people objected to it, but the language seems so natural to us that it's hard to resist it. Moreover, the language of warfare helped

underpin the logic of emergency under which lockdown was to operate. Yet this military mode of thinking about bodies is not central to the Hippocratic tradition, nor the Galenic one which followed. One finds it here and there, for example in the work of Thomas Campanella and Thomas Sydenham, but the major framework for a long time concerned a balance between the four humours. Disease was then a sign of a lack of physiological balance rather than physiological warfare, and re-balancing was part of the healing power of nature. This has its parallel in the political discourse concerning the body politic, which also focused heavily on the idea of a 'balance', either balancing between the classes, or the balance of powers, or balance of forces. The body politic might suffer from pestilence, or consumption or weakness, but these are indications of an imbalance. The key point is that the idea of war against disease does not really become central until the second half of the nineteenth century, at which point balance and healing were overtaken by ideas about war and conflict. What's known as the 'germ war theory of disease' emerged out of the research of Pasteur in France and Koch in Germany. It also became part of the immunological literature that emerged in the very late nineteenth century, in the work of Metchnikoff and others.

In relation to self-regulation in what you call the modern sense, I don't agree with you about it being discovered in the nineteenth century. Yes, as a physiological idea, it gets talked about in the nineteenth century, but self-regulation was one of those 'self-x' terms that emerged in the seventeenth century, not least through the influence of Locke and the general bourgeois notion of selfhood, out of which we see the emergence of ideas about self-formation, self-ownership, self-government, self-reliance, and many of the other 'self-x' terms, including the one we are discussing, self-regulation. Only in the nineteenth century does self-regulation become a physiological idea.

It's worth noting here that the concept of 'self' is one of immunology's key terms, along with 'system', but it is precisely this focus on selfhood, the idea of an immune self and the idea of the body having a process that is inherently geared towards defending the self, that meant immunology for years simply denied that an autoimmune disease was possible. The idea of the body turning against itself was anathema. The term for this, coined early in the history of immunology by Paul Ehrlich, was 'horror autotoxicus', literally a fundamental horror at the very idea of self-toxicity. Ehrlich proposed this at the very end of the nineteenth century, and it dominated immunology for decades. After all, to confront the idea of autotoxicus would be to confront the very possibility of self-destruction, an issue which too many people like to avoid, since to confront it would be to confront the death drive.

One last point on this. The truth to always remember is that behind Smith's notion of self-regulating systems lies the hidden hand. Very rare was it then, or is it now, for self-regulation to be imagined without such a force. This applies to self-regulation across the whole range of its applications. When Smith was teaching at Glasgow in the 1760s, James

Watt was working there on the inefficiency of Newcomen engines, and the two became friends. By the time the *Wealth of Nations* is published, Watt was finishing the development of a feedback system to enable the regulation of steam. This steam engine was understood to be of revolutionary importance, often taken to be the beginning of the industrial age, and people came from miles around to see it. Why? Because it was thought to be a self-regulating system. But what name did Watt give to this feedback system? The centrifugal Governor. Behind every supposedly self-regulating system, we should always look for the governing force. The genius of liberalism is to make this force appear invisible. In one sense, the project of critical theory has been to make such force visible, to spell out how the system is being governed. But I also mention Watt because you refer to cybernetics, and it's worth remembering that this term has its roots in the ancient Greek word *kybernetikos*, referring to the 'steering' of a ship, which comes to be rendered in the Latin as *gubernator*, and then in English as 'Governor'. The point is that not only should we be looking for the cracks in the system, but we also need to determine its governing force, to make visible the forces behind it.

SK: Perhaps this is a similar question to the question of systems, but where do we go now with the field of immunology? If critical theory must use the theories of immunology, how can we make use of them?

MN: There are some incredibly important developments taking place within immunology which I think are politically useful. As immunology emerged as a medical science, throughout the postwar period, some immunologists increasingly started to try and imagine the immune system in conjunction with the nervous system and the hormonal system. It took some time to develop and went under different names at different points, but has increasingly in the last 30 years coalesced around the idea of psychoneuroimmunology. As a field it is interested in the immune system in connection with the neurological system, but also in connection to the psychic field. It's an important development because its central claim is that we can't understand immune processes without understanding neurological processes, but that we also need to connect this idea to the psyche. This field has generated some interesting works, which you can see in the title of books such as *The Inflamed Mind*. What is at stake in this is the possibility of connecting immunity with the idea of nerves, and 'nerves' in the double sense of the physiological nervous system, on the one hand, and a psychically nervous reaction, on the other. In relation to the body, this is generating new and exciting insights into the autoimmune disease, to take us back to a point we have already mentioned in that it connects the autoimmune disease to the death drive via the idea of the nervous state, often understood through a range of other related terms such as burnout, exhaustion, stress, breakdown. One of the last things Freud said not long before he died was that the psyche is somatic, but it just doesn't actually know it. This then allows us to think through the question of security and the body politic: the possibility of imagining the body politic's overreaction in the name of security as a product of the nervous state, the state on the verge of a nervous breakdown. In effect, it allows us to get a political purchase on two ideas – the nervous state and the immune state – and to think of these in terms of the state's overreaction in the name of security, to the point where the state starts destroying its own body politic. The immune state and the nervous state combine in a suicidal politics.

Philosophically speaking, plenty of thinkers have had things to say about the suicidal state, but the work has been restricted to historical periods or reactionary movements. Foucault, Virilio, Deleuze and Guattari, for example, have all talked about fascism as essentially suicidal, and I pushed this idea in relation to fascism in *The Monstrous and the Dead*.[9] My point in *The Politics of Immunity* is that it is if there is any critical purchase on the idea of a suicidal state, it should not be restricted to fascism, but applied to the work performed by the body politic in the name of security-immunity. In seeking to secure itself, it destroys itself. This is our slow death, in the name of security, and why we need to imagine politics differently.

Notes

1. Karl Marx, 'On the Jewish Question' (1844), in Karl Marx and Frederick Engels, *Collected Works*, Vol. 3 (London: Lawrence and Wishart, 1975), 163.
2. Mark Neocleous, *The Fabrication of Social Order: A Critical Theory of Police Power* (London: Pluto Press, 2000).
3. Mark Neocleous, *Critique of Security* (Edinburgh: Edinburgh University Press, 2008).
4. Mark Neocleous, *Politics of Immunity: Security and the Policing of Bodies* (London: Verso, 2022).
5. Peter Sloterdijk, *You Must Change Your Life*, trans. Weland Hoban (Cambridge: Polity, 2013).
6. Roberto Esposito, *Immunitas: The Protection and Negation of Life* (Cambridge: Polity, 2011).
7. Jacques Derrida, 'Autoimmunity: Real and Symbolic Suicides – A Dialogue with Jacques Derrida', in Giovanna Borradori, *Philosophy in a Time of Terror: Dialogues with Jürgen Habermas and Jacques Derrida* (Chicago: University of Chicago Press, 2003).
8. Theodor Adorno, *Minima Moralia*, trans. E.F.N. Jephcott (London: Verso, 2002).
9. Mark Neocleous, *The Monstrous and the Dead: Burke, Marx, Fascism* (Cardiff: University of Wales Press, 2005).

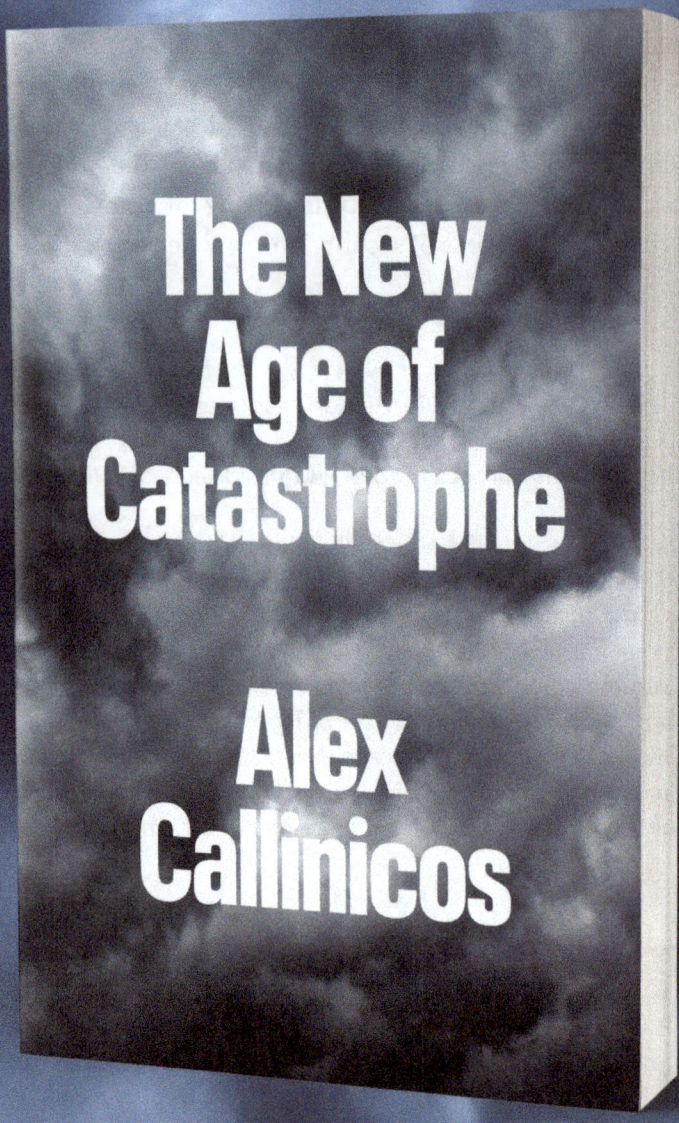

"This splendid new book by one of the world's foremost Marxist thinkers is essential reading to understand the permanent state of emergency that characterises contemporary politics, its history, its causes and the path to an alternative. Callinicos's lucid effort to reflect from a unified perspective on the multiple crises – environmental, economic, geopolitical, social – the world confronts is as intellectually rewarding as it is politically urgent."
Lea Ypi, London School of Economics

"A timely, informative and highly readable commentary for anyone wanting to make sense of the turmoil of world affairs today."
Justin Rosenberg, University of Sussex

PB: 978-1-5095-5417-1 / £17.99 / March 2023

politybooks.com

Transformed formalisms

Nathan Brown, *Rationalist Empiricism: A Theory of Speculative Critique* (Fordham, NY: Fordham University Press, 2021). 272pp., £39.00 pb., 978 0 82329 001 7

Describing the general course of twentieth-century French philosophy, Alain Badiou distinguishes between two major, divergent orientations of thought: a rationalist orientation that promotes a 'philosophy of the concept', following from the works of Léon Brunschvicg, and a vitalist-existentialist orientation that promotes a 'philosophy of life', following from the works of Henri Bergson. In *The Adventure of French Philosophy* (2012), he summarises the historical context in which these two trajectories of thought are set:

> In 1911, Bergson gave two celebrated lectures at Oxford, which appeared in his collection *La pensée et le mouvement*. In 1912, simultaneously, in other words, Brunschvicg published *Les Étapes de la philosophie mathématique*. Coming on the eve of the Great War, these interventions attest to the existence of two completely distinct orientations. In Bergson we find what might be called a philosophy of vital interiority, a thesis on the identity of being and becoming; a philosophy of life and change. This orientation will persist throughout the 20th century, up to and including Deleuze. In Brunschvicg's work, we find a philosophy of the mathematically based concept: the possibility of a philosophical formalism of thought and of the symbolic, which likewise continues throughout the century, most specifically in Lévi-Strauss, Althusser and Lacan.

Badiou goes on to describe how the rationalist trajectory was characterised by the pursuit of a 'philosophical formalism', drawing from the rise of structuralist methods in the social sciences and Lacanian psychoanalysis, as well as from developments in mathematical logic. Adapting the historicist impetus behind the French historical epistemology of science emblematised by the works of Bachelard and Canguilhem to the formalist impetus guiding the structuralist and mathematical-logical horizon, Badiou argues, this formalist orientation would also position itself against empiricist conceptions of science advanced by Anglo-Saxon analytic epistemologies.

> The second point that was retained was that science, far from consolidating empiricism, is *anti-empiricist*. That is the absolute break made by French epistemology from Anglo-Saxon epistemology. We see very clearly with Bachelard, but also with Canguilhem, that not only is science not empiricist, but that it is the principal school of non-empiricism, that it forms the principal critique of empiricism itself. Whether it's a matter of Galileo, Descartes, etc. or even the Canguilhemian conception of the life sciences, it is axiomatic decisions and conceptual constructions that prescribe empirical experimentation, and not the reverse.

Nathan Brown's *Rationalist Empiricism* firmly situates itself within the horizon set by 'the philosophy of the concept', while also contesting the sharp separation between empiricism and rationalism advanced by Badiou's genealogical distinction. At the same time, it develops out of the resurgence of a concern with the problematic of realism within Continental philosophy, as expressed most distinctly in the body of works that have come to be associated with the label 'speculative realism', and with the works and ideas of Quentin Meillassoux, who was himself a student of Badiou. The book rekindles the tradition of French epistemology of science through its elaboration by Althusser and his successors – from Badiou to Meillassoux – to show the inextricability of rationalism and empiricism for a dialectical materialist philosophy.

The result is the distillation of a unique method of speculative critique that hinges on understanding the dialectical intrication between reason and experience, once these are reinterpreted, following Bachelard and Althusser, in their productive, historical dimension: for just as reason realises itself in time in theoretical practices of formalisation and conceptualisation, so experience realises itself in experimental practices bound to historical conditions of technical production. In its historicist aspect, rationalist empiricism is said to be critical rather than dogmatic, insofar as it avoids appealing to an ontological foundation, accepting the Kantian injunction against classical metaphysics. But it is speculative rather than transcendental, insofar as it eschews the

Kantian epistemological foundationalist account of the apperceptive subject as providing the 'ground' of metaphysical enquiry.

In fleshing out the methodological basis and consequences of speculative critique, Brown's argument systematically integrates a variety of theoretical registers: Bachelard's account of 'epistemological breaks' within a historicised epistemology of scientific cognition; Althusser's attempt to secure the distinction between science and ideology through an account of formal theorisation; Hegel's traversal of Kantian transcendental critique in the name of an immanent critique; Badiou's ontologisation of set-theoretical mathematics via Cantor's detotalisation of the infinite; Meillassoux's absolutisation of contingency as providing a speculative materialist answer to Hume's problem of induction; the relation between the process of separation and the commodity form in Marx, etc. The result is a work of philosophy of astonishing breadth, rekindling the systematic ambition of philosophy to think the integrity of scientific ('the True'), political ('the Good') and artistic ('the Beautiful') 'conditions' of philosophy, to use a term again borrowed from Alain Badiou. Above all, Brown's project can be understood as generalising the lessons of the historicised epistemology of science and appropriation of structuralist methods in philosophy elaborated by the Althusserian school and its descendants, the better to think its implications for philosophy and its scientific, artistic and political conditions.

In the Introduction to the book, Brown unpacks the central dyad that organises the title: rationalism aims to think what has to be thought, while empiricism aims to think what is the case. At the same time, these tasks are mutually delimiting and thus inextricable, insofar as what is the case constrains what has to be thought as it must traverse the latter. Understanding this link is coeval with a historicising jettisoning of any foundationalism that would postulate thinking as the transcendental ground establishing the *a priori* conditions for what has to be thought, or else postulate sensory-phenomenological givenness as the ground of what is the case. The passage from transcendental to speculative critique demands a 'transmutation of our epistemological values', leading to a conception of reason unbound from any transcendental foundation, as well as a conception of experience unbound from all appeals to 'givenness.'

To realise this historical 'ungrounding', Brown follows Bachelard and Althusser in reconceiving the dialectical structure of scientific cognition in its relation to ideology. Understood as a diachronic movement of revision and formalisation, science appears not as an ahistorical 'mirror of nature', but rather as 'a field of recursive, historical self-interrogation.' Within such a processual, recursive conception, reason is not the *a priori* bedrock of 'transcendental ideas', but the self-revising protocol of conceptual generation and formalisation in the construction of theoretical frameworks, syntactical systems and deductive axioms-laws; experience is not the fulcrum of our sensory intuition or phenomenological receptivity, but the historically situated space of techno-scientific production and experimentation through which theories are measured against the real. Scientific cognition thus unfolds in the historical-dialectical interplay of these two dimensions, where reason subtracts itself from what is the case through the construction of new formal systems and theoretical-conceptual frameworks, while experience in turn constrains what must be thought through the invention of new experimental techniques for constructing and testing models, specifying the conditions of application and success of a theoretical framework. As Brown puts it:

> The integration of this knowledge into scientific theory will then depend upon the capacity to coordinate rational and empirical values: the testing of speculative theory against experimental outcomes, the consideration of experimental outcomes within the framework of existing formalisms, or the transformation of those formalisms to accommodate empirical findings.

Following Bachelard again, Brown indicates how such a conception of science is continuous with a relational ontology and realist epistemology, affirming that the entities tracked by science cannot be conceived in terms of self-identical substances, but describe a probabilistic and uncertain order 'that reaches a certain threshold of stability, but that also never freezes into unchanging self-identity.' Analogously, a concept cannot be conceived in bottom-up terms, as derived from atomistic 'simples' (Descartes), but must be understood as always involving a relational nexus forming 'a complex of concepts and experiences.' This last point merits some reflection, since it touches on a delicate problem inherent to the tradition of French epistemology of science. One of the central contentions advanced by Badiou in *The Concept of Model* in 1968 is that a 'materialist epistemology' that takes mathematical formalisation to be the mark of scientificity does not merely separate the realm of formal theories from the domain of experience and concepts. Rather, the relation between form and content becomes itself enfolded into the dimension of formalisation, in terms of the relation between syntactical theoretical systems, semantically linked to model-structures that specify a domain of interpretation for a theory. Within Brown's reconstruction, it might appear thus that the separation between the theoretical and the experiential aspects of theory underemphasises how both fit within the horizon of mathematical formalisation as inherent to scientific practice.

In any case, Brown proceeds to argue that the inextricability of reason and experience is not merely legible within scientific cognition but can and must be generalisable within a systematic program for philosophy. The first part of the book expands on the historical lineage of the relation between reason and experience in philosophy since the beginning of the modern period; Chapter One explores how, already, early modern rationalism and empiricism constituted themselves in relation to each other by admitting of 'exemplary exceptions' to their respective methodological constraints. In particular, Brown focuses on the Cartesian 'wax thought-experiment' and Hume's extrapolation of the 'missing shade of blue', to show how just as reason must rely on perceptual experience to ground the order of pure thought, so experience must go beyond the domain of what sensible intuition discloses to explain the articulation of impressions and ideas. Indeed, just as Descartes must exceptionally appeal to the flux of sensory determinations and the perception of qualitative changes when providing a retroactive temporal genesis of the *cogito*, so Hume must grant the mind the capacity to form an idea of a missing shade of colour, thereby contravening the empiricist strictures according to which all ideas must follow from corresponding impressions. But rather than proving their internal and mutual incoherence, Brown argues, these examples testify to the inextricability of reason and experience incumbent upon rationalist and empiricist epistemologies.

> Unthinkable within phenomenology, and prior to the program of transcendental idealism, Absent Blue Wax delivers the outside of rationalism to the outside of empiricism and lets them mingle in their mutual exteriority … It is the interruption of experience by reason, and the extrapolation of reason from and yet beyond experience, that is at issue in the rationalist methodological pole, while it is the experience of reason and also the exposure, by empirical science, of what cannot be experienced that is at issue in our empiricism.

Brown goes on to illustrate how the coordinated movement of interruption and extrapolation that articulates a rationalist empiricism becomes explicitly reinscribed in a materialist register in Meillassoux's analysis of the 'arche-fossil' and the problem of ancestral statements incumbent upon such analysis, which leads to the 'paradox of manifestation': while science is bound to experience, it discloses through empirical enquiry a world withdrawn from all correlation to the subject manifestation. Attending to this paradox requires extending the pursuit of a historical and dialectical conception of scientific knowledge against all forms of epistemological and ontological anti-realisms, against both 'correlationism' and 'subjectalism'. The dialectical resolution of the paradox at the heart of the modern philosophical moment, Brown argues, is the major achievement of Meillassoux's project: the compatibilisation of the Cartesian affirmation of the reality of primary properties with the implications drawn from the Humean problem of induction. Following Badiou's attempt to draw the consequences of the Cantorian 'de-totalization of the infinite', Brown affirms Meillassoux's claim that mathematics grants access to the absolute and the disqualification of probabilistic reasoning when arguing for the contingency of the laws of nature. Such a programme satisfies, he shows, the double criteria specified by Althusser as necessary for any (dialectical) materialist practice: (i) the distinction but also possible adequacy between the real and knowledge, and (ii) the primacy of the real over knowledge. At the same time, the suspension of the Principle of Sufficient Reason (PSR) incumbent in the absolutisation of contingency displaces any metaphysical ground or entity in favour of a *principle* of unreason, yielding a materialism than is not dogmatic but properly speculative in scope.

The second part of the book develops the dialectical kernel of the project, providing a novel reading of Hegelian speculative idealism, assessing its limitations and appropriating its central lessons, constructing an approximation to Hegel's *Logic* for the purposes of developing a de-substantialised and non-transcendental account of speculative thought. Brown distils what he names 'Hegel's *cogito*' at the outset of the *Logic*, where the indeterminate immediacy of pure being in its indiscernibility from nothingness implies the determining mediation of thought: '"*thought is, thought exists*", being is determined as thinking being – and thought is the mediation that, by determining being, makes it negative and thus turns it into the movement of contradiction: becoming.' It is thus the very (discursive) articulation of pure being as indeterminate immediacy, and its paradoxical (in)determination as indiscernible and so logically identical with nothingness, that implies the existence of thought at the beginning of the *Logic*.

Now, this particular argumentative manoeuvre merits some cautionary reflection: that is, the claim that we find Hegel's '*cogito*' as implied already in the germinal dialectic between being and nothingness, and the concomitant derivation of becoming that follows. For Brown's gesture requires that we retroactively notice the determinacy and mediation of thought as implicit in the indeterminate immediacy of being. But Hegel explicitly outlaws any appeals to intentions or subjective acts to ground the absolute difference between being and nothingness; while the agency of thought must in the last instance be derivable from the movement of the *Logic*. Brown's argument, however, suggests that the determinacy of thought involved here is not that of the 'thinking-self': the Hegelian *cogito* can neither be identified with the Cartesian *cogito* of apodictic knowledge, nor with the Kantian 'I' or transcendental subject of apperception. Brown argues, 'by detaching the categories from "their abstract relation to the 'I'" in order to address "what they are in themselves", Hegel's *Logic* eliminates the transcendental standpoint necessary to constitute a priori conditions of possibility.' What is at stake then is the consolidation of a desubstantialised agent of thought in immanent critique, for which thought is its own subject. Put differently, thought does not belong to a subject, nor conforms to the *a priori* conditions of a subject that engages in conceptual activity as a result: thinking is the immanent experience of thought as overcoming the separation between the *a posteriori* and the *a priori*, and which understands contingency as the progressive derivation of thought's necessary determinations. In this regard, Brown's reading follows contemporary readings of Hegel as a sublating of the dialectic between freedom and determinism, conceiving of necessity itself as the becoming and retroactive determination of contingency:

> There is no thinking of that which is prior to the immanent experience of thought, its movement. And thought is unthinkable as posterior to the movement of such experience. Thought is; thought exists: this fact displaces the opposition between the a priori and the a posteriori because it involves the rational experience of thought, as it takes place.

Brown rearticulates the relation between contingency and necessity, resisting the 'double annulment of time' described at the end of the *Phenomenology* (as Absolute Knowing) and the *Logic* (as Absolute Idea), supplanting the necessity of contingency for the movement of contingency as the becoming of necessity. For Hegel surreptitiously brings the movement of conceptual negativity to rest by grounding the groundless fulcrum of contingency and time under the Idea of the 'Whole', in order '[t]o seal the Absolute as the negation of the very movement of negation ... merely declare, by fiat, that the restlessness of the negative which is the becoming of the concept can grasp itself without the very means of its self-comprehension.' In turn, Brown argues, speculative materialism reaffirms the restlessness of the negative, the dissolution of the 'I' and the groundlessness of temporal being as contingency, in what amounts to a resolute rejection of the Principle of Sufficient Reason, still adhered to by absolute idealism. This finally implies a re-articulation of the ontological difference between being and beings, now understood in terms of the distinction between the necessity of contingency (universal-ontological principle) and the contingency of beings (particular-ontic determination).

The book's third part deploys the methodological framework and the re-inscription of the ontological difference to show how rationalist empiricism conceives of its scientific, artistic and political 'conditions'. Brown illustrates the 'complexity and precision of science's ontic operations' in unison with the 'ontological questioning of philosophy'. He focuses on the problem of measure and measurement, tracing the historical redefinition of the concept of the kilogram since the nineteenth century. This history not only provides anecdotal illustration of the historicity of scientific concepts, but reflects the displacement of intuitive self-evidence inherent to the dialectic of formalisation and experimentation outlined in the introduction. Furthermore, it shows the process by virtue of which science overturns the metaphysical order of self-identical substances, by positivising a probabilistic order of uncertainty and contingency within its ontic operations, again in continuity with the absolutisation of contingency and the concomitant de-absolutisation of natural law incumbent upon speculative materialism.

Brown shows how rationalist materialism becomes continuous with a 'materialism of the idea', as expressed in the digital photographic work of Nicolas Baier. Performing a materialist 'inversion of Platonism' different than the Nietzschean vitalist transvaluation of the dialectic, in Baier's work the formal kernel of the intelligible is not divided from but accessed through the technical externalising process of the sensible itself, i.e. what Brown names, drawing upon Whitehead, a '*technics of prehension*'. He subtracts the operational kernel from Whitehead's specific relational process ontology, focusing on how processes of transition and concrescence organise how the ideal becomes exteriorised through the technical mediation of the photographic medium. He exemplifies this dynamic across a series of Baier's work, in continuity with the generalisation of the scientific dialectic between formalisation and experimentation, and drawing from a variety of additional registers: Plato's dialectic between the sensible and the intelligible, Lacan's relation of the image and the real in the gaze, Stiegler's account of the coevolution of technics and the human in the exteriorisation of ('tertiary') memory, and so on.

Brown then goes on a historical detour that refers us to the central role of the concept of structure implicit in Plato's cosmological genealogy in the *Timaeus*. Above all, the concept of structure appears as the 'Rosetta stone' binding the discourses of ontology, epistemology and methodology. Brown attends to the ambiguity latent in Plato's account of Ideas (*eidos*): in his earlier works designating at once the immutable character of the intelligible forms, but here describing the genesis of the elements by the demiurge, and thus the materialisation of the Idea. These elements, insofar as they are geometrically composed of triangular forms, are non-sensible assemblages or assembled forms, subject to generation and destruction; diataxis becomes the fulcrum mediating metaphysics and physics, the purity of the idea and the becoming of bodies, the rational and the empirical.

The last three chapters jointly explore the political consequences of rationalist empiricism, and in particular how it leads to a reappraisal of certain core tenets in dialectical materialism. Brown explores in more detail how Hume's problem of induction and Meillassoux's positive appropriation of it through absolutisation of contingency becomes articulated in the practical-political sphere in relation to Badiou's account of post-eventum Truth: how does the contingency of the eventual emergence of the subject of truth accommodate the horizon of emancipatory politics? Using the example of the sequence and implications of the collective action organised around the Occupy Oakland movement, he insists on the disruptive, subjective force of the event as shattering the empirical order of 'what happens', while also upholding an empiricism of the encounter and an 'aleatory rationalism' in which contingency is forged by a 'groundless synthesis of encounter and decision'. In sight of the undecidable tension between the thesis that such a sequence implied real change and the possibility that nothing finally happened, it would be interesting to see how Brown's argument might appear in light of Badiou's more nuanced theory of change in his re-elaboration of the theory of the event in *Logics of Worlds*.

Brown critically and constructively addresses the efforts of the collective *Theorie Communiste* to rework Althusser's account of structural causality. Secularising Spinoza's account of the relation between substance and the modes, capital unfolds as an immanent process of detotalisation or as an internal scission of the capitalist world. In doing so, it undermines the specific conditions of production and agency in the historical sphere; capital is but is a perpetually dividing structure that reconfigures its parts and relations, understood in analogy with how Spinoza's substance is formally distinguished by an infinity of attributes and modes without itself becoming ontologically divided. Brown follows the TC's communisation theory, which attempts to overcome the programmatist history of the left: just like rationalist empiricism involves the dialectical interplay between theoretical formalisation and technical experimentation, so communisation concerns the dialectical interplay of class struggle, through which the proletariat becomes at once a disruptive force in relation to the structure of capitalist reproduction and, at the same time, identifies itself within such structure as a class.

The final chapter provides an analysis of Marx's account of the 'process of separation' (*Scheidungprozess*) within the theorisation of labour, where 'the concept of separation is the key to understanding the genesis of capital, its subsumption of social relations, and the tendential decline of its historical mechanism.' Emphasising the undertheorised distinction between separation and alienation, Brown argues that the former concept does not rely on the logic of exteriorisation implied by the latter, but describes a formal process central to Marx's method of analysis, which secures the passage between the theoretical and historical parts of *Capital*. In the last instance, this approximation enables Brown to find within Marx's account of separation an expression rationalist empiricism that 'must grasp history theoretically, and theory historically', and which is deserving of the name of 'science'.

Rationalist Empiricism is a work of exceptional breadth and scope, articulating the concerns and ambitions proper to the post-war French Althusserian school and its descendants, as well as contemporary philosophical questions concerning the possibilities for dialectical materialism today. More than this, it opens a space for an unprecedented dialogue concerning the pertinence of structuralist methodologies in contemporary materialisms. Indeed, while the lineage of Brown's book discusses the appropriation of structuralism in the social sciences and psychoanalysis within the French post-war tradition, contemporary Anglo-Saxon philosophy of science and mind has likewise rekindled the prospects for epistemological and metaphysical realism through the development of structural methods, for example, in James Ladyman's brand of ontic structural realism, by way of an information-theoretic understanding of structure derived from Daniel Dennett's account of 'real patterns'. An encounter between these two traditions would allow us to interrogate, above all, the role of mathematical-formal languages in ontological-epistemological theorisation and, in particular, in defining a concept of structure suitable to explain the relation between articulation between scientific theorisation and the world across its discursive, sensory and technical dimensions.

Another possibility opened by *Rationalist Empiricism* concerns the consequences that follow from the critique of 'givenness' characteristic of not only modern concept-empiricism, but also of those philosophies that reify sensory-phenomenological experience as a fulcrum of pre-theoretical understanding. The pursuit of a historical conception of scientific practice that overcomes the conflation between causal and epistemic factors while accounting for the relation between theoretical and experimental practices as they unfold historically forms a common thread binding post-Sellarsian naturalisms in the analytic tradition to the ambitions of the French historical epistemology of science that Brown follows. Rather than simply disavowing givenness at the expense of eliding the role that experience plays in mediating our knowledge of the world and ourselves within it, both traditions suggest that we can and ought to theoretically formalise the dimension of givenness itself. That is, we must fold the receptive dimension of experience into the dimension of structure itself, to show how our theoretical and experimental practices remain grounded in ostensive operations of indexing, measurement and stabilisation, through which cognitive systems represent and intervene in nature and themselves within it.

A coordinated assessment of the legacy of the French school of historical epistemology of science and its incarnation within current philosophical materialisms in relation to contemporary Anglo-Saxon structural realisms in the philosophy of science and mind would thus begin by interrogating how the operation of mathematical formalisation leads to divergent concepts of 'structure', through which ontological and epistemological theorisation construes the relation between subject and world. Seen in this broader context of philosophical questions and tasks, *Rationalist Empiricism* comprises an essential contribution to a living philosophical tradition, but is also an intervention that opens a path for unprecedented encounters between schools of thought that have for too long been kept isolated from each other as a result of obsolete disciplinary boundaries.

Daniel Sacilotto

Art's social forms

Louis Menand, *The Free World: Art and Thought in the Cold War* (Farrar, Straus and Giroux: New York, 2021). 857pp., £30.00 hb., 978 0 37415 845 3

During the past decade there has been an intensified debate in mainstream art criticism about the tension between art's freedom and free speech. In this debate art's freedom has been accused of being under severe threat by, on the one hand, 'cultural Marxists' concerned with identity politics and social justice, and, on the other, by alt-right fascists' promoting a nationalistic art and culture. Both, it has been argued, threaten art's freedom. But what is meant by this concept here? Although art's freedom together with free speech is a given in liberal western democracies, how can this concept be understood? More specifically, is the freedom of art as pure and cleansed of all connections to a societal ground as its liberal defenders try to argue?

From the standpoint of western philosophy, art's freedom – or rather its autonomy – can be traced back, for example, to Friedrich Schiller's *Kallias Letters* (1793), written to his friend Gottfried Körner a few years after the French revolution. Here Schiller constructs an analogy between beauty – represented in art – and the autonomy of the free will as formulated in Immanuel Kant's moral writings, making beauty into 'freedom in appearance'. This idea that art gains autonomy through its form, which then becomes an image of freedom, continues throughout modernity in writers, thinkers and intellectual movements as different as *l'art pour l'art* and the Frankfurt School, Oscar Wilde and Theodor Adorno, including influential American art critics in the Cold War period like Clement Greenberg and Harold Rosenberg.

Another way of interrogating the idea of art's freedom is to focus on the country that has been more than any other historically connected to the idea of freedom, and on a period in its history when this was particularly the case: the USA in the time of the 'free world'. The latter is a term mainly associated with 'The Truman Doctrine', derived from a speech by the then president, Harry Truman, in the spring of 1947, which is often regarded as announced the beginning of the Cold War. The speech is partly reprinted in Louis Menand's latest book, *The Free World: Art and Thought in the Cold War*. Truman famously characterises liberal democracy as a way of life distinguished by 'free institutions, representative government, free elections, guarantees of individual liberty, freedom of speech and religion, and freedom from political repression', in contrast to the way of life of the totalitarian state that 'relies upon terror and oppression, a controlled press and radio, fixed elections, and the suppression of personal freedoms'. The task that Menand sets himself is to investigate the art, culture and thought that was produced in this geopolitically tense historical moment. It's a huge object of study so it is no surprise that the book spans 800 pages. But it has a sharply defined timeframe and geographical location: from the introduction of Truman's doctrine to the end of the Soviet Union in 1991, all viewed from the standpoint of the USA. Despite this scale, most examples in the book cover the 1950s to the 1970s, which is also reflected in that it opens with a chapter on the end of the Second World War and ends with a chapter on the final days of the Vietnam War.

Written in 18 poetically titled chapters – 'Object of Power', 'The Free Play of the Mind', 'Northern Songs' and so on – the book digs into art practices, intellectual movements and cultural phenomena such as Action Painting, New Criticism, the Civil Rights Movement and underground paperback publishing. Although North American phenomena – and this is one of Menand's main points about art and thought in the free world – these ideas and thoughts are transatlantic in nature, mostly because of the way the Second World War ended, and therefore must include France, England and their colonies and former colonies. The title of each chapter effectively functions as an aphorism that Menand unfolds or argues for through a method explained in the preface as containing three parts: firstly, 'the underlying social forces – economic, geopolitical, demographic, technological' of a period, secondly, 'what was happening "on the street", how X ran into Y', and thirdly, 'what was going on in people's heads'. The result of this rather classically chosen method is that most chapters begin with well-chosen statistics on, for example, the number of students enrolled at a university within a certain decade, the number of technological apparatuses a middle-class family owned in the USA in 1955, how many countries were colonies and how many were liberating themselves, and then moves on to specific individuals (primarily men), such as John Cage, James Baldwin, Jean-Paul Sartre, Andy Warhol and George Orwell, to name only a handful of those whose lives are unfolded in minute detail in the book.

The chapters are not structured chronologically or thematically. Rather each says something specific – sometimes contradictory to other chapters – about art and thought in this period. Menand, a staff writer at the *New Yorker*, lets the Chekhovian and creative writing class slogan, 'show, don't tell', lead him. The consequence is an almost novelistic book in which the reader sees Baldwin walking the streets of his childhood in Harlem and, later in life, hears him speak as a renowned writer to fellow writer as well as woman abuser Norman Mailer in a café in Paris in the mid 1950s. Menand makes the reader feel the smell of Jackson Pollock's paint, follow the thoughts of Claude Lévi-Strauss on the boat to New York and experience the fraught love affair between Isaiah Berlin and the Soviet censored poet Anna Akhmatova as if standing in the doorway.

Menand's method is standard in journalistic reportage and mainstream biographical storytelling. It ascribes to a logic that the parts make up a whole. As such it stands in contrast to the method propagated by Karl Marx in his critique of political economy, or to Walter Benjamin's thesis on art criticism in romanticism, as well as to Max Horkheimer's idea of critical theory, in which the entry point of a study is the concept, or as Marx famously puts it, a method in which one goes from the 'abstract' to the 'concrete', where the concrete is not the given but the determination of the abstract. Menand is not a Marxist or a critical theorist, so it is not surprising that he does the opposite, at least at the level of each chapter, where biographical details, colour of clothes and other minute details are pushed to the forefront to tell something. But at the level of the composition of the entire book, Menand structures the chapters in a way which creates something similar to the procedure of going from the abstract to the concrete. This makes the book more worth reading. 'Empty Sky', 'Northern Songs' and 'Vers La Libération' are, on the one hand, intimate stories about

George Kennan, the diplomat behind The Truman Doctrine, the Beatles' arty and cheeky interviews and the articles by Betty Friedan that led up to the second wave feminist movement in the USA in the mid 1950s; on the other hand, these chapters are also titles or aphorisms that together make out a more abstract and often conflicted idea of the concept of art's and thought's freedom in the Cold War. Since people, rather than themes, move in and out of different chapters, and in that way connect them – Jasper Johns, for example, appears in one chapter in relation to Cage and Cunningham, and turns up in another on Warhol and pop art simply because he attended the latter's well-known parties – the book also constructs a coherent and meaningful narrative between individuals and events that would not necessarily have been thought together before. Menand also says he wrote the book to understand his childhood and early adulthood. Not dissimilar to how an analysand creates a narrative of their childhood in the psychoanalytic session, here it is the historian of ideas, Louis Menand himself, who lies on the couch and reconstructs the years of his early life. The question is: are the reconstructions true?

Apart from the essayistic composition of the chapters, the strength of Menand's method of showing rather than telling, as well as his bricolage composition of chapters, is the surprising but illuminating way in which he often brings together two ideas or lines of thought. For example, in the chapter 'The Human Science', he places Lévi-Strauss' concept of culture as structure – and in effect Structuralism as a new discipline in the USA concerned with how things get their meaning and function in a system of signification – next to the major internationally touring exhibition *The Family of Man*, curated by MOMA's director Edward Steichen in 1955. *The Family of Man* was curated like a photo-essay with all kinds of photos and techniques placed non-hierarchically next to one another, not dissimilar to how signification in Lévi-Strauss' structure takes place via function and place. '*The Family of Man* was sometimes edited according to the venue. ... But the overall design required balance, and the fact that, apart from country and photographer, there was no identifying information about the pictures depoliticized most of the images. Every image was generic – which, of course, was the point.' In other chapters Menand simply juxtaposes two persons or phenomena next to one another to make a point. Some of these have been brought together before. In 'Emancipating Dissonance' Menand, like uncountable art historians before him, situates John Cage, Merce Cunningham and Robert Rauschenberg next to one another to say something about a specific atonal method in composition, painting and choreography making. In 'Commonism' he puts the analytical philosopher of art Arthur C. Danto next to Andy Warhol. Other combinations are more unusual, like when he opens one chapter with John F. Kennedy's speech on freedom after the Berlin Wall had fallen and continues without much comment to Isaiah Berlin's two concepts of liberty, before then tying these ideas of freedom together with new printing technologies, such as the soft back book and its utilisation by underground publishers of erotic books. Each phenomenon in Menand's book has been written about on its own before, but by simply situating them next to one another, without much comment or explanation, Menand manages to say something new about how he understands the idea of freedom in this period.

But what is this concept of art's, culture's and thought's freedom? Whereas speeches by politicians like Truman or Kennedy are in the book, as well as accounts of the main philosophical concepts in the liberal tradition on freedom, such as Berlin's *Two Concepts of Liberty* from 1958 alongside Sartre's and other postwar conceptions of freedom, Menand's concept of art and culture's freedom is to be found elsewhere. Firstly and primarily, the idea of freedom Menand writes about appears in the many artistic and philosophical methods or procedures shown in the book. In chapter after chapter Menand unfolds, in a clear prose, artistic and philosophical thoughts and procedures of the artists and thinkers he writes about: from Franz Fanon's distinct ideas of freedom's relationship to culture and domination in his 1956 article, 'Racism and Culture' – 'As long as one group is subaltern, no genuine culture can be produced.' – to Cage's transformation of Stockhausen's 'serial composition' and Rauschenberg's and Johns' 'figural art that was anti-illusionistic'; from the scattered and fast-forward pace of Beat literature to the elitist yet universal addressee of the writings of Susan Sontag. Or George Orwell's socialist concrete style of writing as a critique of managerial capitalism: 'Orwell made jargon, formula, elision, obfuscation, and cliché the enemies of liberty and democracy and the symptoms of creeping to-

97

talitarianism.' Seen from this angle, freedom for Menand is to be found in the making of new forms, compositions, procedures, methods and choreographies. In other words, his is an understanding of freedom as closely related to *form* as that encountered in both Schiller's and Adorno's writings on art.

Secondly, Menand's understanding of freedom is to be found in the infrastructures or ecological systems of art and culture: the material and institutional conditions needed for paintings to be shown, novels to be read and philosophers to be published. Menand draws a picture in which the university (from its meritocratic system in the 1950s to its managerial transformation from the 1970s onwards), independent journals and publishers, specific visas and exchange programmes for emigrants in the post-war years, as well as a flourishing art market and cheap housing, were conditions for the emergence and development of the artistic, cultural and philosophical methods accounted for in the book. As such Menand's concept of freedom is relative, far from *l'art pour l'art*.

The main way in which Menand's study differs from others of this period, apart from its non-academic way of presenting research, is that it invites contradictions and tensions in the people, movements and thoughts that are scrutinised. New Criticism's method of close reading, with proponents like Cleanth Brooks and T.S. Eliot, was not separated from society as they liked to think, but conditioned by a racist and non-democratic southern American ideology: 'In short, American New Criticism was founded by writers associated with a reactionary political and religious program, and under the aegis of a poet and critic, Eliot, who believed that modern society was, in his words, "worm-eaten with Liberalism".' Following Benjamin Piekut and other art historians, Menand also shows how Cage, whose musical scores were open for interpretation by anyone according to his anarchist ideals, nevertheless despised the versions of them by Charlotte Moorman and Nam June Paik.

Despite his attention to such tensions and contradictions, Menand tends to idealise the culture of this youth, which is understandable considering the post-liberal times in the USA in which it was written. Menand writes about the differences between, for example, Aime Césaire's idea of freedom and Baldwin's or Arendt's or Orwell's understanding of totalitarianism, but writing about less canonised artists and thinkers would have brought the antagonisms more to the surface. How can, for example, Angela Davis' and the Black Panther's critique of prisons, Herbert Marcuse's understanding of freedom and sexual liberty, and Yvonne Rainer's transformation of Cage's score be excluded from a book on art, culture and thought in the Cold War? Although Menand mentions how the USA publishing system censored books due to explicit sexual content, he downplays this in favour of the big formalist experiments of the time. This emphasis on the 'good' stuff makes the book melancholic, romantic and untruthful at times. I think that this also has to do with the form and method that Menand employs. His juxtapositions or montages want to please or reconcile, unlike Benjamin who also deployed montage as a way of radically showing rather than telling.

The main problem with the book is, however, the almost completely neglected aspect of capitalism's transformation during this period, how this change is related to the decolonisation and liberation movements taking place in parallel, and how they conditioned the understandings of freedom that can be found, for example, in Friedrich von Hayek's Darwinist writings. As Quinn Slobodian among others have demonstrated, the Cold War years cannot be understood without seeing the emergence of supranational and partly undemocratic institutions like the IMF and the World Bank in parallel to the process of decolonialisation. By not taking these into account, it is as if Menand, from his divan, doesn't go deep enough into his childhood, into the darker conditions of the 'free world' that also paved the way for the emergence of a neo-liberal undemocratic world order. To understand the state of art's autonomy and freedom after 1991, the rise of fascism as well as the social justice movements of the past decades, these larger transformations of capitalism's structure and institutions need to be taken into account.

Josefine Wikström

Thought without thinkers

Timothy Bewes, *Free Indirect: The Novel in a Postfictional Age* (New York: Columbia University Press, 2022). 336pp., £28.00 pb., 978 0 23119 2972

A bold question motivates Timothy Bewes' *Free Indirect*: Is a non-subjective thought possible? Bewes looks for an answer in recent developments in the novel. His contention is that the novel is a mode of thought which operates not only beyond the ideas represented within it – those of a narrator, protagonist, character or author – but also beyond novelistic form itself. Form is only the first of many common literary concepts with which Bewes dispenses in his remarkable reexamination of novelistic thought. In fact, according to Bewes, very few existing concepts can help us grasp the fundamental reconfiguration of the novel's relation to reality that has potentiated, in his words, '*a thought that cannot be inhabited subjectively.*'

One name that Bewes proposes for this reconfiguration is 'postfictional aesthetics'. If fictionality is the logic whereby the novel maps onto but does not coincide with reality, postfictional aesthetics identifies a breakdown of this logic, such that characters and situations no longer simply typify or index aspects of the world but directly constitute forms of relation. But to phrase it this way is to suggest a periodisation – fictionality and its aftermath – that Bewes immediately complicates in his pursuit of a fine-tuned analysis of the limits of fictionality. In the central terms of *Free Indirect*, these limits are set by what Bewes, borrowing from David Armstrong, calls the 'instantiation relation'. By instantiation, Bewes means the function by which any normative discourse makes an entity serve as a case of a larger category, as when fiction is understood to schematise or exemplify some aspect of reality. In the instantiation relation, then, the novel makes sense of the world by tempering its indeterminacy in forms. For Bewes, however, only in the gaps between what is instantiated in the novel is it able to think what Lukács called 'the fundamental dissonance of existence'. Without the instantiation relation, that is to say, novels' ideas can only exist as negations of themselves, or in Bewes' preferred terms, in their 'interstices'.

To articulate the novel's unique kind of thinking, Bewes turns to one of its distinctive innovations: free indirect discourse. The opening lines of Virginia Woolf's *Mrs. Dalloway* provide a well-known example:

> Mrs. Dalloway said she would buy the flowers herself. For Lucy had her work cut out for her. The doors would be taken off their hinges; Rumpelmayer's men were coming. And then, thought Clarissa Dalloway, what a morning – fresh as if issued to children on a beach.

Where do these words come from? They constitute what Ann Banfield calls 'unspeakable sentences', mixtures of direct and indirect speech that evince an indistinction between the consciousness of the narrator and that of the character, if not a thought completely unattributable to any subject. Though the title suggests otherwise, *Free Indirect* is not a book about such ambiguities of free indirect style, nor an argument that it or any other narrative device is capable of evading the aesthetic ideology of instantiation. On the contrary, it is only worth paying attention to free indirect style, Bewes claims, because contemporary thought has witnessed the 'universalisation' of its inner logic, the separation of thought from thinker.

Free Indirect is therefore not concerned with the logics of instantiation or representation, but rather with a kind of relationality that persists at the edges of fiction after the collapse of literature's ability to produce meaningful categories. For this reason, it is not possible to recognise the persistence of thought that Bewes claims for the novel within existing interpretive paradigms, which he identifies with the help of Rancière's 'regimes'. Whereas the representative regime secures a relation between word or image and reality, the aesthetic regime both expands the realm of what can be aesthetically expressed and inaugurates a rift in representation that makes it prone to irony and the sort of second-order judgement endemic to the vagaries of implication. Most prominently authorised by Flaubert, the aesthetic regime relies on the instantiation relation, that is, what is formalised or made manifest in the novel precisely by remaining left unsaid ('show' rather than 'tell', the unstated love between Frédéric and Mme. Arnoux that one gathers simply from the atmosphere of the sitting room in *A Sentimental Education*). The resulting ambiguity anticipates and requires the work of interpretation to render its meaning legible, leaving some critics to wonder whether *Madame Bovary*, to take another example from Flaubert, is a stupid novel or a novel about stupidity.

In the contemporary novel, however, Bewes identifies a kind of thinking which is increasingly inaccessible to the practices of criticism or paraphrase that rely on such rifts within representation. The narrator-author of Rachel Cusk's *Transit*, for example, simply presents the disparate episodes of her life without the slightest attempt at synthesis or even the suggestion that one is possible. The ghostly voice of J. M. Coetzee's *Elizabeth Costello*, to take Bewes' preferred example, may interject a thought, but only if it is just as soon disproven in the narrative itself. But since these novels no longer think in the mode of instantiation, how do they think in its absence? What can a critic say about a work when its thought does not deign to appear in the text?

At this point, Bewes leads his readers into the jaws of a profound paradox: how can the novels that most exemplify the present be those that reject the logic of exemplarity itself? Another way of asking this question would be to ask how to historicise the thought of a moment at which historicisation – including the conceptual work whereby parts are related to wholes, instances to their historical 'moment' – appears untenable. For the critic, this poses a difficult problem, since to say that works in which the instantiation relation does not obtain also instantiate their era is already to reestablish the very relation whose abandonment they express.

Bewes tarries as patiently with this critical impasse as he does with the novels that induce it. Their insistence on irresolvable difference comes to a head in the final section, where Bewes shows that the thought of such novels – irreducible to form, the interpretive possibilities of criticism, or the thought expressed within the novel itself – is like that of cinema in the work of Deleuze: it is a thought unthinkable by us, a thought in which the universe thinks itself. At this point it becomes difficult not to ask: what good is a thought if no one can think it? Or more to the point: why write a book about a kind of thought that it can't think?

Perhaps for Bewes it is enough simply to suppose that such a thought exists. This might still seem a bleak prospect for criticism, but there are plenty of moments when *Free Indirect* becomes more than an elaborate exercise in its own futility. The irony is that, by confronting these and many other paradoxes of contemporary criticism head on, Bewes has made the present newly thinkable (so much so that one might well suspect that if the logic of fictionality was indeed to break down, and with it the practice of critique as such, it would be impossible to write a book like *Free Indirect*). In tracing the autonomisation of thought from thinker, Bewes makes significant headway not only in conceptualising the contemporary novel, but also in identifying the theoretical problems that have made that task so difficult.

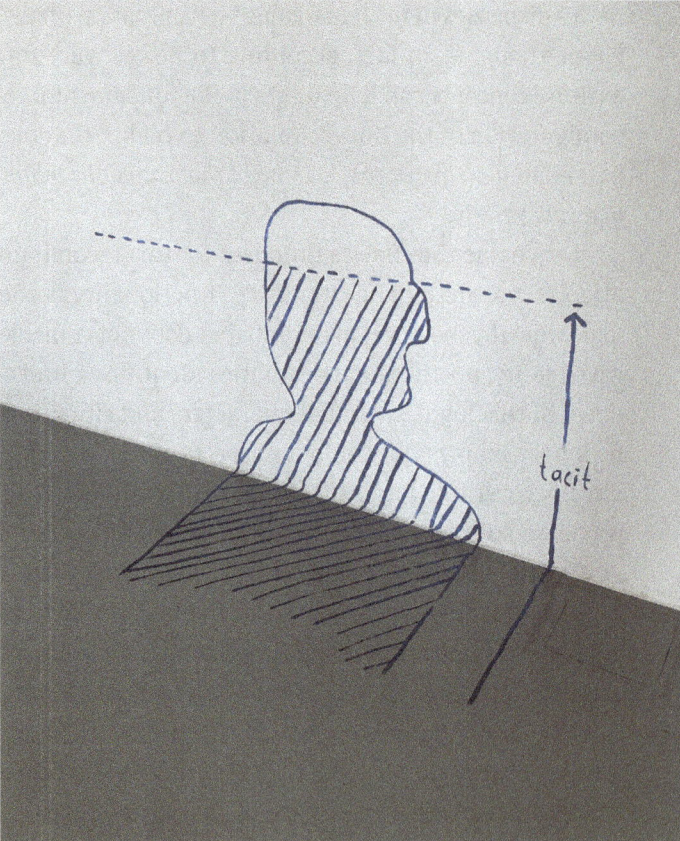

In the terms of *Free Indirect*, however, it remains impossible to theorise contemporary novelistic experiments (and the novel as such) because their mode of thought cannot be instantiated. Far from lamentable, Bewes suggests, this is novelistic thought at its purest; because it is irreducible to an example of or an isolable proposition about reality, it is able to make difference itself immanent to the novel. Bewes thus reads the contemporary novel as nothing short of an overcoming of perspective and point of view, the guarantors of form as much as of ideology and subjectivity. For Bewes, this has always been the promise of the novel – whether in the dialogic quality that Bakhtin praised in the works of Dostoyevsky or in the possibility of an 'ultimate futility of man' that the novel made visible to Lukács – though only recently has such a promise been actualised.

In a discourse (novel theory) obsessed with its own obsolescence, it will likely come as a surprise to encounter a book that not only refutes its object's death but even suggests its apotheosis. If it is indeed an apotheosis, however, it is of a very particular sort, which is to say, it is only an apotheosis if one assumes that the escape from ideology at which Bewes says the novel is arriving is not in fact simply another version of it. Little in *Free Indirect* compels one to share this assumption. Its fantasy of fleeing subjectivity is perhaps most troubling when the book's argument for a novelistic thought beyond the instantiation relation also insists that it be understood as a version of intersectionality, envisioned by Kimberlé Crenshaw as resistance to 'static representations of people's identities'. There is much to be contested in such a comparison and the suggestion that an aesthetic practice or a mode of thought can autonomously achieve an 'essence' which somehow exists outside the histories that have produced such identities, even if in the speculative realm of a non-subjective literature. The most symptomatic version of this claim comes in an 'interlude' in which Bewes likens the instantiation relation to the practice of 'profiling' – from racial profiling to the Cambridge Analytica case – without recognising that the objectification and 'absolute heterogeneity' with which he credits an escape from such practices can just as easily be seen as the historical outcome of their justification.

For anyone familiar with Bewes' earlier work, it might come as a surprise that these problems are never posed in terms of reification, and further that the problematic of reification has all but disappeared from *Free Indirect*. As an earlier essay of Bewes' attests, the instantiation relation is clearly a close relative of reification, one that lacks its cousin's rigorous articulation of commodification and the division of labour. Without these historical reference points, *Free Indirect* must seek its escape from thought as conceptuality and schematisation rather than from the historical structures that produce it as such. Even so, the thought Bewes attributes to the novel intimates that provisional escape from commodification and instrumental reason whose last refuge Adorno located in the aesthetic realm. In such a reading, Bewes could be credited with an impressively innovative method of tracking down, albeit in an unrecognisable form, the utopian dimension of the novel, if not of art more generally. Since the novel's utopian promise is not 'inhabitable', however, whatever hope it preserves is not for us.

Carson Welch

Who cares?

Boris Groys, *Philosophy of Care* (London and New York: Verso, 2022). 106pp., £9.99 hb., 978 1 83976 492 9

Boris Groys' *Philosophy of Care* is comprised of twelve short, pithy sections that plot an abbreviated history of mainly Western philosophy from ancient to modern times. Also included are two diversions into Russian intellectual thought, Groys being an expert on Soviet-era art and literature, as well as a philosopher and media theorist. The course he steers from Socrates and Plato to Hegel, Nietzsche, Kojève and finally to Heidegger, while selective, is a familiar Western philosophical narrative of how the subject negotiates its relation to mortality and immortality through transcendent organising principles, whether God, History, Being or the Future. But, in another sense, the course steered is strikingly unfamiliar given its reframing in terms of care and self-care and the question of health.

Groys' use of the terms care and self-care is unrelated to their common parlance in current art theory and practice in which they infer specific historical lineages: respectively, socialist feminisms' calls to revalue the contribution of social reproduction to labour power, and pedagogic well-being practices in activist struggles, e.g. the Black Panther Party in the 1960s/70s. However, since at least 2016, self-care has become a kind of mantra for middle-class millennials and art workers in relation to increasingly competitive and exploitative forms of labour in neoliberal capitalism. Self-care has come to mean anything from spa treatments and gym work-outs to going for a walk. While Groys briefly refers to alternative therapies, diet and tai chi in his introduction, his philosophy of self-care seeks to transcend biopolitical systems of care, though he also acknowledges its reliance on their management of illness, death and the 'after-life'.

In fact, Groys' ultimate quest in this treatise on self-care is to tease out the possibilities of the 'after-life' in a post-historical secular era. He begins by making a distinction between the living physical body and the symbolic body. Both bodies involve care. The physical body is tended to by the medical profession. Individuals also take care of themselves without any guarantee that the medical or alternative treatments they opt for will enable good health. The symbolic body is administered by archives, documents and images, all of which preserve its material 'after-life'. However, self-care in Groys' philosophical meditation goes beyond administrative maintenance. It is equivalent to self-assertion, an aggressive form of self-sovereignty that attempts to disengage from and transcend the institutions which, in maintaining functional health, repress the true life of the individual. The philosopher, who is in effect the main character of this little book, seeks freedom.

Beginning with Socrates, Groys examines how in the ancient Western world sovereign self-care was assured by the eternal gaze of divinity. This guarantee allows Socrates to take up the meta-position of contemplation of the soul. Rejecting personal self-interest, Socrates prepares for death in a contemplative mode that avoids struggle and competition. In a familiar reading of Plato's story of the cave in *The Republic*, Groys recounts how the philosopher, in moving out of the darkness towards the eternal light of truth, performs a fearless act of self-assertion in the face of death. To become truly fearless, 'the subject of self-care has to insist on the validity of his or her personal evidence – even against the judgement of the Church or the scientific community'. Although Groys uses the feminine pronoun here, the philosophical discourse of negation that he engages with in this book has an exclusively male patrilineage.

Rather than the soul, Hegel contemplates History, 'here understood as a process of revealing freedom as the essence of human subjectivity'. For Hegel, the terror unleashed by the French Revolution signals the end of history when 'the human spirit will establish its own law'. However, in the post-revolutionary state, this ideal is dethroned by 'reasonable institutions' who suppress self-sovereignty by administering to the preservation of life. In secular post-revolutionary society, the afterlife is maintained by the museum, the archive, libraries and monuments, with public institutions taking on the 'divine' role of caretaker responsible for the distribution of care between physical and symbolic bodies. In Groys' narrative, the physical body comes off as weak in its dependence on biopolitical systems of care to maintain its health and extend its life. He cites Canguilhem's notion that illness is a lack of biological confidence. As opposed to this exhausted body, the subject of self-care is one whose vital energies resist longevity and mere survival in a push for 'great health'. Nietzsche is the exemplar here, his striving for 'great health' being directed towards the afterlife, the future generations that would come to read his books. Surmounting his often ill psycho-physiological body, Nietzsche invests in the immortal life of the symbolic body and the promise of eternal return.

While Groys continually oscillates between this *uber* form of self-care and the biopolitical management of care, his emphasis on self-sovereignty intimates that his sympathies lie with the philosopher's sacrificial investment in the immortal life of the symbolic body at the expense of the mortal one. Therefore, it was puzzling when, later in book, he accuses Hannah Arendt, the only female philosopher who gets a look in, of being nostalgic for a time of great men of genius when he had seemed to be advocating for such singularity. Had I been mistaken? An online interview affirmed my initial view: 'As I write in my book, to be healthy means not to fear being ill. If I protect myself from an illness, that means that I am already ill. That is an actual ground for rejecting the masks, vaccination, etc.'

There are further baffling moments when the dialectic between self-care and care begins to slacken and blur, while still being maintained. Claiming that in the post-historical state, everyone is recognised to the same degree, not as equals, but as consumers, Groys asserts that the philosopher as sage is the only one not interested in consumption. '[T]he emergence of the sage signals the transcending of the opposition between care and self-care, the sage finds satisfaction in the anonymous work of care knowing it will continue in the future'. The philosopher as sage works like a machine. However, the modern opposition between the human as machine and the human as animal reinstalls the dialectic: while the system of care works to sustain the health of its workers, for man as animal, self-sovereignty, not longevity and survival, is the supreme value. The idea of animal self-sovereignty leads to a meditation on Bataille, whose desire for expenditure through an excess of energy can be viewed as a reaction to the heterogeneity of the crowd. Once everyone, in theory at least, has a voice, how does the philosopher assert his singularity over and above the repetitive and consumerist rituals of everyday life?

Groys tracks the development of what he calls the 'divinised public' in Kojève's philosophy. Kojève's way out of the deadlock of Hegel's master/slave dialectic, in which the two are locked in a cyclical battle, is to assert that history is moved by the individual desire for public recognition. Rather than corporeal desires or desire as negation, the desire for the desire of the other – a very Lacanian idea – forms the modern basis of self-sovereignty. Considerable attention is given to the motif of care in Heidegger's *Being and Time* and the self-assertion of *Dasein / Isness*. The conflict between institutional care and self-care is repeated here. While modern *dasein* is imprisoned and controlled by technology and institutions, self-care is resistance to 'becoming a thing in the world controlled by others'. As might be expected from a philosopher-art critic, Heidegger's essay 'The Origin of the Work of Art' (1935-6) makes an appearance here. The contrast between authentic existence and mere things is mapped onto the revelation of the truth of peasant life inferred in Van Gogh's famous painting of his shoes and the cleaning of mere objects by a 'charwoman'. The aristocratic form of self-care is always premised on there being invisible others who maintain the labour of life in domestic and related public spheres. However, Groys makes a u-turn here and reconfigures Heidegger's 'charwoman' as performing a modern mode of self-care in the museum: her maintenance reveals the truth of avant-garde art objects as 'things that present themselves as they are to the gaze of the spectator'. What outside the sphere of art is a mere commodity, e.g. Marcel Duchamp's *Bicycle Wheel* (1913), in being contemplated as art, acquires an 'after-life', a form of immortality.

From here out, the aim of Groys' meditations becomes clearer. A digression on the philosopher Nikolay Fedorov, who was part of the Russian cosmism movement, delivers the idea of a radical museumification of life, i.e. that all the people who ever lived should be placed in museums to preserve their immortality. Museum conservation becomes the technology of eternal life, the charwoman, its (Socratic) medium. As opposed to Foucault's critique of biopower which Groys defines as partial and limited, this would be total biopower in which everything is absorbed by care. That this is the only reference to Foucault, who spent much of his time exploring care of the self from ancient to modern times, is a glaring omission. Perhaps Foucault's work might have opened up too many questions about the relational field of self-care practices, whereas Groys' objective is to ascertain the health risks of immortality.

The most ubiquitous absorption of everything into care occurs in the online presentation of the self, which Groys terms self-design, a concept he has been writing about since 2008 in various essays in *e-flux*. Revamped as a form of self-care, self-design functions as a protection against the heterogeneity of contemporary life. Designing itself to be liked by a social gaze that has supplanted God and eternal gaze, the symbolic body performs a form of mimicry that protects the real body that lies behind it. At first it seems as if Groys is advocating this as a form of communal self-care, but then he posits that the prison-house of being trapped in cycles of self-design needs to be escaped. Asking what are the revolutionary conditions that could effect such an escape, he moves into a final meditation on physician and philosopher Alexander Bogdanov.

Unlike most of the cryptic book which assumes some familiarity with Western philosophy, here Groys gives a more detailed explanation of Bogdanov's notion of how all societies operate according to cycles of egression and degression: the former being authoritarian centralised forms of social organisation; the latter, dispersed forms which Bogdanov describes as skeletal. Self-design is a form of skeletal protection. But rather than the multiplicity of self-design resulting in greater flexibility, the societal skeleton becomes 'even more inflexible and ossified'. This, Groys infers, is where 'we' are now, the only escape from which would be a highly centralised, egressive, revolutionary moment. Here Groys seems to diverge from the singularity of self-sovereignty, suggesting that this revolution could involve patients taking power over the system of medical degression and transforming it in their own interests for their own health.

However, the health Groys has in mind does not stem from the collective empowerment of patients. He instead concludes by recounting a short story by Bogdanov, 'Immortality Day' (1912), about an immortal scientist called Fride who, bored with endless repetition, chooses to be burnt at the stake to regain mortality. Groys' interpretation is that this death fails to lead him out of the prison of degressive repetitions. By contrast, Bogdanov himself died, Groys claims, in a truly egressive manner: convinced of the potential of blood transfusions to enable immortality, he gave his blood to an ill young woman, saving her life, while ending his. This strange conclusion is both allegory and summary of Groys' notion that sovereign self-care involves a sacrifice of life oriented towards a future after-life.

Given Groys' approach, it is not surprising that, as well as a lack of engagement with Foucault, he does not mention feminist philosophies of care, such as Carol Gilligan or JC Tronto. An image of society as a complex relational field in which care-givers and receivers negotiate the conflicts between dependence and independence, vulnerability and power, is the antithesis of self-sovereignty and contemplation of the after-life. Ultimately, while a provocative and sometimes brilliant revamping of Western philosophy in terms of care and self-care, especially in relation to the internet, the unmarked sovereign self is universal Man and 'great health' is his universal Truth.

Maria Walsh

International law and capitalism

Ntina Tzouvala, *Capitalism as Civilisation: A History of International Law* (Cambridge: Cambridge University Press, 2021). 276pp., £85.00 hb., £22.99 pb., 978 1 10849 718 3 hb., 978 1 10873 955 9 pb.

At the heart of the post-World War II international order was a legitimating narrative premised on the idea that the world system was no longer imperial; it had now become a community of equal states. This meant that international law established a framework for shared peace and prosperity grounded in multilateral institutions that imposed constraints on all and that, over time, could eliminate the remaining distinctions between historic colonisers and colonised. Furthermore, such arrangements amounted to the progressive spread of basic rights protections around the world. This spread moved from the global centre, especially the United States and Western Europe, to the global periphery in ways that lifted all boats.

Unfortunately, twentieth- and twenty-first-century reality diverged dramatically from this narrative. Today's global order is one of sustained economic and political inequalities across states, alongside violent interventions targeted at those in the periphery. The result is the dramatic enrichment of some and impoverishment of others precisely along many of the old imperial lines.

Given this, left-leaning efforts – in scholarship and in political practice – to critique the role of international law in such developments have proliferated. But to put it somewhat bluntly, they have at times followed two tracks, each of which have their own limitations. The first approach is to emphasise argumentative openness and the potential embedded in the law. Such lawyers and critics argue that, while international legal frameworks may re-inscribe modern hierarchies, legal arguments can be employed against the grain to challenge existing modes of domination. The problem, however, with this approach is that in essentially embracing argumentative flexibility, it can fail to confront why time and again international legal regimes reinforce rather than dislodge structural inequalities (see especially the work of Aslı Bâli). At its worst, it can collapse into a version – albeit far less self-congratulatory – of the progressive account, with continued investment in the idea that if left-leaning lawyers are creative enough perhaps they can use established international legal doctrines for transformative ends.

The second approach is to be far more skeptical of international law's progressive potential. Since its long-term effect is to sustain global hierarchies and entrench new modes of empire, these arrangements essentially facilitate the interests of the powerful masquerading in the guise of neutral rules. A challenge for this orientation is that many international legal instruments still impose real checks on nation-state authority. Indeed, in recent decades the principal promoters in international affairs of the idea that international law is 'not law' have been right-wing proponents of powerful security states. These elites use a version of the same critical argument to contend that, precisely given the flaws of the international legal system, states should be able to pursue their security objectives unconstrained by international legal limitations. Thus, too much skepticism up-front of international law can unwittingly re-entrench the authority of dominant nation-states and aid their reduction of global relations to a violent security competition among them.

In the context of these dilemmas, Ntina Tzouvala has written a remarkable new book, *Capitalism as Civilization: A History of International Law*. The book is a trenchant examination of how international law participates in the reproduction across time of fundamental global hierarchies. In the process, it offers an essential pathway for avoiding the pitfalls embedded in both of these orientations. It does so through an innovative materialist reading, one that links international law to global capitalist development without simply treating the law as a mechanistic outcome of economic processes.

According to Tzouvala, one cannot appreciate the double-sided quality of international law – how it holds out an inclusive promise and yet sustains real subordination – without locating it in the history of capitalism. In particular, she highlights how global capitalist development has two embedded tendencies. On the one hand, it involves a limitless expansion to subject all populations to the imperatives of capitalist accumulation. But on the other, this expansion is never totally homogenous. Rather, it is structured in ways that are inevitably uneven, with 'under-development' and extractive exploitation the product of capitalist spread rather than a result of 'insufficient contact'. For Tzouvala, international law is one of the central sites that navigates this tension between inclusion and inequality. She demonstrates this through a sustained exploration of the legal term 'standard of civilisation'. The term was employed by European legal actors in the late nineteenth and early twentieth centuries as a benchmark for assessing whether non-European polities were worthy of proper membership in the international community and thus for legitimating colonial control.

But Tzouvala argues that the standard of civilisation is not best thought of as a concrete doctrine, one that during the era of decolonisation would in fact be repudiated by lawyers and jurists. Rather, at its core is an argumentative practice that survives in international law down to the present. This is because the standard of civilisation emerged as one way for European officials to manage a world of expanding but unequal global capitalist development. In this way, civilisational claims swung between two logics, mirroring the inclusive and the hierarchical contradictions in capitalism itself. And these logics remain active in contemporary international legal argument. The first, a 'logic of improvement', emphasises the idea that the promise of legal equality can be achieved through domestic reforms and capitalist market transformations. The second, a 'logic of biology', 'constantly negate[s] such a possibility', by always presenting the non-European world as marked by 'unchangeable characteristics' that necessitate various forms of supervision and provisional sovereignty.

In this way, Tzouvala offers an historically compelling and analytically powerful distillation of precisely why international legal frameworks carry progressive and utopian aspirations while repeatedly reinforcing global hierarchies. She further demonstrates how this oscillation between improvement and biology – conditional inclusion and sustained inequality – operates in practice through four case studies drawn from the long twentieth century. Chapter 2 explores the emergence of the standard of civilisation in the years up to and including World War I. Chapter 3 examines its function and argumentative tendencies within the League of Nation's Mandate System. Chapter 4 details the International Court of Justice cases and opinions during the era of decolonisation regarding Apartheid South Africa's responsibility to Namibia (then South West Africa) under the Mandate System. And Chapter 5 argues for the persistence of this oscillating logic even now. Tzouvala does so by focusing on U.S. legal arguments about occupied Iraq and doctrinal justifications for the use of force in its Global War on Terror, especially the idea that states in the periphery can be subject to military action if they are 'unwilling and unable' to root out terrorist bases on their soil.

The result is a work that makes a number of essential scholarly and political interventions. For starters, it powerfully reframes left-leaning critiques of international law. Tzouvala compellingly questions the utility some left lawyers find in international law's argumentative malleability. According to her, such an approach ignores the material connections between legal argument and capitalist development. It fails to appreciate how that very indeterminacy is built into the repeated argumentative patterns of conditional inclusion and persistent subordination. Thus, to imagine that one can genuinely alter structural hierarchies by using tools embedded in the law's 'logic of improvement' is an inherently self-defeating project.

Yet, this materialist analysis does not suggest that one should simply repudiate international law as a terrain of legal-political struggle. Instead, it means treating international law as 'numerous sets of arguments, institutions, and patterns with all their ambiguities, contradictions, and aporias'. The radical critic has to assess the argumentative patterns in various settings as well as how they connect to the reproduction of capitalism. The goal then becomes finding political and legal avenues to contest the underlying logic of each instantiated pattern, for instance by highlighting how established practices sustain racial capitalism or undermine meaningful self-determination. For instance, in the context of the GWOT (Global War on Terrorism), Tzouvala sees proposals to expand who gets to say whether a state is 'unwilling and unable', for example by moving the site of decision-making from the U.S. military to the UN Security Council, as a version of conditional inclusion. Instead of challenging the logic of improvement and the existing argumentative patterns, it simply cloaks them in multilateral legitimacy and so must be resisted.

All of this embodies a grounded way to engage with international law without falling prey to either liberal fantasies of progress or hawkish security dictates. It also opens an entire agenda for critical empirical and normative inquiry. In following Tzouvala's lead, it suggests the real utility of mapping out the variety of other argumentative patterns in law as well as how they relate to material conditions. Such an exercise becomes a concrete way of building a more comprehensive theory of international law. It also aids a radical politics vis-à-vis the international legal system, by delineating whether and how established argumentative moves reinforce structuring hierarchies.

Such avenues for study and action underscore a second significant contribution of the book. Tzouvala's approach meaningfully pushes forward materialist analysis of international law. A real reason why left-leaning politics and critique, particularly in the U.S., has tended to fall into the two camps mentioned above has much to do with a general deemphasis on materialist accounts. Without a grounding in underlying economic structures, international law has either appeared free floating and indeterminate or simply a reflection of nation-state power and rivalry. But one reason why U.S. scholars especially have tended to avoid materialist, including Marxian, interpretations has been a conventional wisdom that such interpretations fail to reckon with law's flexibility – its openness to competing arguments and unexpected doctrinal outcomes.

Tzouvala's book compellingly grapples with these concerns. She does so by skillful weaving into her analysis theoretical reflections on everyone from China Miéville to Antony Anghie. Beyond that, Tzouvala's overarching approach redirects focus away from fixed legal doctrine to underlying argumentative patterns. Rather than framing the law as offering clear formal embodiments of deep-rooted economic structures, she highlights how legal logics are tied to the very contradictions inherent in capitalism. In this way she rejects the routine claim in the U.S. legal academy that materialist analysis cannot reckon with indeterminacy. Instead, Tzouvala's approach shows how, only by grounding international law in a study of capitalism's internal tensions, can one make sense of *why* international law has such indeterminacy in the first place as well as chart out where the argumentative boundaries nonetheless reside. This is a deeply insightful move, one that upends traditional debates around materialist frameworks.

Finally, the book also usefully illuminates how imperial structures can remain even after the formal end of colonial empire. Tzouvala does this by demonstrating the linkages between empire, capitalism and international law. If a liberal internationalist would argue that the repudiation of explicit 'civilisational' claims highlights a break with the past, Tzouvala shows how the persistence of underlying argumentative logics sustains both new modes of capitalist and imperial development. In this way, she is able to capture why today's inequalities are not simply a holdover from a colonial past, which in time will be overcome. Rather, to the extent that the same unequal capitalist development proceeds apace – alongside the connected logics of improvement and biology – one can find real continuity despite the postwar ruptures in the global system. Moreover, one can also appreciate how these continuities are reenacted in the present and so ongoing rather than unfortunate holdovers from the bad old days.

Capitalism as Civilization is a book filled with essential reflections for the study of both law and capitalism. If anything, I finished it wanting more, in particular how her mode of analysis would apply to other corners of international law. But again, this may ultimately be Tzouvala's challenge to her readers and to those committed to finding levers for disrupting the dominant structures of international economic and political order. What Tzouvala provides is not only a striking rereading of international law over the last century. She also offers a powerful model for how to integrate law and political economy in ways that recognise contingency while still centring the structural constraints that shape all emancipatory projects.

Aziz Rana

Subversive agency

Jill Godmilow, *Kill The Documentary: A Letter to Filmmakers, Students, and Scholars* (New York: Columbia University Press, 2022). 224pp., £94.00 hb., £25.00 pb., 978 0 23120 276 3 hb., 978 0 23120 277 0 pb.

Jill Godmilow's *Kill the Documentary: A Letter to Filmmakers, Students, and Scholars* is a curious object. Although published by Columbia University Press, it is not quite an academic text. Unlike most of the theoretical volumes that have been written on documentary film in recent years, Godmilow's is neither concerned with retracing its history, nor in contributing to the scholarly research on the genre, developing consistent categories of its modes, methods, styles or contexts. Instead, the author declares in the first pages of her introduction that she 'intend[s] to be as provocative and subversive as [she] can' in order to 'advocat[e] for a cinema whose trustworthiness and usefulness is dependent not on documentary's pedigree nor pornography of the real, but rather on the strength and the performance of its ideas.' Far from pretending to any kind of scientific neutrality, Godmilow's text is clearly committed to a cause: that of sensitising her readers to the political element of perception and the agency of the forms that mediate reality.

Bill Nichols, who wrote the preface, reads the book accordingly as a 'bold, provocative manifesto'. Yet Godmilow's conversational, unflinching, sometimes ironic tone should not be taken as gratuitous or grandstanding. Rather, it expresses a long-time indignation about the way many official or commercial documentary formats tacitly claim to represent reality in its immediacy, as a positive given. The problem she points at is not only that such claims are spurious, as 'what we normally think of as "the real" in documentary films is a construction, made up of how well the look and sound of the film *simulates* the actual.' This crucial aspect, which has already been emphasised by many independent filmmakers and critics before her, certainly is an important objection against hegemonic claims to neutrality. But what she considers even more problematic is that such an idea of documentary as transparently showing reality 'as it really is' conceals the moral and ideological underpinnings on which it often relies. Far from being as neutral and innocuous as they pretend to be, conventional documentaries not only oversimplify the real by obliterating the multiple frictions, ambiguities and inequalities of society, but also posit a certain reality – that of privileged white middle-class citizens of the so-called first world – as its normative core. They produce 'an egotism that eternally places the citizen/viewer at the centre of the universe, looking out into the represented world, discovering the problems of other peoples. It's a kind of cultural imperialism, as if your knowledge exempts us from having had any part of the damage we find there.'

Capitalising on the genre's general association with trustworthiness and sobriety, such documentaries are thus instruments to keep the dominant power structure of society intact: '[they] ask you to go there to that landscape and, once fascinated with what you find there, to keep watching, anxious for more, and finally find some kind of resolution of the problems presented. The doc asks you to enjoy, weep, celebrate, have pity, gasp, perhaps dread, and finally be released from care when the credits roll.' Her most telling example is the PBS documentary series *The Vietnam War* – an imposing, 18-hour television opus that, while meticulously retracing the chronology of the conflict, reflects an utterly uncritical attitude towards the hegemonic imperialist understanding of history and actual politics which it depicts.

Godmilow's harsh criticism of such conventional documentaries – she also calls them liberal documentaries, or 'dawkis' ('documentary as we know it') – resonates strongly with certain philosophical and critical writings from the early Frankfurt school, especially Adorno and Horkheimer's remarks on the culture industry. Although the two philosophers did not address the documentary specifically, their critique of the culture industry's 'inherent tendency to adopt the tone of the factual report', through which it 'makes itself the irrefutable prophet of the existing order' (*Dialectic of Enlightenment*), applies to documentary, whose peculiar relation to reality is implicit in the understanding of the genre, even more than to other entertainment formats. According to Adorno and Horkheimer, the products of the culture industry resort to a certain fetishised idea of objectivity, akin to that heralded by positivism, understood as a separate sphere of cold facts dissociated from their social and subjective mediation which grants them a meaning. Such an idea of objectivity *qua* factuality is furthermore associated with standardised formal features, which make the constructedness of their mediations pass unnoticed, and sanction a normalised perception of the real. 'Each statement, each piece of news, each thought has been preformed by the centers of the culture industry', writes Adorno in *Minima Moralia*. 'Whatever lacks the familiar trace of such pre-formation lacks credibility, the more so because the institutions of public opinion accompany what they send forth by a thousand factual proofs and all the plausibility that total power can lay hands on.' The problem Adorno and Horkheimer raised is thus not only that cultural products under capitalism have turned into consumer goods like any other and are moulded according to the same market criteria which adapt to the fashion of the moment. The problem is also that they produce, by dint of the recurrent reiteration of the ever-same patterns and common tropes, a harmonised, all-encompassing imagery of reality in which the latter appears as a coherent, impenetrable whole. By overshadowing any trace of uniqueness through clichés associated with allegedly consensual values, they stifle the antagonisms of society under an ideological veil of coherence. The products of the culture industry are thus not only perfectly aligned with the reigning power structure in capitalist society; they also endorse its hegemonic claim for universal validity.

Like Adorno and Horkheimer, Godmilow carves out the interrelations between the recourse to conventionalised forms – the presumed direct relation with the real of documentary formats – and the political significance they take on in society. Hence, she does not consider documentary forms as isolated, interchangeable entertainment objects, but as expressions of society and interventions into its becoming. Documentary is thus for her to be regarded in its dialectical relation to society rather than through categorial filters. Like Jacques Rancière, according to whom 'the privilege of the so-called documentary film is that it is not obliged to create the *feeling* of the real, [which] allows it to treat the real as a problem', Godmilow is not so much interested in the differentiation between documentary and other audiovisual works than in the stance they all take vis-à-vis reality. She thus upholds the importance of producing documentaries able to crack open the rigid imagery and to subvert common perceptions of reality, so as to problematise its all-too-obvious or natural appearance through defamiliarisation, shifts of angles and other subversive artistic strategies.

As such, it is first and foremost necessary to see through the political agency of forms: how is reality comprehended and approached through documentary? Does the latter take on an affirmative position, or does it challenge normalised ideas about society? How do filmic configurations generate an impression of evidence and immediacy, or, contrariwise, open an access to novel perceptions that subvert our conceptions of the real and invite us to engage in social change? How can a specific truth-content be disclosed through particular framings or montage? How can documentary film problematise reality today, a reality that is itself widely saturated by images and sounds?

As an independent filmmaker, Godmilow has been raising such questions about documentary through artistic means for over 40 years. Her experimental documentary *Far from Poland* (1984), for example, does not simply document the Solidarity movement in Poland from a seemingly neutral perspective, as many journalistic formats do. Neither is it an activist film in the usual sense of the term. Instead of informing her audience about factual events or transmitting a clear message, it drags the spectator into a sort of reflective spiral, which problematises not only the ways that diverse media formats and politicians generalise and instrumentalise highly complex situations, but also her own position as an independent filmmaker from the left. Mixing various media footage, restaged scenes of real and fictional interviews and sequences featuring the filmmaker herself with her partner or a group of friends in their private home, the film complicates its subject matter rather than explaining it. Through the montage of heterogeneous materials, critical reflections about the difficulty to grasp the imbrications of reality and the images and sounds supposed to mediate it, the complexity of reality itself during the cold war and the intertwinements of personal life, artistic practice and political action come to the fore. Rather than stabilising a meaning, *Far from Poland* multiplies the questions that arise from the very idea of documentary filmmaking and appeals to the spectators' own critical capacities. Another of her works, *What Farocki Taught* (1996), takes on a completely different form: it replicates Harun Farocki's *Inextinguishable Fire* (1968), which she considers as one of the most powerful subversive non-fiction films of the twentieth century. Farocki's short film approaches the Vietnam War through a thorough Marxian deconstruction of the impact of capitalist organisation (the universalised division of labour) and values (the unquestioned pursuit of efficiency and profit) in modern warfare and politics. Godmilow not only appropriates Farocki's oeuvre by reproducing the exact script, its Brechtian tone and style, but also actualises it by adding colour, resorting to American actors instead of the original German actors playing Americans, and transposing it into a US-American context.

Both films are inherently political insofar as, through a thorough work on form, they disturb commonsensical ideas about reality and its relation to the images and sounds that mediate it. Both address the viewer directly and appeal to her critical assessment. The same is true for her book: Godmilow addresses her reader directly as viewer of documentary formats, rational interlocutor and potential filmmaker of 'useful' (in the sense of subversive, critical, engaging) films whose aesthetic, formal and political choices will inevitably intervene in the very shaping of the perception of reality. She calls such subversive works 'post-realist' films. 'The post-realist film', she writes,

> is an antispectacular form that refuses documentary transparency, evidentiary arguments, classic narrative structure, psychological explanations, and the sympathetic identification systems that posit us/them symmetries. ... Most important, postrealism always addresses an audience that does not yet exist but that could be produced through understanding provided by the film's experience. ... The postrealist film comes in many forms, but always seeks to crack the code of the status quo, to drill even small holes in our social *imaginaire*, our naturalized worldview that suggests what is understood as normal, reasonable, commonsensical, and generally accepted by all.

Godmilow's notion of postrealism, diametrically opposed to what Adorno and Horkheimer called the 'pseudo-realism of the culture industry', shares many characteristics with certain Marxist concepts of realism. Undoubtedly, it draws on Brecht's idea of realism outlined in *Popularity and Realism*, according to which

> Realistic means: discovering the causal complexes of society / unmasking the prevailing view of things as the view of those who are in power / writing from the standpoint of the class which offers the broadest solutions for the pressing difficulties in which human society is caught up / emphasising the element of development / making possible the concrete, and making possible abstraction from it.

Like Brecht, Godmilow emphasises that the political potential of art to address reality directly – in her case, primarily non-fiction film – lies in its ability to unravel gridlocked ideas about reality through formal constructions, to incite the viewer to reflect on their own position in society and to intervene in its course. Likewise, Alexander Kluge's claim that 'the motive for realism is never confirmation of reality but protest' and his idea of an 'antagonistic realism', which conceives of reality as a complex, historically-developed construction, in which the factual is constantly mediated through the society which confers it meaning and the subjective feelings, projections and attributions which actualise it, has much in common with Godmilow's conception.

To be sure, Godmilow does not situate her critical writing on a conceptual level. Much more important for her is to grasp the intelligibility of the forms themselves. Hence, she provides an impressively wide range of examples which not only include experimental documentary films from different contexts and periods – including Luis Buñuel's *Land of Bread* (1933), Želimir Žilnik's *Black Film* (1971), Chick Strand's *Fake Fruit Factory* (1986) and Camilo Restrepo's *La Bouche* (2017) – but also feature fictions, poems and conceptual artworks. Herein lies the specificity and refreshing nonconformity of her book: it pushes the reader not only to see through the ideological premises of conventional formats, but also to delve into the multiple configurations that generate subversive experiences. Through her readings, comments and perceptions, it becomes very clear that such configurations are not ready-made formulas to be emulated but particular formal inventions for specific situations. Hence, she insistently encourages her readers to read, watch and criticise as many works as possible and to invent their own artistic means. Significantly in this respect, Godmilow also calls her book a handbook, including a comprehensive 'tool-kit' full of references and practical instructions.

In a way, Godmilow's obstinate belief in the subversive potential of artistic forms recalls the affirmative stance of militant artists in the periods of the historical avant-gardes or the crisis-laden 1960s and 1970s, which, for some, might seem dated or outworn today. Yet her persistent faith in the importance of developing critical awareness and in the agency of art to intervene into reality despite the omnipresent 'capitalist realism' in the global neoliberal society radiates a compelling force.

Stefanie Baumann

Governing the non-human

Thomas Lemke, *The Government of Things: Foucault and the New Materialisms* (New York: New York University Press, 2021). 299pp., £80.00 hb., £25.00 pb., 978 1 47980 881 6 hb., 978 1 47982 993 4 pb.

Cars that measure and signal fuel efficiency, expanding markets for weather derivatives, and 'vital systems security' infrastructures, among other similar developments, indicate significant transformations in contemporary governmentality at varying scales. New materialist strands of thought have been developing novel understandings of these more-than-human operations of power for several decades by rethinking the ontological categories, epistemological enclosures, political impasses and ethical dogmas of anthropocentric modes of analysis and critique. Thomas Lemke's *The Government of Things* is a welcome addition to the corpus. By inviting new materialist scholars to think with rather than against Michel Foucault, as has customarily been the case, this book unlocks fruitful directions for analysing how power operates in contemporary societies.

One of its biggest successes is the extensive and clear explanation of new materialist thought, particularly its three most highly influential strands: Graham Harman's object-oriented ontology (OOO), Jane Bennett's vital materialism and Karen Barad's diffractive materialism. Lemke provides a helpful and detailed outline of this profuse and diverse body of scholarship representing different intellectual traditions and orientations. He explains that new materialisms are united in proposing a new valuation of matter as productive and dynamic rather than inert and passive, an agentive subject rather than simply subject to (human) agency. This ontological recasting of matter's perceived torpidity also invites a political reorientation wherein power analysis is not restricted to human communities. Furthermore, new materialists endeavour to construct an ethical framework premised upon the gordian entanglements of people and things, whose relations are shaped by 'mutual depend-

ence and exchange'. Epistemologically, they endeavour to remove disciplinary barriers by combining insights from the natural sciences with social scientific and humanistic research.

Lemke's book responds to a dual preoccupation with the possibilities and foreclosures of new materialism's theoretical bearings. On the one hand, Lemke supports 'the new materialist call for a critical reconsideration of matter and materiality'. On the other hand, he has some reservations. Namely, he suggests that new materialists tend to overstate their departure from 'old materialism'. He points out that 'materialism was always engaged in renegotiating and updating its agenda in confronting its counterpart ... in this perspective, materialism as a "revolution in thought" is not breaking news but business as usual.' Furthermore, he suggests that in their quest for interdisciplinarity, new materialists tend to take for granted the truth content of recent developments in the natural sciences. This ends up re-entrenching scientific foundationalism. Relatedly, some strands of new materialism consider critique a limited and essentially negative endeavour. This, for Lemke, suggests a circumscribed understanding of the dynamism and richness of different traditions of critical theory. Finally, he finds that political questions tend not to be addressed directly in the new materialist literature he surveys. He recommends that new materialist ontology take a more robust 'analytics of power that draws on the tradition of critical theory and is informed by a political agenda for change.'

The book takes stock of an impressive range of recent and canonical literature in new materialisms, science and technology studies, action-network theory, and governmentality studies. In the first section, Lemke's critical attention is mainly focused on the works of Harman, Bennett and Barad, with each of the first three chapters examining one strand. Of the three, Lemke appears most polemical with regard to Harman and object-oriented ontology (OOO). OOO proposes that the materiality of matter is essentially opaque and inaccessible through analytical and scientific enterprises, and the only way to access it is through aesthetic practices. Furthermore, it articulates a flat ontology wherein no hierarchies exist among objects, living or non-living. Considering anthropogenic climate change, Lemke rightly quibbles with this idea. A clear hierarchy of effects must be maintained so that theories of being can possibly address and mobilise to redress the human toll on the environment.

Throughout the second section of the book, Lemke most regularly engages with Barad's diffractive materialism and her three-part critique of Foucault: that (1) he does not adequately theorise the relation between 'discursive practices and material phenomena'; (2) his theories of power privilege the social; and (3) he is essentially an anthropocentric thinker. In responding to Barad's concerns, Lemke posits that Foucault's understanding of government 'exceeds a concern for an anthropocentric ethics and forms of (human) subjectivation to analyse the relationalities that connect and separate humans and nonhumans.' He elaborates on the 'government of things', a notion that Foucault introduced in the 1978 Lectures at the Collège de France, published in English under the title *Security, Territory, Population*.

In articulating what Foucault may have meant by the 'government of things', Lemke focuses on the lecture dated February 1, 1978. In this, Foucault works through an early modern treatise on government by Guillaume de la Perrière, noticing how it marks a shift from a territorial notion of government to the 'government of things'. Lemke quotes Foucault:

> The things government must be concerned about, La Pèrriere says, are men in their relationships, bonds, and complex involvements with things like wealth, resources, means of subsistence, and, of course, the territory with its borders, qualities, climate, dryness, fertility, and so on.

From this excerpt, Lemke extrapolates a Foucauldian ontology of matter. He argues that Foucault did not propose an ontological distinction between 'human' and 'thing'. Instead, he understood the production of this difference (as well as the normative roles assigned to them in politics and morality) as an 'instrument and effect' of the art of government itself. For Foucault, Lemke concludes, to govern thus means to govern things – human and nonhuman – according to their natures and based on their relations. At several points throughout the book, Lemke acknowledges that Foucault does not elaborate much on the idea of a government of things. Instead, his thinking around the notion of the dispositive, technologies and milieu provides additional sites where Foucauldian entries to new materialism can be discerned.

Those familiar with the *Security, Territory, Population* lectures might come away from this section of Lemke's book wondering about the relative absence of an engagement with Foucault's analysis of biopolitics. After all, one of his primary preoccupations in these lectures was charting the development of biopolitics as a technology of power aimed to govern the 'population'. In his attempt to distance Foucault's work from critics that reductively read him as only a theorist of biopolitics, Lemke seems to disregard the notion's centrality in Foucault's work altogether. The concern here is not that the conceptual proposal of a 'government of things' departs from an established 'Foucauldian' line of research – Foucault wanted his books 'to be a sort of Molotov cocktail, or a minefield … to self-destruct after use, like fireworks.' Lemke's mission to rescue Foucault from the boxes in which his thought has been confined, and to continue thinking with him in productive ways, is ultimately fruitful. However, acknowledging and interrogating the material(ist) foundations of biopolitics via the inseparability of the *bios* and the *geos* from the molecular to the political might have better articulated the stakes of a new materialist rendering of Foucault's thought.

One of Lemke's central goals in this book is to make a pitch for 'relational materialism' that is also a 'material relationism'. He argues that new materialist scholarship's insistence on agency as an indisputable 'quality of material existence', and their tendency to endorse the truth claims of scientific knowledge, create neo-essentialist ontologies that do not adequately address current governmental operations. Instead, he argues that governance today functions through constant negotiation and delineation of the 'boundaries between the human and nonhuman world' while also calling on the political capacities of 'things'. To that end, governance has a strategic and shifting ontology based on understanding the complex and dense networks among living and non-living entities. While he acknowledges that the outlines of material relationism are still sketchy, a fuller explanation of what he means by it would have better guided the reader towards understanding the political stakes of a Foucauldian approach to new materialism.

Lemke suggests that 'this idea of material relationality reopens the question of the political' in a way that new materialist scholarship has not been able to address. Suppose the subject of politics is construed as networks or relations rather than stable living or non-living entities. In that case, it might be possible to organise a political theory around 'more just or egalitarian human-nonhuman encounters'. In charting this, Lemke gestures at, but does not meaningfully engage with, the work of Jacques Rancière, whose theoretical injunctions inform Bennett's vital materialist theory of democracy. In *Disagreement*, Rancière argues that politics happens when the already-existing 'distribution of the sensible' is disrupted by the spontaneous actions and unruly utterings of the demos.

Notwithstanding the anthropocentric biases of Rancière's theory of politics, it proposes an underexplored angle through which the political stakes of Lemke's project could be expressed. He wants the analytics of a government of things to open up a 'political space of contestation, disagreement, and dissent' that can chart 'alternative, and possibly conflicting, trajectories of socio-technical futures enacting more-than-human democratic practices.' However, democratic theory ultimately requires a theory of action, if not agency, wherein demands for a new distribution of the sensible can be made. The government of things explains how contemporary governments contain and rule through the dense relationalities of living and non-living entities. Still, it doesn't provide a framework for understanding how more-than-human networks and relations can act politically to produce meaningful change.

In the book's final chapter, Lemke works through the notion of environmentality, a term that has increasingly been in circulation, to chart a critique of neoliberalism from a Foucauldian perspective inflected by new materialist concerns. An idea put forth by Foucault, environmentality indicates a governmentality that 'seeks to govern the "environment" of human and nonhuman entities rather than operating directly on "subjects" and "objects"'. Lemke suggests that the idea of environmentality apprehends a central characteristic of neoliberal governance, whose practices 'seek to steer and manage performances and circulations by acting on and controlling the heterogeneities and differences that make up a milieu.'

Lemke traces the genealogy of resilience theory from the 1970s onwards to account for the development of an environmental form of governance. It is not a coincidence that increasing awareness of the ecological crisis prompted a move away from equilibrium as the goal of government interventions. The strategy of fostering resilience rather than re-establishing stability 'has come to reorient policies ... to the question of how to support and foster adaptive capacities in uncertain ecologies.' Thus, contemporary governance operates through a neoliberal environmentalism that contains projections of crisis and critiques of capitalism's ecological costs in order to nurture capitalist expansion. Environmental modes of administration can also be detected in vital systems security, informed by 'probiotic' rather than 'antibiotic' approaches to a future in crisis. These strategies 'do not work by an external mode of operation that restricts, modifies, and contains the environmental conditions of human life but rather by aligning, channelling, and enrolling them.'

Thinking with Foucault has long given rise to hermeneutically sophisticated and precise analyses of governmentalities, historical and contemporary. Lemke's examination of environmentality as the mode of operation of neoliberal governance fosters a fecund critical framework that can explain the emergence of new technologies such as vital security infrastructures, ecologically conscious automobiles and weather derivatives. However, it remains unclear whether the conceptual proposal of a government of things can inform disruptive and anticapitalist politics. While Lemke states this as one of his goals, the absence of an examination of the political struggles – such as the Dakota Access pipeline protests, Extinction Rebellion, Fridays for Future, and many others – that continue to advance a more egalitarian alignment of human and non-human relations is telling. Whether the conceptual proposal of a government of things can animate action for meaningful change and explain challenges to the status quo remains, therefore, an open question.*

Deren Ertas

---

* Thanks to Sultan Doughan, Jochen Schmon, and Sam Nimmrichter for their helpful editorial comments and thinking through this piece.

The hidden abode of digital production

Moritz Altenried, *The Digital Factory: The Human Labor of Automation* (Chicago: University of Chicago Press, 2022). 217pp., £76.00 hb., £22.00 pb., 978 0 22681 549 7 hb., 978 0 22681 548 0 pb.

Since the beginning of spring 2022, many countries have witnessed the return to supposedly 'normal' rhythms of life after the closures and restrictions that followed the latest pandemic. During this period, discussions in the Global North have emerged about the 'great escape' (or 'great resignation') from work – where, in the US at least, this connoted an increasingly collective inclination to reject working tedious jobs for very low wages. Summer marked the arrival of 'quiet quitting', an expression deployed to mark both a refusal to perform tasks beyond one's assigned contractual duties and an intention to be less psychologically invested into one's job. These two (real or apparent) trends are restricted only to a very limited section of the working population, for which remote working expanded (and improved) by developments in digital technologies seems to have suddenly unveiled the inherently exploitative character of many existing working arrangements. And yet, what about the plurality of other workers – usually not falling into the already inadequate category of 'white-collar' – whose work has in the last two decades intensified by virtue of the implementation of digital technology and that could not 'quietly quit' precisely because of this?

Moritz Altenried's book, *The Digital Factory*, intervenes in these discussions to unmask many false assumptions that exist about the vast realm of digital labour, its transformations and the effects on its working agents. It is a clearly written and nuanced overview of broad transformations of labour processes in contemporary capitalism, structured around the chosen lens of the human labour that forms an essential part of what is (or appears as) 'automation'. Despite the false promises, optimistic views, and even threats of a world liberated from work by the development of full automation, the capture, organisation and exploitation of people's time and forces still characterise life under capitalism. What the reader finds in Altenried's book is a clearly systematised set of arguments that shed light on the manifold forms of digital labour hidden behind 'the magic of algorithms'. Every technological development, the author points out, displays a strong 'continued importance of human labor'. Most importantly, with his book Altenried manages to individuate and grant voice to a heterogeneous and geographically dispersed army of digital labourers. These include platform crowdworkers shaping a 'distributed bedroom factory', content moderators on social media, search engine 'raters', 'gold farmers' and 'testers' in the gaming industry, not to mention the logistics sector with its temp workers in distribution centres or absorbed within contemporary manifestations of the gig economy (such as the 'last mile' of e-commerce delivery). Altenried lucidly charts the varied ways the work of these labourers has been progressively standardised, decomposed, quantified, overseen and managed for an increased control and efficacy within what he calls the 'digital factory' and its infrastructures.

One of the most important kernels of the book is the idea that, with the development and implementation of digital technologies, the factory – understood here as a labour regime – has exploded or spread beyond the concrete physicality of an industry workshop. As a consequence, the factory has also begun assuming different (and primarily) spatial forms such as the digital platform. The four central chapters comprising *The Digital Factory* and the research areas chosen for its ethnography – logistics, gaming, crowdwork and social media – concretely outline the materiality of the impact of digital technologies regarding more recent forms of labour exploitation allowed by and intensified by digital technologies. In places that often do not resemble traditional workshops, these new forms of control and management of labour processes have some striking similarities to labour relations that 'one might assume only exist in traditional factories'. In this sense, and the argument is solidly presented throughout the book, the reader is often reminded that the factory should never lose its central place for a critical understanding of contemporary digital capitalism, despite its substantial transformations compared to its more traditional physical form.

Two main theoretical axes – or, as Altenried calls

them, 'vectors' – on which the book's chapters spin are the notions of 'digital Taylorism' and 'multiplication of labour'. This latter notion draws extensively upon Sandro Mezzadra and Brett Neilson's work and signifies here 'the heterogeneity of living labor in a time characterized by the increasing coalescing of labor and life, the increasing flexibilization of labor, as well as shifting and overlapping geographies in the ongoing processes of globalization'. But it is with the concept of 'digital Taylorism' that Altenried provides a key tool to understand the foundations and the tendencies of current transformations of labour practices.

To put it succinctly, Altenried argues that as one of main ways to control and manage labour in the era of advanced digital technologies, digital Taylorism – through a combination of software and hardware – opens up further possibilities for the rationalisation, decomposition and surveillance of the labour process in view of increased performances and outputs. However, there are three main differences in contrast to traditional Taylorism, which congeal in characteristics that often emerge in novel and unexpected ways: the plurality of spaces outside the factory as physical unit, the heterogeneity of figures of labour which are in stark contrast with the homogenised mass worker of the Fordist period and, relatedly, the increasing hyperflexibility of employment arrangements that often lack legal protections. In other words, digital Taylorism, as a pillar of the functioning of the digital factory, allows for a level of 'scientific' management and disciplining of the labour process that was unthinkable in Taylor's time. This has to be understood also in relation to a workforce which, due to the proliferation of smartphones and the extension of the mobile internet infrastructure, has increasingly become global and geographically scattered. In this respect, Altenried's problematisation of the concept of 'digital migration' is particularly significant and is used as a conceptual provocation to disengage the definition of migration from its physical referent. The book does an excellent job in exposing the racialised and gendered dimensions of such a multiplication of the figures of labour, its transformed regimes and forms (such as 'crowdwork', where these dimensions emerge with particular clarity).

Altenried's foremost aim is to shed light, as the book's subtitle specifies, on the labour hidden behind digital technologies. In contrast to a more common outline of the labour of the creatives of digital industries (coders, designers, etc.) – a section of the working population at times fetishised by the theorists of so-called immaterial labour – Altenried prefers the path of mapping the wretched of the digital factory. In this less visible section of the labour force subsumed by capital, what becomes visible is the materiality of the exploitation of these workers that is supported and enhanced by algorithmic control, together with the all-too-traditionally tedious and repetitive nature of the tasks required. Gaming testers, for instance, are required to play specific parts of a videogame for hours on end, and the workers who train different types of artificial intelligence (AI) – usually working from countries in the Global South – are logged on to digital labour platforms to categorise pictures or optimise search engine results. Content moderation on social media platforms is a particularly interesting example showing the limitations of automated systems of content selections, since Altenried maintains that the AI is still far from being programmed with the right sociocultural capacities possessed by human beings. The AI, as he clarifies, lacks the cultural knowledge especially when marked by contextual parameters behind language (nudity, hate speech, violence, and so on).

This leads us to a crucial point that the book outlines regarding automation: labour is not completely automated within the world of digital technology. And even when the AI is trained with a view to prospective automation in the future, labour reappears in other forms (and other places) to fill in the needs of the transformations of labour triggered by the implementation of automated processes. By keeping the category of value at its centre, Altenried often directly invokes Marx in decisive moments in the book. Against the spectre of automation, Altenried aptly maintains that 'digital technology can automate many tasks but generates at the same time new tasks and problems that require human labor'.

While charting such an army of hidden digital labourers and their hyperflexible working arrangements, it is striking that Altenried rarely uses the word 'precarity'. The author understands very well that precarity is not a novel phenomenon in the world of capitalist labour. Rather, the casualisation and fractalisation of labour represented by the word 'precarity' denotes contractual arrangements that have existed since the dawn of industrial production, even if their use was temporarily interrupted by the historical parenthesis of the Fordist phase (and only on the Atlantic axis of the US and Western Europe). Hence, Altenried seems to prefer the word 'contingency' to describe working arrangements put in place to satisfy the necessity of real-time supply chains (the book reminds us about, for instance, temp workers hired only for the Christmas season in Amazon's fulfilment centres). Moreover, as Altenried notes, the contingent nature of contemporary supply chains paves the way to a logic of constant acceleration in the management of labouring practices. As he puts it, the accumulation of data regarding working practices, aided by the algorithm, 'allows for a radicalising of Taylor's concepts [and] fulfils a historical wish of scientific management'. The objective quantification to measure qualitatively different types of labour (or sub-tasks) is unmasked by Altenried's ethnography as not in the least objective, yet implemented in order to forge and maintain a sort of hyperexploitative labouring regime.

It is clear that *The Digital Factory* opens up avenues for further research in the field of contemporary political economy. One of those concerns the potential forms of resistance to these newly multiplied forms of labour in the digital factory. The theme is somewhat underexplored in the book, especially in the chapter on crowdwork. However, the emergence of a workforce that unknowingly cooperates on digital platforms, but whose members work as isolated units, makes political organisation particularly challenging. It should not be surprising that a researcher would find it challenging to trace forms of resistance within such a scattered and irregularly employed labour force. Instead, the book offers a valuable analysis of many new (often invisible) forms of exploitation generated, maintained and reproduced by the development of digital technologies. At the same time, Altenried correctly asserts that '[a] crucial dimension of successful struggles will be the development of new tools of digital organising'.

In addition, even though Altenried specifies from the outset that the reconfiguration of space is a crucial dimension to the developments in the world of digital labour mapped in his book, essential transformations in the dimension of time and temporality are also part of such a multiplication of labour and workers. Indeed, Altenried (somewhat obliviously) points out the problem when dealing with the vocational character of certain figures in the gaming sector, the testers, who are taken advantage of to enforce overtime, increasingly blurring the line between life and labour, and progressively accepting disadvantageous conditions of work. For a long time this trick has been part of capital's arsenal to maintain a tight grip over labour.

The significance of *The Digital Factory* is even more clear after the first two years experience of working during a global pandemic. The tendencies in some sectors of digital labour described in the book – whose manuscript had already been completed by the first months of 2020 – have harshly intensified in the past year or so. In a configuration of capitalism where social cooperation is still crucial, but one in which workers are physically distant or digitally not connected with each other, how to organise new forms of resistance to labouring practices under digital conditions? This is the implicit question present throughout *The Digital Factory*. A nuanced enquiry into the current dynamic transformations of labour in digital capitalism, Altenried's book provides a first necessary step in finding ways to answer it.

Yari Lanci

Platforming new conspiracism

Russell Muirhead and Nancy L. Rosenblum, eds., *A Lot of People Are Saying: The New Conspiracism and the Assault on Democracy* (Princeton: Princeton University Press, 2019). 211pp., £20.00 hb., 978 0 69118 883 6.

One thing a lot of people are saying right now – especially after the events of January 6th 2021 – is that the supercharged forces of conspiracy theory and digital communication platforms have reshaped social norms and the operations of political institutions in the post-Obama era. In *A Lot of People Are Saying: The New Conspiracism and the Assault on Democracy*, political scientists Russell Muirhead and Nancy L. Rosenblum provide the first in-depth account of the complex and recursive relations between the global far right, digital media and the ongoing crises of epistemological legitimacy and value faced by knowledge-producing institutions. The book argues that the globally-connected, anti-democratic right has strategically developed 'new conspiracist' tactics that delegitimise opposition parties, knowledge-based institutions and democratic processes and norms.

In order to understand what makes the new conspiracism new, Muirhead and Rosenblum introduce a key epistemological distinction. For them, classic conspiracy theory is best described as 'a proposed explanation of some historical event (or events) in terms of the significant causal agency of a relatively small group of persons – the conspirators – acting in secret'. Classic conspiracy theory, they say, still believes in the epistemic powers of evidence and explanation to reveal the traces of a knowable, causal agency/agent responsible for global events. The new conspiracism, however, has no use for evidence, explanation and causation. Its distinguishing feature is that it is 'conspiracy without the theory'.

Having shed the commitment to theory and explanation, the new conspiracism thrives off 'innuendo, accusation, speculation, plausible deniability, and plain assertion', and 'traffics in sound bites, flow[ing] here and there through the capillaries of public culture'. Think of Trump's famous rhetorical style, which for the authors serves as the book's key example of new conspiracist messaging. The new conspiracism's disavowal of evidence and explanation, according to Muirhead and Rosenblum, means that it is 'satisfied with an allegation being "true enough", rather than true'. If it's *possible* that a child sex trafficking ring is being run out of a pizza joint in D.C., who is to say – and more to the point, who can definitively prove – it is not happening *now*, or has not happened *before*? But if something seems true enough in the present, we must ask how the new conspiracism arrives at a temporal position so universally indifferent to truth claims.

The new conspiracism thrives in the perpetual present and runs on a corrupted program of epistemological nihilism that weaponises doubt and turns it into a foundational virtue. Muirhead and Rosenblum contend that 'their [the new conspracists'] certainty is at odds with skepticism; they are without residual doubt that things are as they represent them', and they show how the new conspiracism pits skepticism against certainty. They also take note of the epistemological paradox at the heart of new conspiracist thinking: the distortion of skepticism-as-certainty, in effect, makes the new conspiracism 'the enemy of skepticism'. In this formulation, the new conspiracism 'doubles down' on skepticism *as* certainty, which 'corrodes both knowledge and skepticism'. The only thing of which new conspiracists can be certain is that their own unflagging skepticism is true in all contexts.

The coherence of the new conspiracism is paid for at the expense of truth. This coherence is, in reality, false, and what is not-false is that which has not been completely disproven (by new conspiracists, of course – never 'experts'). Despite its alleged commitment to unearthing the truth, 'the new conspiracism sets a low bar' when it comes to testing the epistemological core of its claims. From this perspective, truth – or something resembling it in a funhouse mirror – is equated with skepticism toward total falsifiability. As the authors note: 'If one cannot be certain that a belief is entirely false, with the emphasis on *entirely*, then it might be true – and that's true enough'. In a sense, the new conspiracism recasts the absence of total falsifiability in qualitative knowledge as an existential impasse of sanctioning authority ('true enough' – for what purpose, to whom, and when?). As mentioned above in the brief discussion of the temporal indeterminacy of truth claims in relation to the Comet Pizza restaurant in Washington D.C., the veneer of subjunctivity occludes the processes by which the new conspiracism's self-validating truth procedures function. *A Lot of People are Saying* shows how it might be strategically important for countering the global far right's ascendance if we were to more carefully consider how the investment in modal difference can produce epistemo-political effects that are indifferent to truth and falsity. But my point here, drawing on recent work by Luciana Parisi and Alenka Zupančič, is that the new conspiracism is driven neither by skepticism nor certainty, but by a form of epistemic nihilism, fuelled in turn by an autoimmunological turn in reason that has been exploited by anti-democratic politics and social media platforms. As their epistemic values are stripped bare, justified skepticism and incontrovertible proof become equally worthless to the new conspiracist.

In a related register, Muirhead and Rosenblum show how the cybernetic operations of feedback, noise and signal processing have fundamentally altered the protocols and processes of academic work, remediated inevitably by our everyday experiences of simply being online. In a brief discussion of the QAnon movement, the authors observe how that particular conspiracy theory's process 'mimics collaboration and peer review', not unlike the way in which our relatives' endless scrolling through conspiracy-laden memes on Facebook – or our colleagues' entire workdays spent on 'academic Twitter' – now qualify as 'doing collaborative research'. The epistemic processes and protocols of academic/scientific research and exchange, the authors demonstrate, are now reflected across such vernacularly homogenous domains as Reddit, 'academic Twitter' and 4chan.

The new conspiracism's epistemological nihilism is a feature, not a bug, of digital communication platforms. However, Muirhead and Rosenblum do not clearly define 'the new conspiracism'. Instead, we are left wondering if it is a political movement, an ideological stance, a

conspiracy or an ideologically-neutral network effect. I would submit it is the latter. While social media platforms are not central to the book's analysis, Muirhead and Rosenblum clearly think these technologies and the ideologies propping them up have played a pivotal role in enacting and disseminating new conspiracist tactics and anti-institutional beliefs. As they note early on in the book regarding the importance of sowing epistemic and institutional doubt, 'forwarding, reposting, retweeting, 'liking' ... are how doubts are validated in the new media'. This widespread doubt toward 'political parties, the norms of legitimate opposition ... and knowledge-producing institutions like the free press, the university, and expert communities within the government' is produced and disseminated through platforms' approach to epistemic value, a process which substitutes 'social validation for scientific validation'. The (il)logic of the crowd, the libidinal energy of the swarm and the quantitative affirmations from the 'statistical refuse' heaps of the masses, in Baudrillard's terms: *if a lot of people are saying it*, then it is true enough'.

Merging quantitative determinism with populist logic, digital communication platforms reconfigure epistemic value along these popular and emphatically *populist* lines. The truth or falsity of a claim is irrelevant; what matters is how widely it has been disseminated on digital networks and how many 'engagements' it has generated along the way. 'Even the character limit built into Twitter aligns with the new conspiracism's avoidance of evidence and explanation', Muirhead and Rosenblum write, continuing with the observation that 'the medium invites emphatic, unelaborated assertion [since] the internet is the ideal medium for repetition and for signaling identification with others who spread conspiracist narratives'. While the authors are right to observe that in-group signalling/identification and the quantitative logic of platforms shape cultural value and facilitate the spread of new conspiracist narratives, I am less certain that the ideological or political content of these operations is all that important.

The formal limitations of communication platforms produce real-world political and epistemic effects: from epistemic filter bubbles on digital platforms, to for-profit cable news, to paranoia-as-network-effect. With internet trolls baiting our collective ids into explosive outbursts of affect and with armies of bots unleashed on platforms to boost the numbers and provide (in)authentic social legitimation, is it perhaps time that we reassessed the relations between conspiracy and politics in the age of social media? How much longer can faith in techno-reformism hold?

Regardless of political orientation, there is a tendency among the political junkies among us – or perhaps it too is a network effect of sorts – to view the epistemic and political feedback loops generated by platforms through a strictly partisan and, most worryingly, pathological lens. Digital platforms update Richard Hofstatder's famous observation that the paranoid style in American politics operates as its pathological Other, and they recast the problem of pathology as a problem of informatic signal transmission and detection. Partisan extremists and conspiracy theory true-believers, in this view, have been exposed to 'a malady or affliction that differs fundamentally from a healthy engagement in politics and surfaces in trivial and groundless claims made by marginal groups and individuals that can threaten the pluralist consensus of American democracy', as Fenster writes. The problem here is twofold. First, it is an error to assume that the existence of mis-/disinformation online poses an existential threat to democracy – the problem of transmission – even though many scholars and commentators continue believe the best way to address this problem is through the widespread dissemination of true, factual and empowering information (as we know, platforms already moderate content, of course, and the question to ask is this: do you really want corporate entities and governments regulating even more what you see online?). Second, there is a fundamentally anti-democratic undertone to the issue of faulty signal reception that would make Walter Lippmann blush. What kind of anti-democratic position believes that exposure to bad content on digital platforms irreparably and pathologically harms the everyday citizen's ability to make rational political decisions? In this view, the masses are easily manipulated, mobilised to treasonous political action by what they saw on Facebook or the wrong TV channel. This argument in particular informs Muirhead and Rosenblum's account of the rise of the global right. Nonetheless, Hofstatdter's paranoid maladies resurface in the contemporary moment as a concern over digital form, yes, but mostly content, with platforms facilitating the transmission of malignant packets of ideological warfare couched in too-stupid-to-be-believed memes, viral videos and improperly-curated social media feeds. The form that these digitally-mediated signals take is never the point because we tend to focus exclusively on their ideological content. Repackaging these forms with factually true and proper messaging – or content which aligns with our own partisan loyalties which is, one supposes, the same thing – and retransmitting different political signals across the digital transom might help alleviate the pathological symptoms resulting from toxic media exposure. Or so we might think.

With 'the polarized partisan divide now epistemic as well as political', the tendency to write off political opposition as pathological leads one to believe that the proper political loyalties will immunise oneself from such epistemic afflictions as conspiracy theories and dis-/misinformation campaigns. Framing digital platforms' network effects as forms of pathological exposure does a disservice to political discourse and to the foundations of democracy. Such a narrow and anti-democratic framing also reproduces the new conspiracist goal of delegitimising political opposition. Regardless of virtuous intent or its grounding in 'facts', framing political difference as a matter of pathology erodes public trust in institutions. It's clear that modern day conservatism is 'the pure face of negativity' in the sense that it 'rejects the meaning, value, and authority of democratic practices, institutions, and officials'. Yet according to Muirhead and Rosenblum, the ideologically-neutral forces of conspiracism 'help accomplish what conservatives in office cannot: they delegitimize the people and [knowledge-producing] institutions'. The controversial claim here is that the new conspiracism's operations, techniques and network-effects are in fact ideologically-neutral and cannot be pinned to any one political party. It's true that digital platforms create the conditions in which new conspiracism can thrive, but the success resulting from the coupling of new conspiracist goals and tactics with widespread network-effects has little to do with political ideology. The promotion and facilitation of anti-institutional beliefs (of both the right and left variety) on digital platforms is entirely self-serving, as they would like to be the only corporate institutions left in town. In this context, Muirhead and Rosenblum's book is remarkably persuasive in its final argumentative turn: articulating a more robust defence of political and knowledge-producing institutions may very well be the best form of defence against the new conspiracism.

Michael F. Miller

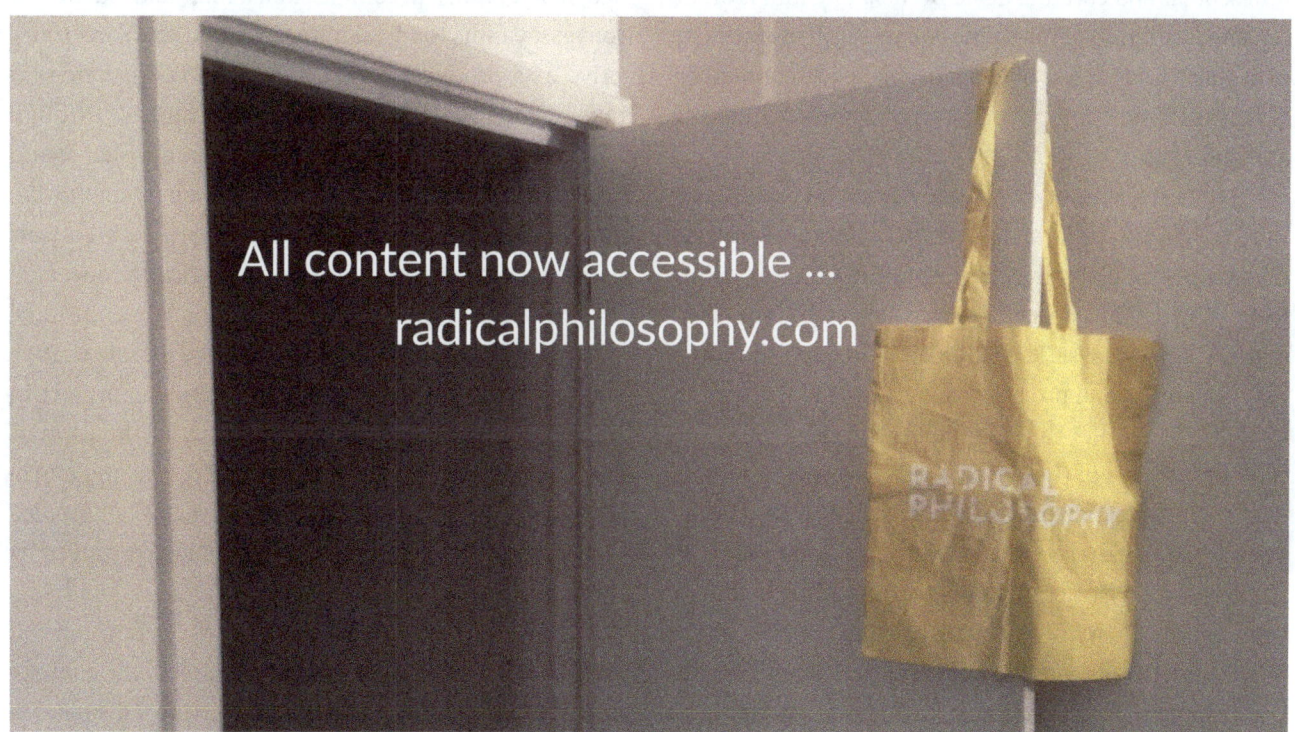

Description of a Self-Portrait
Jean-Luc Godard, 1930-2022
Christa Blümlinger

Shortly after Jean-Luc Godard's death at the end of 2022, the Parisian *Ménagerie de verre*, a private art space primarily dedicated to dance, showed excerpts from the late work of the grand master, in a 'visual and sonorous journey around five films made by Godard between 1999 and 2018'. Planned by his producer Jean-Paul Battaggia and cinematographer Fabrice Aragano, the exhibition organisers had already been involved in the realisation of the last films of the Paris-born Swiss. Four years before his death, and four years after the first 3D-experiment which became his forty-seventh long film, *Adieu au langage* (2018), Godard presented a filmic essay with the significant title *Le livre d'image* (*The Image Book,* 2018), made in collaboration with Aragno and Battagia, as well as the film scholar and curator Nicole Brenez. The film is an intensified variation of his poetic collages, full of contrasts, with which Godard was once again able to use contemporary means to position cinema as an art between literature and painting.

Before its adaptation for television and release in a Blu-ray edition, *Le Livre d'image* was celebrated outside of cinema as a performative event. The film was exhibited at the end of a spacious venue flanked by numerous audio-visual essays. The exhibition, lined with monitors, flatscreens and projections, did not lead through an art space but rather through the backdrops, loggias and rehearsal stages of the Théâtre des Amandiers in Paris. In the almost testament-like *Bilderbuch*, it says: 'Aucune activité ne deviendra un art avant que son époque ne soit terminée' ['No activity shall become an art before its time is over'].[1] With this historical-philosophical sentence Godard seemed to invoke at once the end of the cinema and his own passing. The most outstanding of the founders of the Nouvelle Vague had been articulating the entwinement of film history with his own biography for a long time, and had done so again and again. In a conversation with Alexander Kluge, he associates his birth in 1930 with the beginning of sound film.[2] As for the Nouvelle Vague, he continued to situate it in the middle of the century of film art, for example in his 'documentary film' *Deux fois cinquante ans de cinéma français* (1995).

It is near impossible to outline briefly the multifacted oeuvre of this provocative critic, film-maker, writer and master of editing and montage. Godard has long gone down in film history as one of the most influential authors of short and long films in the most varied genres and formats.[3] These span from narrative films to documentary television series, from collectively produced Maoist 'flyer films' to commissioned films and video clips, from essay films to installations. Godard was sometimes active as a producer, too, in line with his artistic self-image, and, finally, was able to assert himself through a formal gesture of institutional critique which found its way from the Centre Pompidou via the humanitarian organisation Emmaüs and Sotheby's to the New York art market: the mock-ups of his archeologically conceived *Collage(s) de France*, which were originally meant to be curated by Dominique Païni, were offered for sale in 2018 in a New York gallery.[4] From this promising project in the end all that remained was a sketch in the form of objects that were displayed in a controversial and much-discussed exhibition with the title *Voyage(s) en Utopie / A la Recherche d'un théorème perdu* (2006), conceived by the film-maker.

Through the break with classic forms of narration and codes as well as through his re-evaluation of the contemporary, the immediate and the direct, Godard's feature films created new forms of expression. With his companions from the Nouvelle Vague he wanted to demonstrate that one can override conventions such as screenplays and stories while being able to say everything. He achieved this by means of a conscious blending of forms, which, as Marie-Claire Ropars-Wuilleumier noted already in the early 1970s, comes close to the essay: someone speaks, interspersed with the words of another, in a work which is self-referential because it indicates the mechanisms of its production.[5]

Given the variety of his artistic gestures the following can offer only a brief review of a few of the feature-length films that have contributed to Godard's global fame and that still stand for the richness of his innovations. The feature films range from *A bout de souffle* (1959), in which he radically broke with the classic rules of continuity and which also established Jean-Paul Belmondo's career, to the star-studded love drama *Le Mépris* (1963), which, thanks to the involvement of Fritz Lang, secured Godard a symbolic place for himself as the 'Ciné-fils': that is, as one who emerged as the legitimate heir of those Hollywood filmmakers whom a few years before he had praised as 'auteurs' in the pages of *Cahiers du cinema*. Godard's films in this vein extend to the romantic-revolutionary *Pierrot le fou* (1965), shot in Cinemascope, which earned him Louis Aragon's significant acclaim in *Lettres Françaises* – and which Chantal Akerman would repeatedly say inspired her to make films herself – and to the socially visionary image of the ordinary couple in *Week-end* (1967). After a political-collectivist and an educational-televisual phase in the 1960s and 1970s, marked by his work within the Dziga Vertov Group and his collaboration with Anne-Marie Miéville, Godard made a brilliant cinematic comeback with the aesthetically groundbreaking dissolving of filmic movement in *Sauve qui peut (la vie)* (1980). The figurative re-enactments in his radical tableau film *Passion* (1982) mark him out as a master of artistic synthesis, as do the almost polyphonically composed films *Prénom Carmen* (1983) and *Je vous salue Marie* (1985). Among his late oeuvre, which identified him finally as a contemporary *artist*, there is the aesthetically and socio-economically lucid *Nouvelle Vague* (1990), and in *Notre Musique* (2004), a modern history painter simultaneously focused on the abysses of his present and withdrawn in his own garden, while *Film Socialisme* (2010) possessed a melancholic dimension that later acquired a documentary tone.

Godard's essayistic self-reflections, on which my further remarks will concentrate, inherit a literary genre which goes back to Montaigne and runs through to Malraux. Incidentally, references to Montaigne can already be found in the motto of *Vivre sa vie* (1962),[6] and to Malraux, very explicitly, in Godard's video series *Histoir(e)s du Cinéma* (1988–1998). While Godard's much-discussed essayism is inherent in his work, a few examples of his essay films can be seen, in certain ways, to explicate his aesthetic thinking.

Raymond Bellour described the Godardian self-portrait as a form of expression that is specific to film and video, one in which are shown the mechanisms of a writing that chooses the first person singular but does not aspire to a reconstruction of the facts of a life.[7] This form does not follow any narrative but is structured according to thematic categories. It is situated on the side of the analogous, the metaphoric, rather than the narrational, and relies significantly on the montage of elements corresponding to each other. This fragmentary poetics, relying on the expressive power of the images, has often been associated with early Romanticism.[8] In this sense Bellour identifies a form of Godard's generalised self-portraits, that appears from the mid-1970s in films, videos and documentary series through the presence of the film-maker's body, whether through his voice – which in *Ici et ailleurs* (1974) encounters Anne-Marie Miéville's critical response – through the staged handling with audiovisual machines (*Numéro Deux,* 1975), or, after his collective phase, through his appearance again and again as a supporting character in a fiction. It is no surprise that Jacques Bontemps, for example, has recently read *Prénom Carmen* very precisely as a 'disguised self-portrait'

[*autoportrait travesti*], which is close to the pictorial or literary characters of the joker, jester or clown, as Jean Starobinski derives these from Romanticism – that is, emphatically distorted images that the artist sketches of himself and of the state of art. The instruction 'with the body!', which the concert master of the string quartet gives to a young violinist during a rehearsal of Beethoven in *Prénom Carmen*, may stand here for Godard's romantic credo, which corresponds to the playing of the artist of hyperbole 'Monsieur Godard'.[9]

Even though Godard's video essays were often commissioned works, they are of central importance in his oeuvre. Suzanne Liandrat-Guigues and Jean-Louis Leutrat observe in his mostly short essay films the 'laboratory of visual and tonal forms' for his cinema films.[10] One outstanding example of an essayistic short film is the collage of Edgar A. Poe and James M. Cain produced for France Télécom, *Puissance de la parole* (1988), a visually vibrant ode to art in which the expressive power of the film medium is simultaneously radicalised and digitally transcended.

Against this background, some of his projects that have remained on paper alone are also revealing. For example, the never-realised film project *Moi Je* (1973) from the early period that Godard and Miéville dedicated to innovative audiovisual experiments (especially on television) is a hybrid product associated with the elements of text, image, hand and machine.[11] In this encyclopaedic project Godard is concerned to immerse the viewer in a dialectic between the 'social unconscious' (first chapter: 'I am a political person') and the 'machine socialisation' of a social desire (second chapter: 'I am a machine'). The project of this cybernetically conceived film refers to the reflection of the technical and social *dispositifs*, in which film and television are integrated. This machine model is to be understood not so much in terms of a psychoanalytical conception of the unconscious than according to the idea of a 'desiring machine', as theorised by Gilles Deleuze and Félix Guattari. The term aims at the 'capacity for endless connections that extend in all directions'.[12]

As Jacques Aumont put it, Godard can be considered one of the most important contemporary 'theoreticians' of film art:

> If Godard is so essential (and, indirectly, if he is the celebrity that he is), it is precisely because he is the only one to have succeeded in splitting himself between all these positions: an old-fashioned love for movies, adaptation to the media, *aggiornamento* of the representational credo and its marriage with the desire for the imaginary, and finally an up-to-date theoretical position on the very nature of what art is – not only the art of cinema, but simply art, all of art.[13]

Already in *Ici et ailleurs*, but especially from the end of the 1980s, Godard consistently formulates questions that are symptomatic of the modern cinema by means of video and cinematography, and which are condensed in his eight-part magnum opus *Histoire(s) du cinéma* (1988-1998).[14] Some of the films made while Godard was working on *Histoire(s)* bear the traces of this work in their individual montage elements: for example, *Allemagne Année 90 neuf zéro* (1991) and *Les enfants jouent à la Russie* (1993), produced for Swiss television, or the radical self-portrait shot on 35 mm, *JLG / JLG – Autoportrait de décembre* (1994). A series of shorter videos or films such as *The Old Place* (1998) and the recent *Le livre d'image* continue the project of *Histoire(s)*, which Godard condensed once more into 35 mm in *Moments choisis des Histoire(s) du Cinéma*. But the *Histoire(s)* also have a prehistory in an experimental compilation of scenes from *Sauve qui peut (la vie)* (1980), which the film-maker interspersed with other works, such as Eisenstein's *Old and New*. Michael Witt has convincingly demonstrated that the reassembly *Sauve la vie (qui peut)* (1981) serves as a laboratory for *Histoire(s)*.[15]

If Godard writes his polyphonic *Histoire(s)* using video, it is also because this medium allows for a radicalisation of the relationship between writing and image. Here he literally demonstrates that this (hi)story consists not only of image-fragments but that it is also *written*: he sits in front of a typewriter, talks to a friend, consults books from his library in order to form the staccato character of his (hi)stories as a system of overlappings, an endless layering, not only of the video archive at his disposal, but also of language, writing, sound and image.[16]

Through the disjunction of sound and image, there is at the very beginning of *Histoire(s)* a crack in the mirror of the screen, which marks the break between the modern film and classic narration. In one of his early short films Godard shows that the sound film was born from the spirit of ventriloquism: in *Charlotte et son Jules* (1959) he dubs the main male character (Jean-Paul Belmondo) with his own voice, hence contaminating the body image of another through the materiality of his own voice and thus announcing his visual authorship. Later, Godard appears himself in his films, whether in small roles such as in *Je vous salue Marie* (1984), or in the filmic 'letter' *Lettre à Freddy Buache* (1981), where he appears in the reflective pose of a writing film-maker.

The choice of the title of one of his films from the beginning of the 1990s – *JLG/JLG – Autoportrait de décembre* – suggests a conscious form of reflexivity that also refers to the literary tradition: self-portrait, not autobiography, as Godard remarks in the film. This is because in contrast to the autobiographer, the self-portraying person does not know what this self actually is – he is a searcher. Godard's sketch of *Histoire(s) du Cinéma* as a memorial topology of fragments brings to the fore a comprehensive aspiration to overcome the self in favour of a universal theatre of memory that produces unique constellations. His heterogenous collages and montages create a modern form of remembrance, namely, as Karl-Heinz Bohrer describes it, a contemplative act of 'absolute, partly unconscious, in any case not self-directed visualisation of states, mental images, objects of perception'.[17] This contemporary judgement in turn corresponds to a historic consciousness that Jacques Rancière, drawing on German Romanticism, defines as the 'aesthetic regime of art', as a co-presence of forms and experience. Among other things, Rancière described how Godard's *Histoire(s)*, similarly to Rembrandt's paintings, presents film as an encyclopaedia of gestures and as a place of a 'new history', beyond genre, big themes or historic actions.[18]

The *film-writer* works alone; the tools of image and sound are sufficient for him to incorporate found materials. But even in the films and parts of films that Godard shot himself, which required a minimum of collective work, he produces, as Deleuze puts it, an *extremely populated* solitude.[19] When Godard dispenses with a screenplay in his feature films, it is because the already existing world of the actors and the set is a mere starting point for his improvisation and spontaneous shooting. The cinema is for Godard the ideal means for the struggle against loss and loneliness. Perhaps even more explicitly than in other films this thesis is at the heart of *Allemagne année 90 neuf zero*, announced in its subtitle, 'Solitudes, un Etat et des Variations', where the double meaning of 'Etat' indicates both an abstract concept (loneliness as a state) as well as a certain state (the loneliness of Germany).

In his 1995 speech on the occasion of his Adorno Prize award, Godard places cinema besides philosophy, politics and literature.[20] The film, as he says there, is situated in a solitary position, which can be reached by means of the power of its 'eloquent and deep' images. These can do without language because they possess a special expressiveness and historicity. Historicity is to be understood here, first and foremost, in an aesthetic sense. 'I knew Spengler and Husserl, but not Murnau', says Godard about his educational heritage, 'and no one told me that they all lived in the same country as Bismarck and Novalis'.[21] In *Allemagne année 90 neuf zero* the character of the cultured Graf Zelten (Hanns Zischler) embodies Godard's fondness for German Romanticism. This is communicated even more emphatically by means of a semantic idealism, which the film constructs as a world of signs of the ruined and reunited Germany. Faced with the fall of the Berlin wall, Godard chooses a story of the *longue durée* (in Fernand Braudel's sense) over a history of events. This means he chooses (hi)stories of the cinema which he – unlike elsewhere[22] – delimits from (hi)stories of television.

When Godard titles the fourth part (2B) of *Histoire(s)*, *Beauté Fatale*, after the French title of Siodmak's *The Great Sinner*, it is in order to refer to the fatal fact of the cinema that male desire has essentially created the (film) images of women. It is no coincidence that we find here references to Fritz Lang's *Dr. Mabuse*, *M* and Rossellini's *Rome, Open City* as well as Bergman's *Persona*. As with the nineteenth-century novel, the gender difference is the key to the analytical understanding of the narrative cinema: it forms the visual *dispositif* of seeing and being seen.

To write (hi)stories of the cinema for Godard means there is no substitute for the movies, for going to the cinema. Orpheus and Eurydice: that is the fateful gaze of literature on the film, of an Orpheus who must be able to 'turn around, without making Eurydice die'.[23] Godard realises this looking back as the nostalgic memory ritual of a special cinephile. Leutrat and Liandrat-Guigues describe the *Histoire(s)* pointedly as a 'poetic gravestone' that Godard has erected for himself.[24] It is not film history that is shown there but the film in its aesthetic power.

Godard has inscribed his own films and the history of Nouvelle Vague into his *Histoire(s)*. In part 1B we can find a kind of confession of the faith to the cinema as the high art of projection, which is based on the Bazinian idea of the filmic recording as an imprint of the real: 'the image will come on the day of resurrection'. When in part 2A of *Histoire(s)* Godard allows for the appearance of one interlocutor, the critic Serge Daney, he lets him speak but only to make his words become an image. In the reproduction of digital postproduction, a multimedia space emerges, which, although it starts with writing, always leads to visual presentation. With the condensation of film history (including one's own) within a great palimpsest Godard ultimately adopts a Nietzschian position: Godard's *Histoire(s)* inherits the figure of the resurrection and of the overcoming of mortality in a self-image *à la* Nietzsche's *Ecce Homo*.[25]

In the solo exhibition *Voyages en Utopie / A la recherche d'un théorème perdu* in 2006 at the Centre Georges Pompidou, Godard for the first time worked with an art space in the form of a large-scale environment. There a model train emblematised the invention of film as well as the history of the destruction of the European Jews (Lanzmann's *Shoah*) – a constellation of cinema and history, which is also a central theme of *Histoire(s)*. This series of suggestive connections is one among countless that is pursued in the exhibition between films and objects. If Godard's aesthetics is presented here mostly negatively (e.g., through nailed books), its positive energy is in the circulation and networking of knowledge fields, very much in accord with Deleuze and Guattari's desiring machine: 'In desiring-machines everything functions at the same time, but amid hiatuses and ruptures, breakdowns and failures, stalling and short circuits, distances and fragmentations, within a sum that never succeeds in bringing its various parts together so as to form a whole. That is because the breaks in the process are productive, and are reassemblies in and of themselves'.[26] From this perspective, the exhibition *Voyages en Utopie* realises Godard's project *Moi Je* from 1973, namely, 'I am a machine'.

The ruins of the original exhibition present themselves here as a cabinet of curiosities. It bears the signature of the collector who is not interested in an individual portrait but in a constellation. In one of the boxes which served as a mock-up for the *Collage de France* and which is titled *L'alliance (inconscient totem et tabu)*, a portrait of Freud appears next to children's drawings and excerpts of text. Here Godard sets out to follow the traces of the story of his companion Miéville, in order to represent their shared concern for 'the struggle of the image with the angel of text'. These biographemes (in Barthes' sense) about the life of another underlines the renunciation of autobiographical reconstruction. 'Self-portrait, not autobiography', as it says in *JLG/JLG*.[27] A photo of Godard as a child appears there, not as a clear enlarged image but as a blurred portrait that was copied multiple times and visibly reproduced. In a paradoxical double movement, the film-writer and artist creates images of himself which elude a fixed identity. His films, videos, texts and installations thus appear to be an ideal form of *écriture*, as conceived by Marie-Claire Ropars-Wuilleumier: as a theoretical hypothesis, as a pictural writing and montage in the sense of a multi-layered conflict, in which the visual as well as acoustic signs are continuously scattered, so that meanings only ever fluctuate, and are never fixed. 'No activity shall become an art before its time is over': with this Godard also names the paradox of the obsolescence of a medium which had nevertheless served him well in understanding the world.

Translated by Marina Gerber

Christa Blümlinger is Professor of Cinema Studies at Université Paris 8. Her essay 'The History of Cinema, as Experience' appeared in RP *192 (2015).*

Notes

1. This sentence is to be found handwritten in English in Godard's book for the film, printed in a limited edition of 1500 copies: Jean-Luc Godard, *Le livre d'image/image book* (Lausanne: Casa Azul Films/Écran Noir Production, no date), unpaginated.
2. Alexander Kluge, *Blinde Liebe (Eloge de l'Amour), 10 vor 11* (2002).
3. It is impossible to provide here a comprehensive set of references to the still growing literature on Godard, which ranges from biographical studies (Colin MacCabe, Richard Brody and Antoine de Baecque) to detailed exegeses of his oeuvre (Jacques Aumont, Michael Witt) and contextual analyses (David Faroult).
4. See the comments of Dominique Païni in 'Retour sur Jean-Luc Godard' (2010), Service audiovisuel du

Centre G. Pompidou, https://www.centrepompidou.fr/es/ressources/media/nMGLBWZ; as well as Leo Goldsmith, 'Memories of Utopia: Jean-Luc Godard's "Collages de France" Models', *e-flux*, 8 March 2018, https://www.e-flux.com/criticism/241188/memories-of-utopia-jean-luc-godard-s-collages-de-france-models

5. See Marie-Claire Ropars-Wuilleumier, *De la littérature au cinéma: genèse d'une écriture* (Paris: Armand Colin, 1970), 194.

6. 'Il faut se prêter aux autres et se donner à soi-même' [one has to lend oneself to others and give oneself to the self] is a slightly modified quote from Montaigne's *Essais*, (III/ Kapitel X), as Jean-Louis Leutrat and Suzanne Liandrat-Guigues elaborate in their *Godard, Simple comme Bonjour* (Paris: L' Harmattan, 2004), 60.

7. Following Michel Beaujour's analysis of the literary genre as a delimitation from autobiography and in reference to fine art, Bellour's definition of the genre has been very influential in the field of cinema. See Michel Beaujour, *Miroirs d'encre* (Paris: Seuil, 1980), and Raymond Bellour, 'Autoportraits' [1988] in *Entre-Images. Photo, Cinéma, Vidéo* (Paris: La Difference, 1990), 271–337 [translated as *Between-the-Images. Photography, Cinema, Video* (JRP/Ringier, 2012)], and, specifically in relation to Godard, Raymond Bellour '(Not) Just an other Filmmaker', in Raymond Bellour and Mary Lea Bandy, eds., *Jean-Luc Godard. Son+Image* (NewYork: MOMA, 1992), 215–231.

8. See amongst others, Bellour, '(Not) Just an other Filmmaker' and Nicole Brenez, 'Le film abymé. Jean-Luc Godard et les philosophies byzantines de l'image', in Marc Cerisuelo, ed., *Jean-Luc Godard (2). Au-delà de l'image*, dans *Études cinématographiques*, n° 194-202 (Paris: Lettres modernes, 1993), 135–163; and, later, Daniel Morgan, *Late Godard and the Possibilities of Cinema* (Oakland: University of California Press, 2012).

9. See Jacques Bontemps, 'Trois femmes autour de "Monsieur Godard". A propos de *Prénom Carmen*', in *Trafic. Almanach de Cinéma 2023* (Paris: P.O.L., 2022), 360 and 362; and Jean Starobinski, *Portrait de l'artiste en saltimbanque* [1970] (Paris: Gallimard, 2004).

10. Liandrat-Guigues und Leutrat, *Godard, Simple comme Bonjour*, 140.

11. See Michael Temple, 'Inventer un film. Présentation de *Moi Je*' and Jean-Luc Godard, 'Moi Je' (1973) in Nicole Brenez, David Faroult, Michael Temple and Michael Witt, eds., *Jean-Luc Godard. Documents* (Paris: Katalog, 2006), 191 and 195–243.

12. Godard refers in his sketch to the Deleuzian concepts of difference and repetition, but also to the 'machine socialo-désirante', the desiring machine. See Godard, 'Moi Je' and Gilles Deleuze and Félix Guattari, 'Bilan-programme pour machines désirantes', in *Minuit 2* (January 1973), 7.

13. See Jacques Aumont, 'The medium', in Bellour and Bandy, eds., *Jean-Luc Godard. Son+Image*, 213. The idea of categorising Godard's films as 'acts of thinking' or 'theory' was picked up both by Liandrat-Guiges and Leutrat, in *Godard, Simple comme Bonjour*, 221, and by Volker Pantenburg, in *Farocki/Godard. Film as Theory* [2006], (Amsterdam: Amsterdam University Press, 2015). Faroult's contextual analysis of the 'political' Godard considers the interpretation of his artistic practice as 'theory' to be misleading: see David Faroult, *Godard: inventions d'un cinéma politique* (Paris: Les prairies ordinaires/ Editions Amsterdam, 2018), 16.

14. *Histoire(s) du cinéma* (1988-1989) consists of eight parts: 1A: Toutes les Histoire(s), 1B: Une Histoire seule, 2A: Seul le cinéma, 2B: Fatale beauté, 3A: La Monnaie de l'absolu, 3B: Une Vague nouvelle, 4A: Le Contrôle de l'univers, 4B: Les Signes parmi nous.

15. See Michael Witt, 'In search of Godard's "Sauve la vie (qui peut)"', in *NECSUS* (June 10, 2015), https://necsus-ejms.org/in-search-of-godards-sauve-la-vie-qui-peut/

16. Witt has presented probably the most comprehensive archaeological study of *Histoire(s) de cinéma* in Michael Witt, *Jean-Luc Godard, Cinema Historian* (Bloomington: Indiana University Press, 2013).

17. Karl-Heinz Bohrer, *Das absolute Präsens: Die Semantik ästhetischer Zeit* (Frankfurt a. M.: Suhrkamp, 1994), 176.

18. Jacques Rancière, *La fable cinématographique* (Paris: Seuil, 2001), 222f.

19. Gilles Deleuze, *Pourparlers* (Paris: Minuit, 1990), 55.

20. Jean-Luc Godard, 'A propos de cinéma et d'histoire', in *Jean-Luc Godard par Jean-Luc Godard, Les écrits sur le cinéma*, tome 2 (1984–1998), ed. Alain Bergala (Paris: Cahiers du cinéma, 1998), 401.

21. Godard, 'A propos de cinéma et d'histoire'.

22. Jean-Luc Godard, *Introduction to a True History of Cinema and Television*, trans. Timothy Barnard (Montreal: Caboose, 2014). The book goes back to a series of talks that Godard gave in 1978 in Montréal and which was published in 1980 in French.

23. 'Godard makes (hi)stories', Interview with Serge Daney [1988], in Bellour and Bandy, eds., *Jean Luc Godard. Son+Image*, 158.

24. Liandrat-Guigues and Leutrat, *Godard, Simple comme Bonjour*, 21.

25. For Nietzsche's *Ecce Homo* as the book of books, see Beaujour, *Miroirs d'encre*, 320.

26. Gilles Deleuze and Félix Guattari, *Anti-Oedipus*, trans. Robert Hurley, Mark Seem and Helen R. Lane (Minneapolis: University of Minnesota Press, 1983), 42.

27. Jean-Luc Godard, *JLG/JLG et autres textes, phrases* (Paris: P.O.L., 2022), 63.

www.ingramcontent.com/pod-product-compliance
Lightning Source LLC
Chambersburg PA
CBHW082009090526

44590CB00020B/3408